THE GOLDEN LAND ABLAZE

BERTIL LINTNER

The Golden Land Ablaze

Coups, Insurgents and the State in Myanmar

HURST & COMPANY, LONDON

First published in the United Kingdom in 2024 by
C. Hurst & Co. (Publishers) Ltd.,
New Wing, Somerset House, Strand, London, WC2R 1LA
© Bertil Lintner, 2024
All rights reserved.

Distributed in the United States, Canada and Latin America by Oxford University Press, 198 Madison Avenue, New York, NY 10016, United States of America.

The right of Bertil Lintner to be identified as the author of this publication is asserted by him in accordance with the Copyright, Designs and Patents Act, 1988.

A Cataloguing-in-Publication data record for this book is available from the British Library.

ISBN: 9781911723684

www.hurstpublishers.com

Printed and bound in Great Britain by Bell and Bain Ltd, Glasgow

CONTENTS

Introduction	1
1. The Coup	7
2. The Military	37
3. The Ethnic Jigsaw	73
4. The China Factor	109
5. The Politicians	143
6. Myanmar Today—and Tomorrow	175
List of Abbreviations	199
Notes	203
Additional Reading	227
Index	235

INTRODUCTION

This is a tale of hope and despair—and how the leaders of Myanmar's military misjudged the political mood in the country when they seized power in a coup on 1 February 2021. It is also about how the international community failed to realise what really happened before and during the decade of openness which Myanmar experienced from 2011 to 2021. It was not, as many foreign pundits surmised, a 'transition to democracy'. And that was certainly not what the military meant it to be.

Decades of Western sanctions and boycotts had forced Myanmar into the arms of the Chinese, and that dependence had by the early 2000s become so grave that Myanmar military analysts began to state in internal, classified military documents that the country was in danger of losing its independence. Therefore, it had no choice but to open up to the West. But for that to succeed, certain measures had to be taken, such as the release of political prisoners and the introduction of freedom of speech, press freedom and the right to form political parties and non-governmental organisations.

After decades of stifling, direct military rule, elections were held in November 2010 and a new government was formed in March 2011. It did not seem to matter that the election, which the military's Union Solidarity and Development Party had won by a landslide, was fraudulent and that the new president, Thein Sein, was a general who had for several years been a leading member of the junta that had ruled the country since the crushing of a pro-democracy uprising in 1988. Almost overnight, Myanmar turned from being an international pariah to the darling of the Western world. The US secretary of state Hillary Clinton, president Barack Obama, the UK prime minister David Cameron and the king of Norway all went to Myanmar to see for themselves the remarkable changes that were taking place.

But the unprecedented openness that people came to enjoy during 2011–21 did not mean that the supreme power of the military was over. The autonomous status of the military, free from any governmental interference or oversight, had been enshrined in a constitution that had been enacted after a rigged referendum in 2008 and thus before any elections were held. But when the National League for Democracy (NLD), led by Aung San Suu Kyi, the daughter of Aung San, Burma's independence hero who was assassinated on 19 July 1947, won not only the first really free and fair election in November 2015 but also the next election, in November 2020, the generals had had enough of pseudo-democratic theatre. They stepped in, arrested the winners of the election before the NLD and its allies could form yet another government, and the country was placed under the rule of a new junta called the State Administration Council, or SAC for short.

There were protests, and the military opened fire on the demonstrators. But that had happened before—after the initial military takeover in 1962, during unrest in the 1970s, and when a massive pro-democracy uprising was crushed in 1988—and brutal crackdowns had worked on those occasions. After a few days of indiscriminate killings, the protests had fizzled out and people had returned home. But not this time. What had happened during the decade of openness was not a transition to anything, but a transformation of Myanmar society. An entire generation had learned how to use the Internet, to communicate on social media, and to hold workshops and seminars on subjects related to democracy and civil rights.

That, in turn, gave birth to what is called Generation Z and massive opposition to the coup, first by peaceful means and then with armed struggle. The NLD and other political parties have been forced underground, while urban activists have joined forces with ethnic rebel armies such as the Karen National Union (KNU)

INTRODUCTION

and the Kachin Independence Army (KIA) and managed to score some spectacular victories on the battlefield. As one Myanmar observer put it at the time of the coup, 'The military has messed with the wrong generation.' It is unlikely that Thein Sein and the other generals had expected this kind of development when changes were introduced after the 2010 election.

Three years later, Myanmar is still ablaze. The army, which had performed well during the civil wars which have raged in the country since independence from Britain in 1948, is, for the first time, on the defensive. The military has lost control over large parts of the country and a parallel authority called the National Unity Government (NUG), which is made up of MPs who were elected in 2020 and other pro-democracy activists, is active on the international stage.

But, so far, the anti-SAC forces are not well-equipped enough to defeat the much more heavily armed Myanmar army, which, in turn, is stretched out on too many fronts to be able to crush the resistance. And, despite assurances by many foreign, mainly Western, observers, there is no unity among the various Burman and ethnic resistance groups. This is a war that neither side can win by military means, and caught in the middle is the civilian population, which is bound to suffer the most.

Decades of conflict have turned Myanmar, or Burma, once a fairly prosperous country with a fragile but still working democratic system, into a social and economic wreck. I have written this book in order to explain the enigma of military power in Myanmar and to provide interested parties with a better understanding of the many other issues which have led to today's sad state of affairs, and so they will not be misled by shallow analyses and wishful thinking.

But it may not be only doom and gloom. No repressive system lasts forever, and Myanmar's military dictatorship is no exception. Despite all the hardships, Myanmar has a vast pool of talented people of various nationalities who one day may be able to steer their country towards a different reality where they will all be able to live up to their full potential. The long-suffering peoples of Myanmar deserve nothing less, but it will be a protracted struggle which, maybe, has just begun. Only time will tell, and it all depends on what will or will not happen inside the ruling and still remarkably unified military.

Bertil Lintner

Note on names

U, *Ko* and *Maung* are used alternately to mean mister, depending on the rank and age of the man addressed, and his relationship to the speaker. Thus, Nu would be called Maung Nu by his mother, Ko Nu by his friends and U Nu when addressed formally or by subordinates. Daw and Ma are used similarly for women. Daw Aung San Suu Kyi is the formal designation, while Ma Aung San Suu Kyi would have been used when she was younger or by her friends.

Bo and *Bohmu* are military titles for officers which are often carried into civilian life, like *Bogyoke*, which means 'supremo' or 'chief' and is more respectful than 'general', a military designation only. *Thakin* is a title used by the young nationalists in the 1930s (Thakin Than Tun, for instance); it means 'master' and was originally reserved for the British, but the nationalists used the title to show that they were the real masters of their country. Some of the communist leaders, who once were members of the early nationalist movement, are referred to as *thakins* as well. *Saya* means 'teacher' and *Sayadaw* refers to learned Buddhist monks.

Yebaw means 'comrade' and was used by the communists and, until 1988, also within the ruling Burma Socialist Programme Party. Male Shans are titled *Sai* ('brother') and females *Nang* ('sister'). *Sao* and *Khun* are Shan titles originally reserved for the ruling families but later used by military officers in the insurgency. Karens are titled *Saw* (men) and *Naw* (women). *Mahn* is the Pwo Karen equivalent of *Saw*. *P'doh* is used for addressing officials in the Karen rebel administration. Mon males are titled *Nai* ('mister'). The Burmans, Shans, Arakanese, Mons, Karens, Karennis, Was, Padaungs (Kayans), Palaungs and most smaller tribes do not have family names. The Chins, Kachins and Nagas, on the other hand, have surnames as well as clan names.

Myanmar or Burma is another issue that often causes confusion. There is actually no difference between the two terms other than that *Myanmar Naing-ngan* is the formal designation of the country,

INTRODUCTION

while *Bama-Pyi* has always been used in daily speech (and in the original national anthem). The issue is explained in more detail in Chapter Three. Here, Burma is used when the text is about the country before the 1989 'name change', and Myanmar is used when describing events after 1989. Rangoon rather than Yangon is used when dealing with proper names such as the University of Rangoon and in references to books printed before 1989. Towns and regions are referred to by their old as well as new names.

1

THE COUP

It began with carnival-like protests in the streets of Yangon, Mandalay, Mawlamyine, Pathein and almost every city, town and major village across the country. Millions of people took to the streets to voice their opposition to General Min Aung Hlaing and his military, which had arrested the country's elected representatives and assumed absolute power in a coup on 1 February 2021. Youth in fanciful costumes, some dressed as contestants in beauty pageants or as ghosts carrying placards saying, 'the military is scarier than us', 'Use a condom, don't let people like Min Aung Hlaing be born again', and more straightforward slogans like 'Free our leaders' and 'We want democracy, we reject the military coup'. Older protesters, inspired by the youngsters, dressed in pre-Buddhist temple robes, met for religious ceremonies reminiscent of those during Myanmar's fables *nat pwes*, or 'spirit festivals', asking deities for help to get rid of Min Aung Hlaing and other coup makers—and then cast evil spells on them.

At one point, almost the entire nation was on strike. But the situation took a different turn when the military began shooting peaceful demonstrators. Specially trained snipers picked out the youngest in the crowds in order to get their message across. A year later, Min Aung Hlaing even said in a televised speech: 'You should learn from the tragedy of earlier ugly deaths that you can be in danger of getting shot in the head and back.'[1] By then, more than a thousand demonstrators had been killed and more remained in military custody while thousands had taken to the hills to fight against Min Aung Hlaing and his hugely unpopular State Administration Council (SAC).

The current popular revolt, although fiercer and more massive than previous uprisings, is nevertheless following similar patterns to those in the past. The students, always at the forefront of any protest movement, were the first to openly demonstrate against the initial military takeover on 2 March 1962, which marked the beginning of now more than sixty years of military rule. On 7 July of that year, students gathered on the of campus of Rangoon University (it was still Rangoon at that time), speeches were given and the area was declared to be 'a fortress of democracy'.[2]

But the festive atmosphere changed later that evening when the students saw soldiers being deployed along the tree-lined University Avenue, armed with newly issued West German G-3 assault rifles. Then, without warning, they opened fire on the students. Officially, fifteen were killed and twenty-seven wounded.[3] But both neutral observers and students who were there say that the campus looked like a slaughterhouse, where hundreds of potential leaders of society in many fields lay sprawled in death. The man in charge of the operation was Sein Lwin, a 4th Burma Rifleman and one of Ne Win's closest lieutenants, and the orders to kill had come directly from the strongman himself.

In the early hours of 8 July, residents in the capital were awakened by a loud explosion that reverberated through the city. The army had dynamited the historic Students' Union building, reducing it to rubble. David Steinberg, a US Burma scholar, has described the act as 'gratuitous and unnecessary…[the building] had been as familiar a symbol in the secular sphere as the Shwe Dagon Pagoda was a symbol of Buddhism…The student demonstrations and their tragic aftermath were harbingers of continuous trouble the military experienced from the volatile student community.'[4] After the crackdown, radical students went to the base area of the Communist Party of Burma (CPB) to join the armed struggle against the Yangon government while some of the Shans and Kachins joined the movements of their respective ethnic groups.

But the urban anti-government movement had not been totally subdued. In May 1974, the oil workers in Chauk went on strike, demanding higher wages. The unrest spread from the oil fields to Yangon, where the workers at a railway workshop in the northern suburb of Insein also went on strike, over food shortages, rising prices and bad labour conditions. Soon, workers at the Thamaing Spinning Mill and the Sinmalaik Dockyard joined the strike and began pressing political demands as well.

Ne Win responded as he had when the students demonstrated in 1962: he sent in troops who fired indiscriminately on the workers. Officially, twenty-eight were killed and eighty wounded. Independent sources put the death toll at about a hundred. Hundreds were arrested—and universities as well as colleges were closed since the students had demonstrated in support of the striking workers. The government blamed the unrest on 'unscrupulous elements from the outside who had created disturbances'.[5] No attempt was made to understand the deeper causes of resentment against the military authorities.

The superficial calm, sustained by the army's firepower, lasted until December. U Thant, the general secretary of the United Nations, had died in New York on 25 November. He was perhaps the best-known and most respected Burmese citizen internationally. Because of the long-standing animosity between the brilliant statesman and intellectual, U Thant, and the general who ruled at home, the government sent no official delegation to receive the coffin when it arrived by air at Yangon. The authorities had planned to bury it in an obscure cemetery on the outskirts of the capital. The students, almost inevitably, seized the opportunity to launch large scale anti-government demonstrations.

As the funeral procession moved towards the proposed burial site, the students snatched the coffin and carried it away to the university campus. Buddhist monks joined in and gave U Thant the rites appropriate for someone who had achieved distinction—and the students then buried him near the Shwe Dagon. The violence and the subsequent arrest of hundreds of students and monks provoked demonstrations all over Yangon. The marchers, many of whom were young, were cheered and applauded by ordinary townspeople as they chanted anti-government slogans. The government responded by declaring martial law on 11 December. When the students defied the order, the troops opened fire. The official casualty toll was ludicrously low: five killed, seventy-four wounded and 1,800 arrested. Students who participated in the demonstrations claim that 300–400 of their comrades were gunned down that day in Yangon.

After the December 1974 demonstrations, hundreds of young people took to the hills, where they joined a resistance force led by Bo Let Ya, one of the Thirty Comrades, heroes of the independence movement in the 1940s. But in Yangon, the movement continued underground. In June 1975, on the first anniversary of the labour strike, students and workers decided to rise against the military regime. Kyaw Gyi was one of them:

> Secret contacts had been established between us students and the workers. We had decided to march again on 11 June and many of us gathered at the Shwe Dagon on the night before. We camped at the pagoda—but were awoken at five the following morning when soldiers and policemen stormed in. 213 of us were arrested, half of them were under twenty, some as young as thirteen. We were trucked away to Insein Jail where we were interrogated for about two months. I stayed there for four years before I was released.[6]

It was during the unrest in the 1970s that the military and its secret police, euphemistically called the Military Intelligence Service (MIS), refined the brutal ways in which they dealt with dissidents. Kyaw Gyi says he was forced to kneel on sharp pebbles while he was constantly hit and beaten. An almost perverted form of torture commonly employed was known as 'the motorcycle':

> A military intelligence officer would order me to 'get on the motorcycle'. When I said I could not see one, he'd beat me, point at an empty space on the concrete floor and shout: 'There it is, don't you see?' Then I had to stand at a half-crouch and pretend I was riding a motorcycle, making all the engine noises and all that.

> Intermittently, the officer would rap me with his bamboo staff and shout comments such as: 'You didn't stop at the red lights! What's the matter with you? You don't obey the laws!' It went on like that until I thought I was going mad.[7]

A similar form of torture was called 'the helicopter' and was basically aimed at making the victim dizzy by forcing him to spin around with outspread arms. When he lost his balance, he was beaten and then ordered to commence spinning. More brutal forms of torture included electric shocks and forcing the prisoners to drink their own urine. The purpose of the torture was never to extract information from the prisoners but to return them to their families as wrecks—and thus serve as a warning to others. But that did not always work. When these young people were released, some of them took to the jungle, where they joined the insurgents, the CPB or Bo Let Ya's non-communist resistance. Among those who remained behind in Yangon, preparations began for the next round of anti-government activity, which was scheduled to coincide with the 100th anniversary of the birth of Thakin Kodaw Hmaing, a national hero who had inspired the pro-independence movement in the 1930s. Tun Myat participated in that movement:

> Our intention was to launch a general strike on his birthday in March. But our underground movement had become so heavily infiltrated by military intelligence agents that the plans leaked out. There was only a relatively small demonstration on the campus in Yangon and 130 of us were arrested before anything dramatic could happen. I spent two years in Insein Jail after that. We were all tortured. 'The motorcycle' was very common. A friend of mine was also stripped naked and told to climb a tree. Half-way up, a policeman poked a stick up his anus and ordered him to shout: 'Release the arrested students!' and 'Lower tuition fees!', the slogans of our movement. It was all terribly humiliating.[8]

The aborted Thakin Kodaw Hmaing movement was the last attempt to organise student protests in Yangon in the turbulent 1970s. The killings, the arrests and the torture of detainees appeared, after all, to have cowed most of the pro-democracy activists into submission. But the superficial calm lasted only until the end of the 1980s, when the next round of protests erupted.

It began in March 1988 with a brawl in a teashop in one of Yangon's suburbs and escalated into massive, anti-government street demonstrations. Scores of protesters were killed and at least a thousand were arrested. In June, more demonstrations shook Yangon and the riot police, the dreaded *Lon Htein*, brutally crushed the demonstrators. A curfew was imposed and universities, colleges and schools were closed.

But that did not put an end to the protests. People had had enough of more than two decades of military dictatorship and economic hardship—and word had spread across the country that there would be anti-government protests on 8 August. At eight minutes past eight on 8 August 1988, the dockworkers in Yangon port walked out. That was the auspicious moment, and as soon as the word spread that a strike was on, masses of people began marching towards the city centre. The *Associated Press* reported:

> Marching behind red flags, symbolising courage and waving portraits of 1940s national hero Aung San, young students, women, monks and other Rangoon residents...called for democracy and economic reform. "You couldn't see the end of it," said a twenty-two-year-old British student...Georgina Allen said she saw "solid flanks" of organised unarmed demonstrators clenching their fists, cheering and clapping their hands as they marched along a main street in Rangoon.[9]

And demonstrations were held not only in the capital. In every city, town and major village, millions of people took to the streets to vent twenty-six years of pent-up frustrations with the one-party regime of the Burma Socialist Programme Party (BSPP), a party set up and dominated by the military. People marched in Mandalay, Meiktila, Sagaing and Shwebo in the north; Pathein and Hinthada in the Irrawaddy delta; Bago, Toungoo, Pyinmana and Minbu in the central plains; Mawlamyine, Myeik and Dawei in the south-east and Kawthaung on the southernmost tip of the nation; Taunggyi in Shan State; and even as far north as the Kachin State capital of Myitkyina. Those who lived outside urban centres arrived in lorries and bullock-carts to participate in the demonstrations. The country had never before seen such a massive, nationwide uprising which also included all segments of society: young and old, laymen and Buddhist monks, Christians and Muslims, students and peasants as well as rich and poor.

The euphoric atmosphere in Yangon prevailed all day as speakers took turn to address the crowds from makeshift platforms which had been erected at major intersections. At 11pm there were still thousands of people outside the Sule Pagoda in the city centre. At 11.30, trucks loaded with troops suddenly roared out from behind the nearby City Hall. Those were followed by more trucks as well as Bren-carriers, their machine guns pointed straight in front of them. Spontaneously, the demonstrators began singing the national anthem.

Then, two pistol shots rang out—and the sounds of machine-gun fire reverberated in the dark between the buildings surrounding Bandoola Square. People fell in droves as they were hit. The streets turned red with blood as people 'scattered screaming into alleys and doorways, stumbling over open gutters, crouching by walls and then, in a new wave of panic, running again,' Seth Mydans wrote in the *New York Times*.[10]

Richard Gourley, who was in Yangon on that fateful Monday, reported for the *Financial Times*: 'Eyewitnesses saw armoured cars driving up to demonstrators and opening fire indiscriminately, challenging official claims that they were using only moderate force. Some witnesses reported seeing demonstrators carrying dead protesters over their heads as they marched through the streets.'[11]

Shooting also occurred in Sagaing on 9 August. On that day, students marched towards the local police station to demand the release of other students who were being detained there. The demonstrators were joined by a large number of peasants from surrounding villages. By the time they reached the police station, the crowd had swelled to about 10,000. At the police station, someone in the crowd—believed by local people to have been an agent provocateur—threw stones at the police, who responded with gunfire. When a male student stood up to urge the crowd not to react violently, he was immediately shot and killed. A monk repeated the student's plea. Five bullets hit him before he died and fell to the ground. When the monk fell, a female student shouted: 'Be calm! We're not afraid to die!' She was shot as well.[12]

There was a moment's silence—followed by automatic gunfire. The one who began shooting indiscriminately into the crowd was Thura Kyaw Zwa, the chairman of the Sagaing Division People's Council. He was blasting away with his Sten gun and hundreds of people were hit. Between 200 and 300 demonstrators were killed on the spot, while others died in hospital or elsewhere. According to doctors, most of the dead and wounded had been hit from behind as the crowd rushed away.[13]

The title *Thura* in front of Kyaw Zwa's name means 'hero', a distinction he had earned when he was an army officer fighting communist rebels in upper Burma. Local people in Sagaing say that he used to kill even small children, arguing that they were 'the seeds of communism'. Thura Kyaw Zwa was but the most extreme example of former and still serving army officers who filled the posts of the BSPP administration out in the provinces. The Burma Broadcasting Service described the massacre 'as an attack by 5,000 demonstrators against the town's police station', and in order to prevent the police station from falling into the hands of the mobs, shots were fired. It was learnt that thirty-one people were killed and thirty-seven others wounded in the incident.[14]

In the Shan State capital of Taunggyi, seventy-two people were shot while attending the funeral of a young female demonstrator who had been killed.[15] In Mawlamyine in the south-east, forty-seven people including four monks were killed, and about twenty wounded when the military fired on the demonstrators. There were also shootings in Bago, Myitkyina, Hinthada and Pathein, as well as in other towns.[16] No one knows exactly how many people were killed during and in the aftermath of the 8.8.88 demonstrations, though doctors who later managed to flee the country believe that at least 3,000 people were gunned down when the army opened fire on demonstrators all over the country. But that did not put an end to the protests. On 26 August, Aung San Suu Kyi addressed several hundred thousand people in a public appearance outside the Shwe Dagon Pagoda in Yangon. A general strike was proclaimed, and the country ground to a halt.

THE COUP

Ne Win, who had resigned from the presidency in 1981, relinquished his last official post, that of chairman of the BSPP, at a congress in June. His successor as president, his right-hand man San Yu, also stepped down from his post. Sein Lwin, who had led the massacre of students in 1962, was appointed successor to the presidency as well as the BSPP chairmanship, but amidst daily demonstrations against the regime, he was forced to resign after only seventeen days in power and was succeeded by Dr Maung Maung, a military historian.

That, however, made no difference. The military was solidly behind Dr Maung Maung and no one wanted one of Ne Win's old henchmen, not even a semi-civilian, to rule the country. The demonstrations continued and the local administration all over the country was in the hands of strike committees—until the military, led by General Saw Maung, stepped in on 18 September, not to seize power but to shore up a regime overwhelmed by popular protests. And this time, the crackdown was carried out in a more systematic way than in August. About a thousand people were gunned down as soldiers with guns at the ready, armoured personnel carriers and other military vehicles moved in perfect formation into town centres. It was all over after three days of killings and mass arrests.

A junta called the State Law and Order Restoration Council (SLORC), with Saw Maung as its chairman, took over from Dr Maung Maung. The 1974 constitution was abolished—and so was the Burmese Way to Socialism. Perhaps in order to soften criticism from the outside world, the SLORC pledged to introduce a market-oriented economy—and it also said that elections to a new parliament would be held as soon as 'law and order had been restored'.[17] SLORC chairman Saw Maung stated that 'the Defence Forces have no desire to hold on to state power for a prolonged period'.[18]

It was also announced that the one-party system had been abolished. The BSPP reinvented itself under the name the National Unity Party (NUP), while the democracy movement led by Aung San Suu Kyi—and former army chief General Tin U, who had been released from prison during a general amnesty in 1980—

formed the National League for Democracy (NLD). Other groups took advantage of the new laws, and within a couple of months, there were more than a hundred parties, most of them political of different shades and persuasions, among them organisations representing the ethnic minorities.

But not everyone was convinced that the military would, as it had said, hold free and fair elections and then hand over power to the winning party.[19] After the formation of the SLORC, nearly 10,000 mostly young pro-democracy activists fled to the border areas, where they hoped the ethnic rebels would provide them with guns and military training. On 5 November, they formed the All-Burma Students Democratic Front (ABSDF) and vowed to take up arms against the SLORC.

However, these rebel groups—Karen, Mon, Karenni and Pa-O—were unable to give the urban dissidents more than a handful of weapons. None of the ethnic groups could match the strength of the CPB, which had about 10,000–15,000 troops under its command and controlled a 20,000-square-kilometre territory along the border with China in the north-east.

During the decade 1968–78, CPB had received massive support from China, and although that had been sharply reduced after the death of Mao Zedong in 1976 and the rise of Deng Xiaoping and his new, non-revolutionary foreign policy, the party still had vast quantities of Chinese-supplied arms and ammunition. Despite government claims of a 'communist conspiracy' during the 1988 uprising, there was at that time no linkage between the anti-totalitarian pro-democracy movement in central Burma and the orthodox, Marxist-Leninist CPB.

A situation which could have been potentially dangerous for the SLORC arose in March and April 1989, when the hilltribe rank and file of the CPB—led by its military commanders, who also came from the various minorities in its north-eastern base area—mutinied against the party's ageing, mostly Burmese, political leadership. On 17 April, ethnic Wa mutineers stormed the CPB's headquarters at Panghsang on the Yunnan border, seized the armoury and forced the old leaders to flee across the border to China. The former CPB's army soon split along ethnic lines

THE COUP

and formed four regional resistance forces, the largest being the United Wa State Army (UWSA).

Ethnic rebels along the Thai border sent a delegation to Panghsang to negotiate with the Wa component of the former CPB. The possibility of a linkup between the four former CPB groups and the ethnic rebels along the Thai border as well as the urban dissidents in the ABSDF caused alarm bells to ring in Yangon. Consequently, the central military authorities reacted faster, with more determination, and with much more to offer than the Thai-border-based ethnic rebels. Within weeks of the mutiny, Khin Nyunt, the new head of military intelligence, now called the Directorate of the Defence Services Intelligence (DDSI), travelled to the border to meet the former communist commanders, and alliances of convenience were forged between the Burmese military and various groups of mutineers.

In exchange for promises not to attack government forces and to sever ties with other rebel groups, the UWSA and the other three CPB mutineers were allowed to continue to control and administer their respective areas and to retain their weapons. They were also granted unofficial permission to engage in any kind of business to sustain themselves. And 'business' in the former CPB area inevitably meant opium and its derivative, heroin. As a result of the 1989 ceasefire agreements, Burma's opium production skyrocketed. According to US government reports, the 1987 harvest for Burma alone yielded 836 tons of raw opium; by 1995, the production had increased to 2,340 tons. The area under poppy cultivation soared, from 92,300 hectares in 1987 to 142,700 in 1989 and 154,000 in 1995.[20] Within a year of the mutiny, there were also more than twenty new heroin laboratories in the former CPB areas east of the Salween River.

After those ceasefire agreements with the mutineers had been agreed upon, several ethnic groups which had depended on the former CPB for supplies of arms and ammunition entered into similar accords with the military. The first was the Shan State Army (SSA), on 2 September 1989, followed by smaller groups of Palaung, Kayan and Pa-O rebels. The main blow to the ethnic resistance came when the powerful Kachin Independence Army

(KIA) entered into a ceasefire agreement with the military on 24 February 1994. Ironically, at a time when almost the entire population had turned against the regime, thousands of former insurgents rallied behind the SLORC. The threat from the border areas was thwarted and the regime was safe. Only the KNU continued to fight against the SLORC, but with tens of thousands of troops freed from combat duty elsewhere in the country, the military could concentrate their efforts on attacking Karen bases along the Thai border, most of which were captured in the early 1990s. ABSDF was also on the run, and many of its fighters went into exile in Thailand.

Meanwhile, elections were held on 27 May 1990, and the voting turned out to be free and fair. Aung San Suu Kyi had been placed under house arrest and the entire top leadership of the NLD was in jail, while Khin Nyunt's DDSI had arrested thousands and put them behind bars in a crackdown that began in July 1989 and lasted for several months. But the problem from the military's point of view was that the NLD, even without its leadership, won a landslide victory, capturing 392 of the 485 seats in the *Pyithu Hluttaw*, or parliament, while the NUP got only ten.

That was hardly surprising, because the 1990 election should not be seen as an 'ordinary' election; it was a referendum where the NUP stood for the old order and the NLD represented the people's desire for change. It was for or against the NUP, and that was for most people an easy choice. The change of the name from BSPP to NUP fooled no one. The NUP had inherited the buildings and machinery of the BSPP, and its entire central committee consisted of second-rung ex-BSPP leaders with close army connections. Its chairman, Tha Kyaw, was a former 4th Burma Rifleman and ex-minister. Thura Kyaw Zwa, the butcher of Sagaing, was appointed local NUP leader in Bago, to where he had moved and where he probably felt safer after what he had done in his hometown.

But there was also a third factor: the ethnic parties. Although loosely allied with the NLD, they wanted to highlight the aspirations of the country's non-Bamar nationalities. Significantly, the Shan Nationalities League for Democracy won twenty-three

THE COUP

seats and became the second-largest party, followed by the Rakhine Democratic League, which secured eleven seats.

It was obvious, from the military's point of view, that the rules had to be rewritten. On 9 January 1990, Saw Maung had said at a meeting between the central junta and its local divisions held at the office of the commander-in-chief:

> We have spoken about the matter of State power. As soon as the election is held, form a government according to law and then take power. An election has to be held to bring forth a government. That is our responsibility. But the actual work of forming a legal government after the election is not the duty of the *Tatmadaw* [the military]. We are saying it very clearly and candidly right now.[21]

Drafting a new constitution was not an issue before the election. On the contrary, Saw Maung even lashed out against the NLD for raising the issue of a constitution—which some of its activists were doing at the time. In a speech on 10 May 1990—two weeks prior to the election: 'A dignitary who was once an attorney-general talked about the importance of the constitution. As our current aim is to hold the election as scheduled we cannot as yet concern ourselves with the Constitution as mentioned by that person. Furthermore it is not our concern. A new Constitution can be drafted. An old Constitution can also be used after some amendments.'[22] That 'dignitary' was former attorney-general U Hla Aung, who was close to the NLD and, at the time, researching constitutional issues for the pro-democracy movement.

DDSI chief Khin Nyunt, however, had made a curious statement on 13 April 1990, just over a month before the election. According to him, 'The Cabinet cannot be formed just after the election...the Cabinet is to be formed in accordance with the constitution.'[23] That day, *Reuters* quoted a diplomat in Rangoon as describing the statement as 'the first categorically saying that the military won't hand over power until a constitution is in place...it is the fist showing through the velvet glove'. Khin Nyunt, as head of intelligence, probably knew more about public sentiments than any of the other members of SLORC. He had begun to realise that the NLD was going to win—and this was the way out of the looming predicament.

The official response to the NLD's election victory came on 27 July 1990, when SLORC issued 'Announcement 1/90' declaring that 'it should not be necessary to explain that a political organisation does not automatically obtain the three sovereign powers of legislative, administrative and judiciary powers by the emergence of a people's assembly'.[24] Only SLORC had the right to those powers—and 'the representatives elected by the people' would merely be 'responsible for drafting a new constitution for a future democratic state'.[25]

More than sixty-five elected legislators were arrested for asking the military to respect the outcome of the election and NLD offices all over the country were closed. Another twenty MPs elect fled to either Thailand or India, where some of them linked up with the ABSDF and their ethnic rebel hosts. At a grand ceremony at the Karen rebel headquarters at Manerplaw on the Thai border on 18 December 1990, six MPs elect proclaimed the formation of the National Coalition Government of the Union of Burma (NCGUB), which also came to include representatives of the ethnic rebels and other dissidents.

The NCGUB was headed by Sein Win, a first cousin of Aung San Suu Kyi. His father, Aung San's elder brother Ba Win, was among those who were gunned down along with the independence hero in the Secretariat building in Yangon on 19 July 1947. But that was Sein Win's only political credential. He was a mathematician who had graduated from the universities in Yangon and Hamburg and later taught in Sri Lanka and Kenya. And it soon became clear that no foreign country was going to recognise the NCGUB. The desperate move to appoint Sein Win prime minister of the jungle-based government reflected the dire straits into which the once mighty NLD had fallen.

In the end, the assembly which was elected in May 1990 turned out to be not even a constitution-drafting body. Instead, about a hundred of the 485 MPs elect had to sit together with 600 other, non-elected representatives who had been handpicked by the military and draft that new constitution. It was a process that lasted for years, but Saw Maung did not oversee it, as he resigned in April 1992 and was replaced by his deputy, Gen Than Shwe. But that purge was not really political in nature. Saw Maung had become increasingly erratic—some would argue he had gone insane. His public speeches were incoherent and rambling, covering subjects such as dying tomorrow and sightings of Jesus in Tibet. He had also been seen at a military golf course in Yangon screaming 'I am King Kyansittha!' in a reference to one of the rulers of the ancient Bagan empire whose name means 'the remaining soldier' or 'the one who was left behind'.[26] Saw Maung died in oblivion and obscurity in July 1997.

Assisted by foreign PR agencies, the SLORC was given the new, more palatable name the State Peace and Development Council (SPDC), on 15 November 1997. Than Shwe remained junta chief, and began to further consolidate his power. The old dictator, Ne Win, had died on 2 December 2002, mourned by no one, not even the military officers whose godfather he once was. Seeking to avoid the fate of his predecessors Ne Win and Saw Maung, Than Shwe decided to appoint not one, but three successors. The secretary of the SPDC, Gen. Thein Sein, would become president after a sham election that was planned for November 2010. Another general, Shwe Mann, would head the military's own political party, the Union Solidarity and Development Party (USDP), which was formed twelve years after the 1988 uprising, the subsequent collapse of the BSPP and the poor performance of the NUP in the 1990 election. A weak and less-than-competent general, Min Aung Hlaing, was designated to take over as head of the military.

Everything seemed to be going to plan—when a new and unexpected bout of unrest shook Yangon. There had been sporadic demonstrations throughout the early 2000s, but no large number of ordinary people had dared to take to the streets. But then, during August, September and October 2007, thousands of monks marched through the streets of Yangon and elsewhere to show their displeasure with military rule. The international media began to refer to the movement as 'the Saffron Revolution' because of the saffron-coloured robes that Buddhist monks wear. That was actually a misnomer, as Thai, Lao, Cambodian and Sri Lankan Theravada monks wear such robes, while, in Myanmar, monks' robes are a dark, crimson colour rather than saffron. But it was a catchy name, and the movement received worldwide publicity.

Few foreign journalists were allowed to enter Myanmar at that time, but the Internet had arrived and still photos as well as videos of monks marching with banners which read 'Non-Violence' in Burmese reached the outside world. Young people also joined the marches, and, for a while, it seemed like another 8.8.88 uprising was about to break out.

But that did not happen. Once again, troops were dispatched to put an end to the marches. The number of monks and laymen killed is not known, but the military authorities admitted that thirteen had died. Exile sources put the figure of dead at 138, while at least a thousand were arrested.[27]

After crushing the monks' movement, it was time to adopt the constitution that had finally been drafted—just as the country was reeling from a cyclone called Nargis. The storms and the rains devastated the Irrawaddy delta, the country's rice bowl and home to millions of farmers. At least 130,000 people died and 2.4 million were made homeless or affected in other ways.[28] It was the worst natural disaster since the December 2004 tsunami, which caused destruction in countries around the Indian Ocean.

At first, the SPDC refused to accept any foreign assistance or help going to the victims. The official newspaper, the *New Light of Myanmar*—which until April 1993 had been the *Working People's Daily*—assured its readers that, despite the images being sent out of the country by what it called 'destructive elements', hunger could not be a problem, since farmers can gather edible water plants or 'go out with lamps and catch plump frogs'.[29] Only after severe pressure from the international community, including the United Nations, did the regime allow some aid to reach the victims. But all efforts were supervised by the military authorities, and the movement of aid workers was severely restricted.

A referendum was carried out on 10 May 2008, and it was clear before it was even held that it would be approved—and, regardless of the outcome of coming elections, secure a leading role for the military. There had been no critical discussion of its contents and most people had not seen the document they were supposed to vote for or against. There were even talks of criminal penalties for opposing the referendum, creating a climate of fear.

The referendum was postponed only in the forty-seven worst-hit townships in the Irrawaddy and Yangon Divisions and, if official figures are to be believed, there was a 99 per cent turnout and 92.48 per cent voted in favour of the charter. Two weeks later, voters in the Irrawaddy and Yangon Divisions affirmed the new constitution with a resounding 92.93 per cent, the *New Light of Myanmar* reported.[30]

Elections were finally held on 7 November 2010, and the USDP won 259 of the 440 seats in the House of Representatives and 129 of 224 in the House of Nationalities. The NLD boycotted the election because of the strict laws under which it was held. US president Barack Obama said it did not meet 'internationally accepted standards', and the governments of the countries of the European Union expressed similar concerns.[31] But such criticism had no impact on the military's plans.

The SPDC was disbanded, and a new government was formed in March 2011. As decided before the election, Thein Sein was sworn in as the country's president. Then came the surprises: the release of political prisoners and the introduction of freedoms which the country had not enjoyed since the time before the 1962 coup. Many in the outside world were astounded. Was Myanmar really on the road to becoming a democracy?

Western pundits and others began publishing essays attempting to make sense of why the military had taken such 'important steps towards a transition to a democratic civilian government' and how international organisations could 'work with Myanmar in its process of democratisation'.[32] Marie Lall, a UK-based academic, even wrote a book titled *Understanding Reform in Myanmar: People and Society in the Wake of Military Rule*.[33] Other Western writers began referring to Thein Sein as 'Myanmar's Gorbachev' for his seemingly daring moves towards openness and respect for—at least some—democratic values.[34]

The problem all along was that there was no 'transition' and the 'process of democratisation' was not what it seemed. It was all done according to a master plan, which was separate from Than

Shwe's scheme for his succession, and mapped out in a classified document compiled in August 2004 by Lt-Col Aung Kyaw Hla, a researcher at Myanmar's Defense Services Academy in Pyin Oo Lwin.[35] His Burmese-language, 346-page top-secret thesis, titled 'A Study of Myanmar–US Relations', outlines the thinking and strategy behind the actions the military took in 2010 and 2011—and, it should not be forgotten, the military still held supreme power even after the 2010 election. But the establishment of a more acceptable regime than the old junta made it easier for the Myanmar military to launch its new policies, and to have those taken seriously by the international community.

It is, however, unclear whether 'Aung Kyaw Hla' is a particular person, or a codename used by a military thinktank. Anecdotal evidence suggests the latter. The main argument of the dossier is that Myanmar's reliance on China as a diplomatic ally and economic patron, which came as a result of the imposition of sanctions and boycotts by the West after the 1988 massacres, had created a 'national emergency' that threatened the country's independence. It stated that Myanmar must normalise relations with the West after having in place an elected government so that the regime can deal with the outside world on more acceptable terms.

Aung Kyaw Hla, whoever he might be, goes on to argue that, although human rights are a concern in the West, the United States would be willing to modify its policy to suit 'strategic interests'. Although the author does not specify those interests, it is clear from the thesis that he is thinking of common ground with the United States vis-à-vis China. The author cites Vietnam and Indonesia under former dictator Suharto as examples of Washington's foreign policy flexibility in weighing strategic interests against democratisation. If bilateral relations with the United States were improved, the master plan suggests, Myanmar would also get access to badly needed funds from the World Bank, the International Monetary Fund and other global financial institutions. The country could then emerge from 'regionalism', where it depended on the goodwill and trade of its immediate neighbours, including China, and enter a new era of 'globalisation'.

THE COUP

The master plan clearly articulated the problems that must be addressed before Myanmar could lessen its reliance on China and become a trusted partner with the West. The main issue at the time of writing was the detention of pro-democracy icon Aung San Suu Kyi, who Aung Kyaw Hla wrote was a key 'focal point' and 'whenever she is under detention pressure increases, but when she is not, there is less pressure'.

While the report implies that Suu Kyi's release would improve ties with the West, the plan's ultimate aim—which it spells out clearly—is to 'crush' the opposition. The dossier concluded that the regime could not compete with the media and non-governmental organisations run by Myanmar exiles, but if American politicians and lawmakers were invited to visit the country they could help to sway international opinion in the regime's favour. That happened and, as a result, relations with the United States improved rapidly, exactly along the lines suggested by Aung Kyaw Hla in 2004. Myanmar's relations with China and with another, for the West, undesirable ally, North Korea, were high on the agenda when United States secretary of state Hillary Clinton visited Burma in December 2011. She discussed democracy and human rights with the Myanmar officials she met as well, but only after geostrategic issues had been addressed.[36]

In the beginning, the military actually had nothing to fear from taking those steps towards a more open society. According to the 2008 constitution, the 'Defense Services' shall 'be able to participate in the National political leadership role of the State', and it did so by securing the right to appoint 25 per cent of all seats of both houses of the National Assembly.[37] The Supreme Command also appointed the three most crucial ministries: Defence, Home Affairs—which includes the internal security apparatus—and Border Affairs.

Chapter 12 of the charter details the complicated rules for constitutional amendments, which effectively gave the military veto power over changes to the power structure. Minor constitutional changes could be considered by the parliament if 20 per cent of the members submitted a bill. But a tangle of 104 clauses stated that major changes could not be made without the prior approval of more than 75 per cent of all members of parliament, which, in effect, gave the military veto power against any attempt to change the constitution. But even if, miraculously, more than 75 per cent approved of a change, a nationwide referendum then would have to be held where more than half of all eligible voters cast ballots. And the generals stated time and again that it was their duty to uphold and defend this basically undemocratic constitution.[38]

But the plans drawn up by the military failed when Thein Sein and the USDP, despite the liberalisation he had introduced, did not become as popular as expected. Elections were held in November 2015, and, this time, the NLD did participate—and won by a landslide, capturing 255 of 440 seats in the House of Representatives and 135 of 224 seats in the House of Nationalities, or the Upper House. The USDP got only thirty and eleven seats, respectively. Yet again, the choice was basically the same as in the 1990 election. The NLD stood for the desire for real change and an end to military rule—direct or indirect did not matter. The NUP had all but disappeared from the scene and won only one seat in 2015, and, this time, it was the USDP that represented the old order. It was an easy choice. People voted without hesitation for the NLD.

A new government was formed in April 2016. Aung San Suu Kyi could not become president because the 2008 constitution prevented anyone with close relatives who are not Myanmar citizens from having that post.[39] Instead, a new post, that of state counsellor, was invented, and she became the de facto head of the new government, which took over most duties—except the crucial ministries of Defense, Home Affairs and Border Affairs, which remained in the sole hands of the military. As did the military itself, an autonomous entity beyond any kind of parliamentary control or even oversight.

Another blow to Than Shwe's plan to retire peacefully and without risks to himself and his family came when USDP chief Shwe Mann realised which way the wind was blowing. He went his own way and began to reach out to the NLD and Aung San Suu Kyi. Not surprisingly, he was removed as head of the USDP in August

2015 and, in April 2016, was sacked from the party along with seventeen senior party members.

Elections were held again in November 2020 and the outcome was yet another miscalculation on the part of the military. The generals believed that Aung San Suu Kyi and her government had failed to live up to the expectations of the urban middle class and also lost support from the country's many ethnic minorities. That was true—but, again, it was in effect a referendum rather than an ordinary general election. The USDP did not stand a chance. This time, the NLD's landslide victory was even greater than in 2015. The NLD got 258 seats in the House of Representatives and 138 in the House of Nationalities. The USDP's share of seats decreased to twenty-six in the House of Representatives and seven in the House of Nationalities.

A second NLD victory was more than the military could accept. On 26 January 2021, military spokesman Maj.-Gen. Zaw Min Tun held a press conference in the capital Naypyitaw, claiming that the November 2020 election was marred by irregularities and outright fraud.[40] No evidence was produced and his assertions ran contrary to the findings of international election observers, including the Carter Center, the Asian Network for Free Elections and the European Union's Election Observation Mission, all of which declared the elections a success. The EU's preliminary statement noted that 95 per cent of observers had rated the process 'good' or 'very good'.[41]

Three days later, a demonstration was held in Yangon against 'the fraudulent election'. At the time, most observers dismissed it as a 'rent-a-crowd' event and few took the warning signals seriously. But, in fact, Zaw Min Tun during the press conference had refused to rule out a coup when asked about the intentions of the military.[42]

What the military had not expected were massive, nationwide protests against their coup. And, once again, the military misjudged the situation when it decided to use brute force to suppress the demonstrations. A new, politically active and aware civil society had emerged during the 2011–2021 period of relative openness. People had also had enough of direct or indirect military rule, which had been the situation from the 1962 coup to the 2015 election, hence the NLD's massive electoral victories. Aung San Suu Kyi had refrained from challenging the military's political and economic power during her first term from 2016 to 2021, but the NLD's overwhelming election win in November 2020 gave her a strong mandate to push for real democratic change. That could, in turn, have led to the generals risking retribution for the many crimes they committed during their many years in power.

The coup took place on the same day that the new government was due to take office. After the tanks had rolled into Naypyitaw and Yangon, the military declared a state of emergency, detained MPs elect, and declared that a junta called SAC had assumed power. The moves, non-violent at first, were met by the formation of a Civil Disobedience Movement which brought together health workers, civil society activists, bank staff, teachers, civil servants, transport workers and many others. People also began boycotting products sold by military-owned companies and, when millions of people demonstrated against the coup, the protests were live-streamed on social media. At night, people banged pots and pans and sounded car horns to vent their anger with the military's seizure of power.[43]

On 8 February, the Committee Representing the Pyidaungsu Hluttaw (Union Parliament) was formed by elected MPs and claimed to be the legitimate authority running the country. The military responded by imposing a curfew on Yangon, Mandalay and other towns. Gatherings of more than five people were banned—but this was ignored by the people in the streets.

The first signs that a violent crackdown was imminent were discernible the next day. During a demonstration in Naypyitaw, the police fired rubber bullets and used water cannons and tear gas against the protesters. Then a live pistol shot rang out, and Mya Thwe Thwe Khaing, a nineteen-year-old protester, was shot in the head and died. Photographs of her were carried in demonstrations after the shooting, and the festive mood of the first protests began to grow sombre. The generals were not going to listen to reason, and it was becoming clear that they were prepared to use violence to maintain power.

THE COUP

On 22 February, a nationwide general strike was proclaimed and hailed as 'the five twos revolution' after the date 22.2.2021 in numerology-friendly Myanmar. It led to the closure of workplaces, stores and markets. Min Aung Hlaing then went on the air assuring people that everything remained open. In a speech on 25 February, as protests were sweeping the country, he chose to talk about the importance of consuming less cooking oil.[44]

These were surreal throwbacks to the years when the ruling military could say and do whatever it wanted, but those years were long gone. While it was far from the first time the public had risen up against a military dictatorship, what happened after the 2021 coup is vastly different from what happened in 1988, when soldiers suppressed a pro-democracy uprising by spraying automatic rifle fire into crowds of unarmed demonstrators, or from the 2007 Saffron Revolution, which was also quelled by brute force. In 1988, photographers smuggled out rolls of film in their underwear, and while digital media did exist during the Saffron Revolution, usage was limited to a privileged few. Just before the coup, approximately 35.1 per cent of the population had access to the Internet. This was a dramatic increase from less than 1 per cent in 2011, the first year such statistics became available.[45]

The uprising was not only about the detention of Aung San Suu Kyi—she and Win Myint, the president, were taken to prison in Naypyitaw—and the military's attempts to eliminate the NLD. During the decade of relative openness, from 2011 to the coup, people of all ages had become used to an unprecedented level of free expression. They simply did not want to return to military rule. And no one believed the military's claim that the 2020 election was fraudulent. That was merely a thin excuse to justify the coup.

In a draconian move to quell dissent and silence the population, SAC introduced a new cyber-security law that reimposed censorship and stated that social media platforms had to share private information about their users when requested by authorities. But tech-savvy young people in what became known as Generation Z then used different sets of SIM cards, mobile roaming services and VPNs and managed to get around the military's feeble attempts at closing down some social networks and limiting access to others. Police who had opened fire on demonstrators were named and shamed with photos on social media platforms. Arrests of activists, even at night, were recorded, and when a crowd of hired thugs armed with iron rods climbed out of a truck to confront protesters, they were filmed through the windscreen of a car. Footage of people with loudspeakers and placards in wooden boats plying Inlay Lake in Shan State went viral on social media, as did a caravan of motorcycles in the northern town of Namkham on the Chinese border, and video of police joining demonstrations in Loikaw, Kayah State and Magwe in central Myanmar.

Seen in a broader perspective, the coup also put an end to the outdated notion that the military is the only force that can hold the country together. This myth has been perpetuated by military propaganda and further spread by some Western academics and think-tankers.[46] Robert Taylor, a well-known Myanmar scholar, has even gone as far as uncritically quoting unnamed people saying that the old dictator Ne Win was 'an honest, sincere, and dedicated patriot'.[47]

With what the Burma Campaign UK describes as 'incredible bravery and determination', the people continued to resist the coup throughout February.[48] In early March, when people were still protesting in the streets, the military decided to strike back. On 3 March, at least thirty-eight people were killed when soldiers opened fire on large crowds in Yangon and other cities.[49] They also viciously beat four volunteer health workers, and one of them died from his injuries. Local media was also targeted. Several independent news outlets were raided and banned, and journalists were arrested. The next targets were striking workers and trade unions. Hundreds of striking railway workers were surrounded by troops in Yangon, and forced to return to work.

More killings occurred on 27 March, Armed Forces Day. As troops paraded in Naypyitaw, at least 114 people, including a five-year-old boy, were killed.[50] As a warning to the public at large, state television displayed pictures of anti-coup protesters who had been arrested and showed visible signs of torture. One woman's face was so swollen from beatings that she was almost unrecognisable.[51] Reports began to emerge of women being stripped naked during interrogations and then gang-raped in detention centres. Myanmar's military tribunals also went to work, sentencing twenty-eight protesters to death.

But repression breeds resistance. That happened after the massacres of 1962, those in the 1970s and the extremely bloody events of 1988. This time, it was better organised and information more easily disseminated via digital media. On 16 April, it was announced that MPs elect, activists and representatives of the non-Bamar nationalities had formed a National Unity Government (NUG), which they maintained was the country's legitimate supreme authority. It recognised Win Myint as president and Aung San Suu Kyi as state counsellor, and appointed a Kachin lawyer, Duwa Lashi La, as 'acting president'.[52]

On 5 May, the NUG made public the formation of an armed wing called People's Defence Forces (PDF). The resistance moved from the streets of cities and towns to the countryside—and armed struggle replaced peaceful demonstrations. Until then, the civil war had been confined to the frontier areas; now it spread to parts of the country that had not seen any fighting since the CPB was forced out of those areas in the 1970s. And although the PDF were poorly armed and trained, they managed to force the Myanmar military out of large parts of Sagaing and Magwe regions. Ethnic armies scored unprecedented victories and put the Myanmar army on the defensive in Kayah, Chin and Kachin states.

Then, on 27 October 2023, an alliance of three ethnic resistance armies in the north, the Kokang-based Myanmar National Democratic Alliance Army (MNDAA), the Ta'ang National Liberation Army (TNLA, a Palaung group) and the Arakan Army (AA), launched a massive campaign in northern Shan State codenamed 'Operation 1027', following the launch date. The Brotherhood Alliance, as it is called, managed to overrun more than 200 junta bases and confiscate huge quantities of weapons, including artillery pieces and armoured vehicles.

Morale among the Myanmar army's troops appeared to be low, and there were surrenders and even defections. The alliance's military successes in the north encouraged other resistance forces across the country to be more active, and by early 2024, the Myanmar army seemed to be losing ground everywhere.

There are, however, four factors that have to be taken into account when making a realistic assessment of the situation. The first would be the strength of the PDF, and the lack of unity within it. According to a report published by the United States Institute of Peace on 3 November 2022, only 60 per cent of them are armed, and 'mostly with locally produced low-quality arms'.[53]

But the poor performance of the Myanmar army's infantry has been compensated by extensive use of air power. Helicopter gunships and fighter jets have strafed villages and even towns, especially in Kayah and Chin states, where even schools and churches have been destroyed and people of all ages killed. And the PDF does not have anti-aircraft guns and other kind of weaponry capable of resisting such attacks. Civilian casualties, therefore, have been heavy, and hundreds of thousands of people have been forced to leave their homes.

And it seems there is little coordination and no common supreme command. The PDF, perhaps as many as 300 of them, do not appear to be operating in accordance with a well thought-out strategy encompassing the entire country. They seem more concerned with defending and possibly expanding their respective areas. The NUG may be the nominal leader of the resistance, but military action is carried out independently by a multitude of local forces, ethnic as well as purely political.

The second factor is the lack of unity among the PDF's supposed allies, the ethnic armies. Kachin, Palaung and Shan armies claim more or less the same areas in northern Shan State, and there are also territorial disputes between the Shan and the Wa, whose UWSA controls over 20,000 square kilometres of land in eastern Shan State. There are also longstanding territorial disputes between the Shan and the Pa-O minority in southern Shan State.

The most powerful of the ethnic forces, the UWSA, may have provided the MNDAA, the TNLA, the AA and the Shan State Army of the Shan State Progress Party—another resistance ethnic group—with weapons, but it still adheres to a ceasefire agreement it struck with the Myanmar military in 1989 and could not be considered part of some overall resistance. In Kachin State, a local ethnic Shan army is siding with the Myanmar military against the KIA, whose ceasefire agreement with the Myanmar military broke down in 1994. The KIA, in turn, has little or no influence in Lisu- and Rawang-inhabited areas of northernmost Kachin State.

There are several rival Chin armies in Chin State, and the Pa-O in southern Shan State have been involved in fights with the Shan State Army of the Restoration Council of Shan State (RCSS). The RCSS, on the other hand, sticks to a ceasefire agreement it signed with the Myanmar military in 2015, and some of its leaders appear to be more interested in investing in real estate in southern Shan State than in fighting the SAC.

The third factor is the seemingly everlasting unity of Myanmar's armed forces. Despite purges and dismissals since it first seized power in 1962, it has not seen any splits or even inner tendencies that could be viewed as embryonic factions. The military has become a powerful state within a state with its own institutions and privileges for its members. And what is happening now is nothing new. The Myanmar military has been under siege many times during the long history of the country's ethnic and political civil wars, which broke out shortly after independence from Britain in 1948, and it has always persevered in its endeavours, chief of which is to remain the country's most potent institution. Only a decisive split within the military, or much larger defections than those we are seeing now, would cause it to fall from power. No one can predict the future, but there have so far been no signs of any such infighting, or even serious disagreements, among the officer corps or the rank and file.

The fourth factor, which is too often overlooked, is China. Myanmar is of utmost strategic importance to China because it is the only neighbouring country that gives it direct and easy access to the Indian Ocean. China also has other interests in Myanmar, such as resource extraction and, most recently, how to deal with the many cross-border scam centres run by international crime gangs which have been bleeding the nation for years. And, regardless of what the Brotherhood Alliance has said in statements, the recent fighting in northern Shan State has more to do with that than any fight for federal democracy. Billions of dollars have flown out of China and into those scam centres, and this at a time when China is facing an internal economic slowdown.

The main centres affecting China were located in the UWSA-controlled territories of north-eastern Shan State, and in Kokang and adjacent areas to the north. The Chinese were able to deal with the UWSA, which is heavily dependent on China for trade and supplies of everything from guns to food. The Chinese issued a couple of arrest warrants for prominent UWSA personalities, read the leaders the riot act and reined them in.

It was a different story in Kokang and other parts of northernmost Shan State. There, the centres were in areas and at localities controlled by SAC-allied, local militia forces. At first the Chinese put pressure on the SAC to deal with the problem, but apart from deportations of quite a few not especially important people, nothing really happened. The Chinese then sent undercover special branch officers into Kokang, and several of them were killed by the militias—something that really angered the Chinese. Then the Brotherhood Alliance went on the offensive, and the problem was solved.

So did China's security authorities initiate Operation 1027? That is hard to say, but their security services were certainly aware of the plan in advance and did nothing to stop it, and were pleased to see that the alliance attacked several of those centres and forced them to close down. The UWSA has declared that it is 'neutral', but it has supplied the alliance with most of its weaponry. Those weapons are of Chinese origin, and it is hard to believe that the Chinese disapproved of them being handed over to the alliance forces.

By no stretch of the imagination could it be claimed that Myanmar's many resistance armies are a unified force with a common purpose. Since the first military takeover in 1962, Myanmar has been stuck in a vicious circle of repression and resistance—and a conflict that no warring party can win.

At the same time, the enigma of military power in Myanmar has long bewildered many outside observers. How was it possible for the comparatively small army that emerged from the chaos of the years immediately after independence in 1948 to develop into the formidable force that came to dominate state and society for decades after it assumed power in a coup in 1962? And why have all attempts to dislodge it from power failed? That is the crucial question that has to be addressed before any predictions can be made for the future.

2

THE MILITARY

Armed Forces Day, which falls on 27 March every year, is commemorated with a spectacular display of tanks, armoured personnel carriers, trucks carrying or towing artillery and other heavy weaponry, various types of aircraft flying overhead—and thousands of soldiers marching in perfect formation past the grandstand where the commander-in-chief and other high-ranking officers stand to attention.

The 2006 parade was a special occasion because it took place for the first time in the new capital Naypyitaw, or 'the Abode of Kings'. The then commander-in-chief and junta leader, Senior General Than Shwe, declared: 'Our *Tatmadaw* [armed forces] should be a worthy heir to the traditions of capable tatmadaws established by the noble kings Anawrahta, Bayinnaung and Alaungpaya.'[1] Larger-than-life statues of those three warrior kings and rulers of erstwhile empires tower over Naypyitaw's main parade ground as a reminder of the historical heritage on which today's military is based. Or is supposed to be based. A more truthful account of the history of Myanmar's military reveals a very different picture of how it was founded and became what it is today: Myanmar's most powerful institution which has ruled directly or indirectly since it seized power in a coup in 1962.

Modern-day mythmaking can be discerned in the change of the very name of the annual celebrations on 27 March. On that day in 1945, nationalist forces led by Aung San turned their guns against their former Japanese allies, who had invaded the then British colony Burma in 1942. Officially, the Japanese had granted Burma independence on 1 August 1943, but this did not turn out to be the freedom the nationalists had hoped for. The repression was even worse than under the British, and the nationalists contacted their former colonial masters, and the liberation of Burma began.

That element of military history has been gradually changed. In the mid-1950s, 27 March became Resistance Day (Armed Forces Day), a name it retained until a massive popular uprising for democracy in 1988, when it became Armed Forces Day (Resistance Day), and then, under the rule of Senior General Than Shwe, only Armed Forces Day. Three long-dead kings have become role models, not Aung San's and his comrades' struggle for independence in the 1940s.

Most of the young nationalists in British Burma, among them Aung San, were leftists, and their influences came from the communist movements in India and China. In line with that school of thought, they met in a small flat in Barr Street, Yangon, in August 1939 and decided to form a communist party. But because Barr Street is just around corner from Yangon's City Hall, where the British police had a presence, the meeting was moved to a more discreet location, the home of Thakin Ba Hein in Myay Nu Street in Sanchaung, a northern suburb. There, the Communist Party of Burma (CPB) was formed on 15 August.[2] But Thakin Ba Hein, the best-read Marxist among the young radicals, did not become its general secretary. That title was given to Aung San, and some time later, the party decided to send him and his friend Thakin Mya Hlaing (later known as Bo Yan Aung) to Shanghai, where they knew the Chinese communists were strong.[3]

Eager to elude the police, the two young men—Aung San was twenty-five and Thakin Hla Myaing twenty-four when they left in August 1940—stowed away on a ship bound for China in the port of Yangon. But the ship was destined for Amoy (Xiamen in Mandarin Chinese), a coastal city in China's Fujian province,

THE MILITARY

which was occupied by the Japanese. That was not what they had expected, but they found work as English teachers in Kulangsu (Gulangyu), an island within the urban area of Amoy, which served as an international settlement.

Aung San and Thakin Hla Myaing were soon to find out that they were far from safe in Kulangsu. Letters they sent home to their comrades back in Burma were intercepted by Japanese intelligence, who thus managed to track them down.[4] A couple of Japanese agents met Aung San and Thakin Hla Myaing and promised to provide them and their comrades with what they wanted: guns and military training to fight the British. Instead of ending up with Mao Zedong's partisans in the mountains of China, Aung San and Thakin Hla were taken to Tokyo and then to Bangkok, which was not actually occupied by the Japanese. But Thailand had a government that allowed them to operate freely in the kingdom.

Thakin Hla Myaing remained in Bangkok while Aung San returned to Yangon in disguise to recruit men for the independence army they planned to set up with Japanese assistance. Three batches of young leftist nationalists were smuggled out of Burma onboard Japanese ships and brought to Tokyo. A young Burmese drama student in the Japanese capital joined them as well and, by including him, they were now nineteen young men preparing to fight for independence.

Then, in July 1941, a fourth batch of eleven arrived in Tokyo. They came from a rightist, minority faction of the *Dohbama Asiayone* ('Our Burma Association'), the main nationalist movement. Among them was Thakin Shu Maung, later known as Ne Win, the dictator who ruled the country for decades after the 1962 coup. Their arrival caused some concern among Aung San and his comrades, but for the sake of unity, they kept together as much as they could.[5] With the arrival of the fourth and last batch, they added up to thirty young nationalists and, hence, became known in the country's history as 'the Thirty Comrades'. Their leader and instructor was Colonel Keiji Suzuki, the Japanese officer who had apprehended Aung San and Thakin Hla Myaing in Amoy.

After spending some time in Tokyo and undergoing military training on the Japanese-held islands of Formosa (Taiwan) and

Hainan, the group was transferred to Bangkok. They were now actually twenty-eight after the drama student remained behind in Japan and another had died from malaria in Formosa. On 26 December 1941, the survivors gathered for a solemn ceremony in a house in the Thai capital owned by a Burmese doctor. They drew blood from their arms in syringes, and then poured the blood into a silver bowl and mixed it with liquor. All of them drank from the bowl, pledging 'eternal loyalty' among themselves and to the cause of Burmese independence. The Burma Independence Army (BIA) was born, with Colonel Suzuki as commander-in-chief and Aung San as chief of staff.[6]

Recruits were found among Burmese living in Thailand, but the BIA's poorly organised contingents numbered only a few hundred when they, in early 1942, entered Burma on the heels of the Japanese army. Many more though, especially schoolteachers and young nationalists in towns and villages, joined them as soon as they had crossed the border and the BIA soon had thousands of fighters. On 7 March 1942, Yangon was captured with the help of the BIA and the British were driven to the north, and, after heavy fighting, across the border to India in the north-east.

Burma was a colony of many different ethnic groups, and some of them, notably the Karens and the Kachins, remained loyal to the British and deeply resented the Burmese nationalists. With the help of the British, the Karens fought a guerrilla war against the Japanese, and often clashed with the BIA as well. Hundreds of Karens, mostly innocent villagers, were butchered by the BIA, causing a deep-rooted resentment that lingers to this day. In the Kachin Hills in the north, local guerrilla forces aided by the British and the Americans, battled the Japanese. Kachin fighters even prevented the Japanese from advancing north of the town of Sumprabum.

But, before long, the BIA was dissolved by the Japanese and replaced by the smaller Burma Defence Army (BDA), which became the Burma National Army (BNA) after the Japanese-sponsored 'independence' had been proclaimed in 1943. By then it had become clear to Aung San and the nationalists that the Japanese had no interest in saving their country from British colonialism.

THE MILITARY

All that the Japanese wanted was to cut off the supply roads from Burma, through which the British were sending weapons and other supplies to nationalist Chinese forces battling the Japanese in China. Japanese atrocities against Burmese civilians also made the nationalists turn against their new masters.

Thakin Thein Pe and Thakin Tin Shwe, two leftist intellectuals, were sent secretly to Calcutta to let the British know that the nationalists were ready to break with the Japanese. When that happened on 27 March 1945, the BNA was renamed the Patriotic Burmese Forces (PBF), though that name was first used in public during a parade in Yangon on 23 June 1945, which marked the final Allied-Burmese victory over the Japanese.[7]

The British were back, and negotiations for real independence could begin. But Burma was still in turmoil. Thakin Soe, a communist firebrand and diehard Stalinist, broke with the CPB in February 1946, set up his own communist party (Red Flag), and resorted to armed struggle in the Irrawaddy delta. In October that year, the main CPB was expelled from the Anti-Fascist People's Freedom League (AFPFL), a front led by Aung San, and became a vocal critic of the interim administration. The CPB declared that they wanted not the 'sham independence' negotiated with the British, but the establishment of a truly socialist republic. The AFPFL, in turn, was made up of factions that did not always collaborate smoothly with one another.

The Karens were restless and wondered what would happen if Burma became independent—and ruled by the Burmans, who were their enemies even before the British arrived on the scene. On 16 July 1947, they formed the Karen National Defence Organisation (KNDO) to safeguard their interests. A 'goodwill delegation' was sent to London to see if the Karens could have their own, separate nation called Kawthoolei. They were well-received by a few not particularly high-ranking British officers but were given no promises.[8] Even though the Karens had fought bravely against the Japanese, the British did not want to see a break-up of Burma. In fact, Lord Louis Mountbatten, who had led the war efforts in Southeast Asia, favoured Aung San, whom he saw as the only leader capable of keeping Burma together—and that against the wishes of other British officers who wanted Aung San tried for treason because he had joined forces with the Japanese for most of the Second World War.

The fate of the Burman resistance forces had been decided at a meeting in Kandy, Ceylon (now Sri Lanka) in September 1945. A national army should be established consisting of 12,000 men, of which at least 5,200 should come from the PBF, with another 200 PBF soldiers being commissioned as officers.[9] In addition, ethnic Karen, Kachin and Chin units, mostly drawn from the old colonial army but also consisting of men who had fought against the Japanese during the Second World War, would be integrated into the new army, which, according to some historians, became 'a two-winged army, featuring ethnically homogeneous units'—one wing for the Burmans and another for the non-Burmans.[10]

But that left out thousands of former BIA, BDA, BNA and PBF fighters who were not willing to give up their arms. Many of them formed the People's Volunteer Organisation (PVO), which became, in effect, a paramilitary force loyal to Aung San. Other former resistance fighters joined the CPB's Red Guards, which protected its leaders and party headquarters in Yangon's Bargyar Street. And there were more, privately run, militias. According to Mary Callahan, an expert on the Burmese military: 'At the same time, private "pocket armies" were rallying under competing politicians.'[11] The proliferation of guns during the war, Japanese as well as those supplied by the British and the Americans, had made it possible for any influential person to have their own armed force.

Ethnically based armies also emerged in the wake of the Second World War. In the west, U Sein Da, a former Buddhist monk nicknamed 'the King of Arakan', formed an army and began waging guerrilla warfare to regain freedom for Arakan, which had been an independent kingdom until it was conquered by the Burmese in 1785. Muslims living in the same region began propagating in favour of joining the eastern part of the proposed Muslim state of Pakistan. Called *mujahids*, they armed themselves to fight for that cause.

In the east near the border with Thailand, the Karenni, who claimed they had always been independent, proclaimed the United

Karenni Independent State on 11 September 1946. Their claim was based on an agreement signed by T.D. Forsyth, for the British Crown, and Kinwun Mingyi U Khaung, the representative of the king of Burma, according to which 'the state of Western Karenni shall remain separate and independent and that no sovereignty or governing authority of any description shall be claimed or exercised over that state'.[12]

'Western Karenni' referred to Kyebogyi and Bawlake, while the eastern Karenni state of Bawlake had a similar but separate arrangement with the British crown. In reality, however, the three Karenni states enjoyed the same status as the Shan principalities, which were protectorates and as such not part of the actual colony, though still under British supremacy.

In the midst of all this uncertainty, Aung San travelled to London and, on 27 January 1947, signed an agreement with prime minister Clement Attlee.[13] Burma was going to become an independent country, 'within or without the Commonwealth, as soon as possible'.[14] At that time, 'within the Commonwealth' meant having the status of a dominion where the British monarch would remain head of state represented by a governor-general. That practice was broken when India became a republic on 24 January 1950—and stayed within the Commonwealth. In 1947, Burma's political leaders had no desire for their country to become a dominion, which would have incurred the wrath of the CPB as well as many diehard nationalists, so independence at that time meant a republic outside of the Commonwealth.

But before that could happen, Aung San was assassinated. On 19 July 1947, a group of uniformed, armed men burst into the Secretariat, a Victorian-style, redbrick building in central Yangon. They entered a room where the pre-independence cabinet was holding a meeting—and opened fire. The shooting continued for about thirty seconds, and the uniformed men then left the building, jumped into a jeep which was waiting outside and drove away.

Tables and chairs in the meeting room were overturned and soiled with blood. Nine bullet-ridden bodies lay on the floor: Aung San, the chairman of the cabinet; his close friend and erstwhile student leader Thakin Mya; Ba Choe, the former editor of the nationalist *Deedok* journal and now a prominent politician; Razak, a Muslim school principal and politician; Razak's eighteen-year-old bodyguard Ko Htwe; Aung San's elder brother Ba Win; Mahn Ba Khaing, one of the few ethnic Karens who had chosen to participate in mainstream Burmese politics; Sao Sam Htun, the Shan *saohpa*, or prince, of the Shan State of Möng Pawn, who had taken part in efforts to amalgamate the frontier areas with Burma proper; and Ohn Maung, a deputy secretary of the Ministry of Transport, who had come into the room to submit a report just when the assassins struck.

The nation was plunged into grief. Its most competent leaders, who were preparing to run Burma after the British had left, were dead even before the country had become independent. Aung San, the national hero who had led the struggle for independence, was only thirty-two and left behind his wife, Khin Kyi, and three small children: two sons and a two-year-old daughter.

On the same day, the Yangon police arrested U Saw, an older right-wing politician who had been Aung San's main rival for the premiership of independent Burma and charged him with ordering the murders. He was convicted and hanged on 8 May 1948. But doubts remain as to whether he and his gunmen acted alone. It is beyond doubt that some British, who saw Aung San as a traitor because of his alliance with the Japanese during the war, were involved. One of them was Captain David Vivian, who had been selling guns to U Saw, and John Bingley, the British Council representative in Yangon, who U Saw sent letters to after his arrest, asking for money.

Vivian was arrested and sentenced to five years' imprisonment, while Bingley left Burma in a hurry in September 1947 and his whereabouts are unknown. There are also, not surprisingly considering the magnitude and political importance of what had happened, conspiracy theories where Ne Win, one of the Thirty Comrades but not a friend of Aung San, may have instigated the assassinations by telling U Saw that he would become prime minister if only Aung San was out of the way.[15]

U Nu, the deputy leader of the main political party at the time, the AFPFL, took over and became Burma's first prime minister

THE MILITARY

when independence finally came at the auspicious hour of 4.20am on 4 January 1948. In order to appease the ethnic minorities, the post of union president was given to Sao Shwe Thaik, the *saohpa* of Yawnghwe and a prominent leader of the Shans. The timing of the declaration of independence had been carefully selected by the country's astrologers, who even the Western-educated political leaders often consulted. The Union Jack was lowered and the last British soldiers passed the grandstand accompanied by a military band playing 'Auld Lang Syne'.

But rather than enjoying freedom after years of struggle, Burma was thrown into civil war. Without Aung San's neutralising presence on the political scene, the confrontation between internal political and ethnic groups escalated. Thakin Than Tun, the CPB chairman, was Aung San's brother-in-law, and on 12 February 1947, five months before his assassination, he had signed an agreement with the leaders of the Shan, Kachin and Chin ethnic minorities, paving the way for the proposed union of Burma. U Nu, the new national leader, was a devout Buddhist and an outstanding intellectual, but he lacked Aung San's charisma and was hardly the strong ruler the fragile nation needed during its first, difficult years of independence.

The CPB was the first major group to resort to armed struggle after independence. On 2 April 1948, the first shots were fired in what became a communist insurrection lasting until the late 1980s. It began with a skirmish near a small village in Bago north of Yangon and, within only a couple of months, CPB rebels had taken over large parts of central Burma. Troops from the 1st Burma Rifles, one of the units in the newly established post-independence army, joined the rebellion in June and, in July, a faction of Aung San's old militia, the PVO, also went underground and were joined by two platoons of the paramilitary Union Military Police (UMP). In August, 350 officers and soldiers from the 3rd Burma Rifles—led by Bo Ye Htut, one of the Thirty Comrades—went underground as well. Together with other army mutineers, they formed the Revolutionary Burma Army and allied themselves with the CPB.

The armed forces were in disarray, and U Nu's government had to rely on the 4th Burma Rifles headed by Ne Win, which was the only Burman-dominated unit that remained intact and was still loyal to the central authorities—and, somewhat ironically given the historical animosity between the Burmans and the ethnic minorities, units made up of Karens, Kachins and Chins. Naw Seng, a legendary Kachin warrior who had led battles against the Japanese in the northern mountains during the Second World War and later became a captain in the 1st Kachin Rifles of the Burma army, fought against the CPB in the Irrawaddy delta region and the Pyinmana area.

But when Naw Seng was ordered to attack KNDO rebels, who had resorted to armed struggle in January 1949, he and his Kachin warriors switched sides. The Kachins are Christians like many Karens, and Naw Seng had no desire to fight them on behalf of the Burmans. A combined Kachin-Karen force went on a rampage through Burma, capturing cities and towns including Meiktila and Mandalay. Called the 'Upper Burma Campaign', it was one of the most devastating rebel offensives in modern Burmese history. In Meiktila, they took over the air base and got some American pilots who were seconded to the Burmese Air Force to fly them to the hill station of Maymyo (now Pyin Oo Lwin) near Mandalay, one platoon of Karen soldiers in one place and a Kachin platoon in another. From there, they went on to capture Lashio in the northern Shan States and Namkham on the Chinese border.

The outbreak of a Karen rebellion and the mutinies among Burman as well as ethnic regiments had immediate repercussions for the entire structure of the fledgeling Burma army. Lt-Gen. Smith Dun, an ethnic Karen and the commander-in-chief, was dismissed, and so were Wing Commander Samuel Shi Sho, the chief of the air force and also a Karen, and Brig.-Gen. Henson Kya Doe, a Karen who had joined the BIA during the Japanese occupation and after independence had become chief of operations.

On 31 January 1949, Smith Dun was replaced by Lt-Gen. Ne Win, who began building an entirely new army centred on his own regiment, the 4th Burma Rifles. When he took over, Dr Maung Maung, an official, pro-military historian, estimates, 'there were maybe 2,000 soldiers at General Ne Win's disposal, all scattered in decimated, weak battalions and companies'.[16] And U Nu's administration, which Ne Win served, was actually in control of little more than the capital and was therefore aptly referred to as 'the Rangoon [Yangon] Government'—and it was a miracle that it managed to survive.

But massive outside assistance, primarily from India, enabled the authorities in Yangon to rebuild their shattered armed forces. According to U Nu, 'True to his words, Pandit Nehru sent several shipments of arms, without which Burma might never have recovered. Now the unserviceable guns of the combat troops were replaced, and new units raised and equipped. By November 1949, the army, the civilian police, and the UMP felt strong enough to retake towns and villages under rebel occupation.'[17]

While soldiers from the 4th Burma Rifles formed the nucleus of the new army and filled the ranks of the officer corps, many Kachins also joined the military. No fewer than six battalions of the Kachin Rifles were established in 1949–51, followed by a battalion of Kayah Rifles which enlisted Karennis, Shans and other ethnic minorities in the Kayah (Karenni) and Shan States. Many of the new soldiers also came from the Chin minority. Like the Kachins, the Chins were a hardy, warlike hill people who had fought bravely against the Japanese during the Second World War.

Within a few years of the mutinies of 1948 and 1949, the strength of Burma's armed forces had increased to more than thirty thousand, and by 1955, the number was closer to forty thousand. In addition, irregular forces had been drafted into a militia called *Sitwundan* in Burmese, which totalled fifty-two companies and played a large and important part in fighting the insurgents. Burma's passion for raising militias, which began with the PVO, became institutionalised.

The rebels were far from defeated, but they were not going to march into Yangon and overthrow the government. They were on the defensive rather than the offensive and, as victory seemed elusive, their daily struggle was for survival in the areas where they were still holding out. Karen rebels had their strongholds in the Irrawaddy delta region and in the eastern mountains. Smaller bands of Mon rebels were also active in the Thai border areas, and the CPB was active in the delta as well as in the Pegu Yoma mountains north of Yangon, in Sagaing Division in the north-west, and in the jungles and mountains of the Arakan region bordering India and East Pakistan (now Bangladesh).

Thakin Soe's Red Flag communists also had units in the delta and the Arakan mountains. But they were much smaller and less significant than the mainstream CPB. Karenni rebels were active in their area, but were few in number and poorly equipped, as were the *mujahids* in northern Arakan. Naw Seng and his Kachin rebels, however, had retreated into China after being cornered in Möng Ko in north-eastern Shan State in April 1950. Under the terms of independent Burma's first constitution, the Kachins had been given their own state within the union, and most of them seemed content with that—at least for the time being and as long as there was no gross interference in their internal affairs.

But, in the early 1950s, an unexpected threat appeared on the scene in the northern and eastern Shan States, where Shan *saohpas* still ruled their respective principalities. Thousands of nationalist Chinese Kuomintang (KMT) forces, unable to withstand the onslaught of Mao Zedong's communists and cut off from the main force which retreated to Taiwan at the end of the Chinese civil war, crossed into the Shan States and ensconced themselves in the hills surrounding Kengtung and Möng Hsat close to the Thai border.

The KMT recruited soldiers from the border areas, mostly Lahu tribesmen, and gave them military training. Reinforcements were also flown in from Taiwan to the airstrip at Möng Hsat, which had been reconstructed into a formidable air base, capable of receiving C-47 transport planes. The number of KMT troops in the Shan States swelled from an initial 1,700 to more than 4,000, and arms, ammunition and medical supplies were also flown in from Taiwan. This dramatic build-up was a joint venture between the nationalist Chinese government in Taiwan and the United States Central Intelligence Agency (CIA), and the aim was to encircle China and reconquer it from the communists. The 'Secret KMT Army' in the Shan States tried on no fewer than seven occasions between 1950 and 1952 to invade Yunnan but was repeatedly driven back.[18]

Brig.-Gen. Kyaw Zaw, one of the Thirty Comrades and southern commander of the Burmese army, was put in charge of an operation to rid the country of its uninvited guests and fought successfully against them on a number of fronts. The issue was also raised in the United Nations, which, on 22 April 1953, adopted a resolution demanding that the KMT lay down their arms and leave the country. Thousands of KMT soldiers were evacuated by special aircraft and with pomp and circumstance from Lampang airport in northern Thailand—at the same time as more reinforcements were flown in from Taiwan by nightly flights. Thus, the number of KMT soldiers in the Shan States increased to 12,000 by the end of 1953.

The Burmese army failed to defeat the KMT but managed to isolate them in pockets east of the Salween River. The campaign, therefore, was seen as a success, and Kyaw Zaw became a national hero—but also too popular for the egotistical Ne Win. Accused of leaking classified army documents to the CPB, Kyaw Zaw was forced to leave the army in 1956 and officially dismissed from duty on 7 June 1957. No evidence was presented to substantiate the allegations against him, but shortly after his arrest, the army printed an information broadsheet about the campaign against the KMT. It did not even mention Kyaw Zaw. Instead, a smiling Ne Win in a bush hat was there inspecting the frontline troops 'to personally direct operations against KMT aggressors'.[19] Eyebrows were raised in many quarters. Ne Win had not even participated in combat against the KMT; he hardly ever ventured outside Yangon. Every Sunday, he could be seen at the city's racecourse, where he had his own private box.[20]

Rather than fighting the KMT or the rebels, Ne Win and his men from the 4th Burma Rifles spent the latter part of the 1950s building up a power base—and a business empire. In 1951, the Ministry of Defence established the Defence Services Institute (DSI) as a non-profit organisation that could conduct business. The enterprise was controlled by twelve members, all military officers. A general store which distributed consumer goods to members of the armed forces was opened in Sule Pagoda Road in downtown Yangon. There, imported and locally produced goods were sold to army personnel and their families at low prices.

The start-up capital for the project was a loan of 600,000 Burmese kyats, which U Nu's government had provided to enhance the morale of the armed forces. Imported goods were exempt from port fees and import duties as well as domestic taxation. It became a success, and within a few years there were eighteen DSI shops across the country. The institute was able to repay the loan to the government and was soon running its projects independently with its own budget. According to U Thaung, an independent Burmese journalist and analyst:

> The military leaders happy and proud of their achievements learned something wonderful from their business experience. They discovered that a business enterprise without government taxes could yield a great fortune. And the DSI expanded rapidly.[21]

The DSI's second venture was a publishing house whose original purpose was to supply textbooks and writing material to soldiers and their families. It was founded in 1951, and by 1955 it had been expanded into a major stationery store called Aya House. This time, the store was also open to civilians, making it the DSI's first venture into public trade. A new, military-controlled entity called the International Trading House was set up in 1953 with the aim of eliminating civilian contractors in the construction business. Such contractors were allowed to operate, but now they had to go through the army firm, which acted as a kind of middleman, reaping commissions and pay-offs.

Through the DSI, the army soon also owned and controlled Rowe & Co., which sold high-quality foreign goods, the Ava Bank, which was set up after buying up the former A. Scott Bank, the Burma Asiatic Company formed after taking over the East Asiatic Company and, most important of all, the Burma Five Star Shipping Line, a freight service company with a fleet of seven ships.[22] The military also controlled the importation of coal for the railways, electric supplies and inland water transport.

With profits from its own businesses, the military had even funded a newspaper to convey its ideas to the public, the English-language *Guardian*, which had been established in 1955 by Brig.-Gen. Aung Gyi from 4th Burma Rifles, and the pro-military historian Dr Maung Maung. The paper's editor, however, was Sein Win, one of Burma's leading and best-respected journalists.

THE MILITARY

In order to bring greater professionalism into the armed forces, the Defence Services Academy (DSA) was set up in 1955 in Maymyo (now Pyin Oo Lwin). It was modelled on America's West Point and the original classes—or 'intakes', as they became known—were given the basics of parliamentary democracy and received university degrees after four years of training. The recruits came from those who had distinguished themselves as outstanding pupils while at high school. Another training facility, the Officers Training School (OTS), was set up at Hmawbi just north of Yangon. It provided more basic in-service training for officers who were rising through the ranks. A one-year course at Hmawbi was sufficient to receive a commission in the army.

In January 1955, it was decided to integrate the *Sitwundan*—or what remained of it after several units had joined the communist insurrection—into the main army as a type of infantry force which became known as the Burma Territorial Force. But the idea of relying on support from self-sustaining militias was not abandoned. In October that year, the government introduced another paramilitary outfit known as *Pyusawhti*. The programme involved township, village and mobile units and the recruitment involved armed groups led by provincial political bosses, who employed local people as a basis for exercising authority. Their semi-autonomous status created difficulties for state security leaders, who encountered problems in controlling the *Pyusawhti*.[23]

The military was becoming a state within the state, but few Burmese paid much attention to it. After all, the vast majority of the population had faith in the democratic system, the constitution and the rule of law. In June 1958, Ne Win had also declared:

> There may be some of our comrades who find their personal attachments to some political leaders too strong. If they find their personal feelings in conflict with duty, they should resign from the Tatmadaw. We ourselves shall serve the people and uphold the constitution. We should work under any constitutionally established Government. We would also, on our part, request the leaders of the Government to respect the constitution, and call on us to render only those services which are in keeping with it.[24]

So who could possibly think that Ne Win, less than four years later, would stage a coup, overthrow a democratically elected government and establish a brutal military dictatorship that was to last for decades? But the military's first taste of actually governing the country came in 1958. The ruling AFPFL had split into two rival factions, U Nu's main 'Clean AFPFL' and the 'Stable AFPFL' led by two prominent socialists, Ba Swe and Kyaw Nyein. The situation was further complicated by the surrender of two thousand PVO insurgents. They almost immediately formed a legal political organisation, the People's Comrade Party, and proposed to contest the elections under a communist-style programme (the CPB had been formally outlawed in October 1953).

On 26 September, U Nu spoke to the nation over Radio Rangoon and solemnly announced that he had invited Ne Win to 'assume the reins of government...due to the prevailing situation regarding security and law and order'.[25] The nation was stunned. Had a 'parliamentary coup' taken place? The AFPFL had split and U Nu's government had been further destabilised during a vote of no confidence before the announcement. Whatever the reason for U Nu's move, army officers from across the country met in the garrison town of Meiktila south of Mandalay and, on 21 October, adopted a policy declaration titled 'The National Ideology of the Defence Services' with the rather curious subtitle 'The Constitution of the Union of Burma'.[26] A week later, on 28 October, Ne Win inaugurated what was called a 'Caretaker Government' headed by himself and vested with extraordinary powers. The declaration stated:

> Ever since their Conference in 1956 the Commanding Officers of the Defence Services have all thoroughly studied and discussed the National Ideology which must be the ever-fixed guiding star of the Defence Services. After the Defence Services Conference, held in Meiktila on 21 October 1958, they did as first phase in ideological development, unanimously adopt the Statement of the Defence National Ideology and pledged their unfaltering support. With the adoption of this Statement of the Defence of National Ideology, the Defence Services acquired a sense of purpose and direction. A psychological regeneration

took hold of the Defence Services personnel and stirred among the people as a whole. The people, with spirits uplifted, march beside the Defence Services. This is a military and psychological achievement...this change is the result of the decisive leadership of the Government and the firmly established ideological convictions of the Defence Services.[27]

The essence of that 'National Ideology' strongly resembled the *dwifungsi* concept of the Indonesian military. The idea that the military has a 'dual function' in society—both to defend the country and to play a dominant role in politics and economic development as well as in the socio-cultural field of the nation—was first articulated in Indonesia by Gen. Abdul Haris Nasution in a speech in 1958 and later turned into a national doctrine. In accordance with this view, the military is the only institution capable of holding the country together. And it would be prepared to do so, even with the force of arms if the situation in the country was seen as drifting towards what the military would consider chaos.

Ne Win's Caretaker Government included Brig.-Gen. Aung Gyi, Brig.-Gen. Tin Pe, Col Kyaw Soe and several other close associates of Ne Win, mainly from the 4th Burma Rifles. Even if ordinary democratic rules had been set aside, the policies of the Caretaker Government were not entirely unpopular. The streets of Yangon and other cities were cleaned up, the civil service seemed to be more efficient than before, and more rebels surrendered to the central authorities. Officially, 3,618 insurgents 'returned to the legal fold', as the authorities liked to state it, while 1,872 had been killed, 1,959 wounded and 1,238 captured alive.[28] Those figures may have been grossly inaccurate and inflated, but they showed that even the military believed the insurgencies were more or less over, and a propaganda leaflet, produced by the Caretaker Government, stated that Parliament had given Ne Win 'the mandate to restore law and order in the country and also create the conditions that would be conducive to holding free and fair elections as soon as possible'.[29]

Elections were indeed held in April 1960 and U Nu was once again sworn in as prime minister. By the time the Caretaker Government had finished its term in office, it had expanded its initial business enterprises in retail and publishing to include a single coal import license, a hotel company, fisheries and poultry distribution businesses, a construction firm, a bus line that carried thousands of passengers daily between Yangon and Mandalay, and the country's biggest department store chain.[30] The DSI's gains were consolidated into a new entity called the Burma Economic Development Corporation (BEDC), which was set up after an act had been passed in parliament in May 1961. It divided the twenty-five companies owned by the DSI into two groups: some firms would be run under the aegis of the BEDC while the DSI would continue to control others directly.[31]

The prime minister and six board members who were appointed by the president were officially in charge of the BEDC, and some of them turned out to be military officers. While it appeared that the new set-up was subjected to civilian oversight, U Thaung argues that:

> the Act was a big achievement for the army. The DSI would continue to keep the money-making firms in their grip, and unremunerative projects under the BEDC. These groups would work together with the bureaucrats from the Burmese civil service, concerned with providing money, and all of them controlled by the army.[32]

The transformation of the military to a state within the state was nearly complete. Large parts of the economy were in the hands of the army and there were 104,200 men in all three services. But there was a major challenge that the military had yet to address—and that came from the country's many ethnic minorities. To them, it was becoming clear that the 1947 constitution, which was adopted six months before independence, had to be revised, not in order to dissolve the union—that was not what they demanded—but to satisfy their desire to enjoy greater autonomy in their respective areas. But to the military, such thoughts were perceived as a threat which had to be dealt with.

In June 1961, Shan and Kachin leaders met in Taunggyi for what was called an 'All-States Conference'. The delegates issued a statement saying that:

the conference expressed the desire that a National Convention, composed of all nationalities in the whole Union, be immediately called at an appropriate place to ensure the development and prosperity of the Union of Burma; for better and closer relationship of the peoples of the states within the Union; for consultation with one another on the question of equality of all citizens of the Union.[33]

Sao Shwe Thaik, Burma's first president and a prominent leader of the Shans, became a major spokesperson for what became known as the Federal Movement. He submitted a proposal to loosen the federal structure of the constitution, not in order to see the country fall apart, but to strengthen it by giving the frontier areas a larger say in their own as well as national affairs.

But not everyone would be satisfied if those areas were granted only wider autonomy. One of U Nu's promises before the April 1960 elections was to make Buddhism the state religion of Burma, and that was seen by the predominantly Christian Kachins as an open provocation against them and their beliefs. On 5 February 1961, three Kachin brothers—Zau Seng, Zau Tu and Zau Dan—formed a group called the Kachin Independence Army (KIA) with the stated aim of establishing a 'free republic of Kachinland'.[34] But, like *Noom Suk Harn*, a band of young Shan nationalists who had resorted to armed struggle in 1958, it was fairly small and had strongholds only in the Lashio-Kutkai area of northern Shan State. *Noom Suk Harn*'s poorly armed soldiers were based near the border with northern Thailand.

Nevertheless, there were signs of unrest in the frontier areas which could escalate into something bigger if not contained by legal means. In February 1962, the government convened the Nationalities' Seminar in Yangon to address that issue and the future status of the frontier areas, or the Constituent States, as they were now called. All the government ministers, Members of Parliament, heads of the Constituent States and their State Ministers were in attendance and U Nu was hopeful about the outcome of the meeting.

The military had other plans, however. In the early hours of 2 March 1962, troops moved in to take over strategic positions all over the capital. About 2am, U Nu was arrested in his home in Pyidaungsu Lane. Five other ministers, the chief justice and over thirty ethnic leaders were also taken into custody. Among them was Sao Shwe Thaik, who was led away by armed guards, never to be seen again. Another prominent Shan leader, Sao Kya Hseng, the *saopha* of Hsipaw, disappeared within days of the coup. He had attended the parliament in Yangon the day before the military takeover and travelled to the north to visit relatives. Both Sao Shwe Thaik and Sao Kya Hseng are believed to have been extrajudicially executed shortly after their arrests.[35]

The shootout at Sao Shwe Thaik's house on Kokine Road also claimed another victim. His seventeen-year-old son Sai Myee was gunned down as he came running down the stairs and saw the soldiers apprehend his father, and, as his brother Chao Tzang later recalled, 'He was, it could be said, the first of the many thousands of unarmed young citizens of Burma killed with calculated coldness by the military regime.'[36]

Despite the murder of Sai Myee and the disappearances of Sao Shwe Thaik and Sao Kya Hseng, many Burmese still seemed to believe that the takeover in March 1962 would be only a repeat of the 1958–60 Caretaker Government. The international community by and large shared this view—though a rare exception was a CIA analyst who predicted with remarkable foresight as early as in 1951:

> [There is a] current struggle for control of the armed forces between the government and the army commander-in-chief, General Ne Win. For some time, the government has been attempting to undermine Ne Win's dominant personal position within the army. Ne Win may retire completely from the struggle and leave the government in undisputed control. On the other hand, there is a continuing possibility that Ne Win might attempt a military coup, which would lead to protracted violence.[37]

And that was precisely what happened after the coup. The rapid expansion of the armed forces in terms of troop strength throughout the 1950s, the wealth that the officers had accumulated since independence, and, behind the scenes, the military leadership's

THE MILITARY

growing interest in politics meant that Ne Win and his men were prepared to make the move from running a state within the state to taking over the entire state. It did not take long for people to realise that this was not 1958. In sharp contrast to the legalistic approach of the 1958–60 Caretaker Government, when Ne Win had frequently appeared in parliament to answer questions and had even petitioned it to allow him to rule for more than six months, this time the military dissolved the parliament, abrogated the 1947 constitution, and ruled by decree. It was becoming obvious that the military was there to stay and did not intend to hand power back to any civilian government.

The Revolutionary Council, the junta that was set up after U Nu's democratically elected government was overthrown, introduced a new economic system called 'the Burmese Way to Socialism'. But rather than establishing a socialist regime reminiscent of those in Eastern Europe, the Soviet Union, North Vietnam, North Korea or China, Ne Win's rendition saw everything nationalised and taken over by twenty-three military-run state corporations. Military coups were not uncommon in Asia at that time, but the difference in Burma was that the military seized not only political but also absolute economic power. The seeds sown by the DSI had blossomed into an economic system that was entirely in the hands of the military.

While the economies of Thailand and Indonesia, for instance, blossomed because the military entered into marriages of convenience with indigenous plutocracies, Ne Win took Myanmar in a completely different direction. The old business community, which was mainly of Indian and Chinese origin, had their properties and assets seized by the military, driving hundreds of thousands out of Burma into India, Thailand, Singapore and Taiwan.[38]

Burma's new power structure consisted of Ne Win at the top of the pyramid, and under him a stratum of loyal, second-generation officers who had also held positions in the 1958–60 Caretaker Government: Aung Gyi, Tin Pe and Kyaw Soe, all formerly of the 4th Burma Rifles, plus some from the 3rd Burma Rifles and others who had served under Ne Win in the high command in Yangon.

The Revolutionary Council was even referred to by many as 'the fourth burifs government'.

After the student movement had been silenced, at least temporarily, in July 1962, the country's once lively and vibrant press were next in line. Privately owned newspapers were nationalised and several editors ended up behind bars. In their place, the military launched its own daily newspaper, the *Loktha Pyithu Nezin* in Burmese and the *Working People's Daily* in English. At the same time, the military took over the *Guardian*, already an organ for the army, and the left-wing *Vanguard* offered itself for nationalisation.

Meanwhile, the military began to formalise its rule—and its peculiar brand of socialism. In February 1963, the state officially took over the production, distribution, import and export of commodities, as well as the banks. Then, on 28 March 1964, all political parties except the Burma Socialist Programme Party (BSPP), which the military had set up after the coup, were banned and all Buddhist organisations had to be registered with the new government. The military was taking no chances. It had to be in control of everything from commercial activities to the country's political and social institutions.

Ne Win gradually established, at his Ady Road residence on a peninsula in Inya Lake in Yangon's northern suburbs, an almost absurd, anachronistic replica of the old Burmese monarchy. In many ways, it also resembled a Byzantine-style court with intrigues, deep distrust, nepotism and a mixture of bizarre characters and bright young officers. Significantly, one of the few men Ne Win trusted was his Indian cook, Raju, who had served him since the days of the 4th Burma Rifles. Ne Win, always fearful of being poisoned, entrusted only Raju with the task of preparing his food. But even Raju had to taste it first, in Ne Win's presence. Raju always accompanied Ne Win on his many trips abroad, and his closeness to the general gave him unique opportunities to make a fortune. Whenever someone wanted to buy land, build a house or needed a quick government decision on an important matter, a few banknotes in Raju's pocket could open any doors. While tasting the day's meal in front of Ne Win, Raju would casually remark on what he had been paid to say.

THE MILITARY

A nod of approval from the general would mean that a deal had been struck. In this extraordinary way, the cook Raju became one of the most influential power-mongers in the country.

And if the 1962 coup had been meant to prevent the country from being overrun by the insurgents—which was one of the officially stated reasons for the takeover—it turned out to be counterproductive. The rebellion that had broken out among the Kachins in 1961 in areas of northern Shan State spread to Kachin State, and the KIA took over most of the north. The even smaller rebellion among the Shan escalated into full-scale war as several bands grouped together to form the Shan State Army (SSA) in 1964. The first chairperson of its War Council was Sao Shwe Thaik's widow, Sao Nang Hearn Hkam, who had managed to flee to Thailand after the coup.

The Burmese Way to Socialism had, hardly surprisingly, led to economic collapse—and a flourishing black market with neighbouring Thailand. That became a blessing in disguise for some of the ethnic rebels, notably the Karen National Union (KNU), which set up tollgates along the border between Thailand and Burma, where consumer goods going in one direction and minerals and forest products in the other were taxed. With the income generated from the cross-border trade in contraband, the rebels could buy guns and other necessities on what is euphemistically called 'the black market' in Thailand. As a result, the KNU and other rebel armies became much better equipped and more heavily armed than they had been before 1962.

As the year 1968 was ushered in, the civil war took another, dramatic turn. Right after midnight on 1 January, hundreds of men armed with automatic rifles, machine guns and bazookas stormed across the border with China at Möng Ko in north-eastern Shan State and overran the small garrison guarding the place. It was Naw Seng, the Kachin warrior, who had come back, but not, as before, to fight for Kachin rights. He and his Kachin comrades were accompanied by Khin Maung Gyi, a Moscow-educated CPB political commissar—and Chinese volunteers who made up the bulk of the unit that had crossed into this remote corner of Burma. It was the beginning of a grand plan: the Chinese, long wary of the ambitious and unpredictable general who had seized power in Yangon, had decided to give all-out support to the CPB.

A group of 143 Burmese communists had trekked over the mountains into China in the early 1950s and been allowed to stay at Chengdu in Sichuan. But they were not given any material support for their struggle as long as U Nu was the prime minister of Burma. Meanwhile, Naw Seng and his Kachins who had retreated into China—also at Möng Ko—in 1950 had been staying at a people's commune in China's Guizhou province. The Burmese communists, most of whom were urban intellectuals, needed fighting men to go with them into Burma, so the Chinese brought the two groups together. They formed the nucleus of the new CPB that was going to set up a base area along the Chinese border and, from there, push down to the Pegu Yoma and other old base areas in central Burma. But because the new fighting force was still quite small, thousands of volunteers—mostly Red Guards who had become active during the Cultural Revolution—were sent to join them.

During the decade 1968–78, the Chinese poured more aid into the CPB effort than into any other communist movement outside Indochina. Unlike the old units in the Pegu Yoma, who were dressed in Burmese longyis (sarongs) and sandals and were armed with little more than old Second World War-era rifles and shotguns, the new troops in the north-east had new Chinese uniforms with red stars on their caps, and were well-equipped with modern Chinese weapons: semiautomatic and automatic rifles, light machine guns, 12.7mm anti-aircraft guns, 60, 82 and 120mm mortars, and 75mm recoilless rifles. Radio equipment, jeeps, trucks and petrol, rice, other foodstuffs, cooking oil and kitchen utensils were also sent across the border. The Chinese even sent a truckload of detailed military maps, covering all the border areas and parts of central Burma. The Chinese also built hydroelectric power stations at Möng Ko as well as Panghsang, the headquarters of the north-eastern forces. A clandestine radio station, the People's Voice of Burma, was officially inaugurated on 28 March 1971, the twenty-third anniversary of the CPB's uprising, and began transmitting from the Yunnanese side of the frontier in April.

THE MILITARY

Within a couple of years, the CPB had managed to wrest control of a 20,000-square-kilometre base area in north-eastern and eastern Shan State, plus a smaller area along the Chinese border in Kachin State. But the plan to push down to Burma proper and eventually seize power in Yangon did not materialise. The Burmese military soon realised that it lacked the capacity to defeat the CPB in the north-east—so it turned on all the 'old' base areas in central Burma where the communists were poorly armed and ill-equipped. By the late 1970s, all those base areas had been captured, and the CPB became isolated in the areas in Shan and Kachin States which they had captured, but where the party's future, if any, would not lie. After the Chinese volunteers were withdrawn in the late 1970s, the 'new' CPB army consisted mostly of hilltribe recruits for whom ethnic conscience, not communist ideology, was what motivated them to fight.

The fight against the CPB had nevertheless prompted a further build-up of the country's armed forces. By 1976, the number had risen to 160,000, organised in a series of battle-hardened Light Infantry Divisions which were constantly on the move, fighting the CPB or Kachin, Karen, Shan and other ethnic insurgents. But in order to strengthen and preserve military rule, Ne Win also built up one of Asia's most ruthless as well as efficient secret police forces. Military Intelligence Service (MIS) was known throughout the country down to the lowliest non-English-speaking peasant as 'MI' (*em-eye*). Even if executions of political opponents were the exception rather than the rule, anyone suspected of having contacts with opponents of the regime was likely to be arrested and tortured while in jail. The MIS also had its own prison and torture centre, the infamous Yay Kyi Aing ('Clearwater Pond') near Yangon's Mingaladon airport.

The MIS kept a watchful eye not only on the country's ordinary citizens, but especially on army officers with liberal ideas—a surveillance which apart from rotations, corruption and institutionalised brutality contributed to the remarkable cohesiveness of Burma's armed forces—and on the many politicised Burmese exiles living in Britain, West Germany, Thailand, Australia and the USA. Among the Burmese community abroad, no one was ever sure who was an informer and who was not; for many years, mutual suspicion neutralised them as a political force.

The origin of MIS and its methods can be traced back to the Japanese occupation of Burma, 1942–45. Donald Seekins, a professor of Southeast Asian Studies at Meio University in Okinawa, argues that, because of Tokyo's policy of self-sufficiency in its occupied Asian territories, the large numbers of Japanese soldiers in Burma—300,000—essentially lived off the land. The Japanese secret police, the Kempetai, conducted a reign of terror, which was so harsh that even the head of the pro-Japanese puppet government, Dr Ba Maw, had to intercede with the highest military commanders to curb the worst excesses, and eventually, it prompted Aung San and his nationalists to ally themselves with the British.

But, according to Seekins, part of the legacy of the alliance with the Japanese is that the Burmese army adopted similar methods, among them brutal counter-insurgency tactics: 'There are more than superficial resemblances between the Tatmadaw's [the Burmese military] "Four Cuts" policy against ethnic minority rebels (to…deprive rebels of recruits, funding, supplies and information) and the Japanese army's *sanko seisaku* or "three all" policy in China ("kill all; burn all; destroy all").'[39]

It is hardly a coincidence that Ne Win—the architect of the Four Cuts policy—was trained by the Kempetai and other sections of Japan's security forces. Lt-Col James McAndrew of the US military states in his study of Burma's military intelligence apparatus:

> Chosen for both "guerrilla tactics and clandestine activities" and "special" leadership training was the future dictator and long-time strongman, Ne Win. Significantly, this curriculum included intelligence training provided by Kempetai, the brutal Japanese Military Police and counterintelligence organisation. Being selected for training by the Kempetai is more than noteworthy in hindsight, and it must be viewed as an important early demonstration to Ne Win that maintaining coercive intelligence and counterintelligence organisations were essential to maintaining authoritarian rule.[40]

THE MILITARY

The importance of having a loyal secret police service first became obvious to Ne Win and his inner circle just over a year after the 1962 coup. An Anglo-Burmese captain named Kyaw Swa Myint—known as 'Johnny Liars' in English—tried to assassinate Ne Win, whose dictatorship he believed had ruined the economy. The attempt failed and Kyaw Swa Myint fled to Thailand, from where he made his way to Australia. His wife, mother and sisters, who remained in Burma, were jailed and tortured while the armed forces were purged of Anglo-Burmese officers.

By the early 1970s, the military felt it had to formalise its rule. The first step came in 1971, when the BSPP's control over the military was set down in the 'Organisation Rules for the Burma Socialist Programme Party'. Party committees were established within the military and organising committees headed by military officers were set up in the General Staff Office as well as in regional commands, divisions, garrisons, base commands, battalions and companies.[41]

Then, in December 1973, a referendum was held for a new constitution, but the 'voting' hardly met any acceptable, democratic standards. There were two boxes in the polling booths—white for 'yes' votes and black for 'no' votes—which indicated how the people were expected to vote. The boxes were hidden behind a screen, but placed in different corners of the polling stations, and there was a fifteen-to-twenty-centimetre gap between the floor and the screen, so officials could easily see how the people voted.[42] Not surprisingly, 90.19 per cent of the electorate voted in favour of the new constitution, which provided for a one-party socialist state.

When the new constitution was promulgated on 3 January 1974, military officers changed their uniforms for civilian clothes—and Ne Win became the country's president. Despite wording such as 'socialist democracy is the basis of state structure', the military controlled the BSPP and its subsidiary organisations, and the military, the BSPP and the administration was under the control of Ne Win. That was, in short, the actual power structure that had emerged. It was a highly centralised military dictatorship with a paper-thin socialist veneer. In effect, the military had done away with the old social and political power structure and established itself as the new ruling class. It had its own housing, hospitals, shops where they could buy goods which were not available in ordinary stores, and special schools for the children of military officers.

But there were challenges as well. Violence against unarmed civilians in the 1970s combined with the failure of the so-called 'Burmese Way to Socialism' had led to discontent even within the armed forces. A bright young captain called Ohn Kyaw Myint began plotting against Ne Win's dictatorship. Ohn Kyaw Myint was a University of Rangoon graduate who had completed OTS Batch 29 with the best cadet award. He went on to become the personal assistant to the then army chief, Gen. Kyaw Htin. Ohn Kyaw Myint, though, saw what direction the nation was heading in politically as well as economically, and he and his comrades came to the realisation that there was no other solution to Myanmar's problems than to overthrow the Ne Win regime.

But it did not go as planned. The MIS became aware of the plot and, on 2 July 1976, Ohn Kyaw Myint went to the residence of the United States ambassador in Yangon. The young captain told the ambassador about the abortive coup attempt and asked for political asylum—but was turned away and arrested shortly afterwards.

Government media made no mention of the attempted coup until 20 July, when the Burma Broadcasting Service issued a bulletin stating that eleven captains and three majors had been arrested for plotting to assassinate Ne Win and other state leaders. Also arrested were two colonels who were charged with dereliction of duty. Several of those arrested were DSA graduates, which shows the possible extent of the plot.

The trial began in September and, to the surprise of many, former army chief Gen. Tin U appeared in the prisoners' dock. He was charged with having prior knowledge of the coup attempt but failing to inform the military authorities. On 11 January 1977, Tin U was sentenced to seven years hard labour and imprisonment according to the Crime Against the State and High Treason Act. The actual reason for his arrest and punishment is believed to have been that students who had demonstrated against the regime in March 1976 had shouted 'Long Live General Tin U!'

The coup plotters had been asked who they would have liked to see as leaders of the nation if they were to be successful and, apparently, they had mentioned Tin U, who was popular among the general public, and Brig.-Gen. Kyaw Zaw, the army veteran who had been purged in 1956. But arresting one of the Thirty Comrades could have been seen as too extreme even for Ne Win's military. Kyaw Zaw left Yangon just before the announcement of the arrest of Ohn Kyaw Myint and travelled with family members to the north. They crossed the border with China near Namkham—and about a month later, Kyaw Zaw's voice was heard on the CPB's clandestine radio, denouncing the Ne Win regime. He had joined the communist resistance movement in the north-east.

About 200 Tin U supporters were brought in for questioning and, in November 1976, Ne Win announced publicly that more than 50,000 BSPP members and cadres had been dismissed. During the party congress that followed in February 1977, forty-two central committee members lost their seats. On 27 July 1977, Ohn Kyaw Myint was executed, while about a dozen of his co-conspirators were given long prison sentences.[43]

The 'Ohn Kyaw Myint affair', as it became known, was over, but Ne Win realised that, in order to avoid anything similar from happening again, his secret police apparatus had to be strengthened. His intelligence chief for many years was his devoted subordinate Brig.-Gen. Tin U—not to be confused with General Tin U. 'MI' Tin U was trained by the CIA on the Pacific island of Saipan in 1957 and, by 1961, had become Ne Win's aide-de-camp and was almost regarded as Ne Win's adopted son.[44]

At the time, Rodney Tasker characterised MI Tin U in the Hong Kong weekly *Far Eastern Economic Review*:

> He and his MIS colleagues were men of the world compared with other more short-sighted, dogmatic figures in the Burmese leadership. They were able to travel abroad, talk freely to foreigners and generally look beyond the rigid confines of the corrupt regime…although known to be ruthless, he built up a reputation as a gregarious, open-minded, charismatic figure—a direct contrast to some of his mole-like colleagues in the leadership.[45]

But then, in May 1983, the Burmese government suddenly, and totally unexpectedly, announced that MI Tin U had been 'permitted to resign' along with the Home and Religious Affairs minister and also a former intelligence chief, Col Bo Ni. They had been purged ostensibly because their wives were corrupt—a charge that could be brought against any army officer in Burma. MI Tin U and Bo Ni were subsequently jailed—and the entire MIS apparatus purged as well.

The reason behind the move, however, remained a matter for conjecture. It was suggested at the time that the urbane MIS people had become too powerful for comfort and almost managed to establish another state within a state—which threatened Ne Win's inner circle of hand-picked, less-than-intelligent yes-men.

Whatever the reason behind the purge, it had immediate effects on the security situation in the country. On 9 October 1983, twenty-one people, including four visiting South Korean cabinet ministers, were killed in a powerful explosion in Yangon. Three North Korean military officers were behind the atrocity. One of them was killed in a shootout with Burmese security forces, while the other two were captured alive. One of the bombers was executed in 1985, while the third remained in Yangon's Insein Jail until he died from liver cancer on 18 May 2008. His life was spared because he had turned witness to the prosecution and revealed all the secrets behind the planning and execution of the bombing.[46]

Observers at the time believe that the incident would never have taken place if MI Tin U had still been in charge; it clearly indicated that the military intelligence apparatus was no longer what is used to be. A new intelligence chief, Khin Nyunt, was appointed in 1984. His Directorate of the Defence Services Intelligence (DDSI), the successor to MI Tin U's secret police, soon became almost as efficient as the old outfit. Khin Nyunt in many ways also resembled MI Tin U; he was fairly young, relatively bright and he could be exceedingly ruthless whenever this was considered expedient by his mentor, the old strongman Ne Win.

Khin Nyunt, who had served as first secretary in the post-1988 junta, was appointed prime minister on 25 August 2003—and was ousted on 18 October 2004. He was sentenced to forty-four years in prison on various corruption charges but was allowed to serve his time under house arrest instead of behind bars. The entire DDSI was purged in a drive reminiscent of the ouster and purge of MI Tin U and his men in 1983, and many of Khin Nyunt's closest associates ended up in prison. Like the old intelligence boss, Khin Nyunt had built a state within the state, and that was unacceptable for Than Shwe and the top military leadership. It did not help that Khin Nyunt and the DDSI had played an important role in crushing the 1988 uprising, tracking down and arresting pro-democracy activists—and been the architect of the ceasefire agreements that were agreed upon in the late 1980s and early 1990s. He had become too powerful for his own good and had to go.

It would, from the top generals' point of view, be unthinkable to let any elected civilians meddle in such internal military affairs, which explains why they were staunchly opposed to any attempts to amend the 2008 constitution—and why they, in the end, decided to stage a coup and reassume absolute power of the state and all its institutions.

All army officers also know where the skeletons of past atrocities are buried, both in the frontier areas and also in the urban centres, home to an emerging and growing middle class. Min Aung Hlaing is widely loathed across the population for his ruthless post-coup clampdown and killings, and he and his companions know all too well that they either maintain power at any price or land in prison—or worse. As an old saying goes, 'if they don't hang together they fear they will hang separately'. It is a combination of those fears and deeply entrenched economic interests that holds the military so tightly together and not, as some Western analysts have suggested, some underlying sense of patriotism or because officers have been hardened through battles in the field. And that also explains why, so far, no cracks have emerged within the military despite the violent, irrational and seemingly self-defeating orders being handed down by officers and carried out by seemingly unswervingly obedient foot soldiers.

In the old days, the military was also an extremely brutal force committing numerous and often unspeakable atrocities on the civilian population in the frontier areas. At the same time, it was actually quite poorly armed—but, despite all that, a battle-hardened and largely effective light infantry force. Soldiers were constantly on the move, and there were fights against the CPB, the Karen on the Thai border, the Kachin in the far north and other pockets of resistance in ethnic minority areas.

All that changed after the 1988 pro-democracy uprising. The main fear within the Tatmadaw leadership was that disgruntled soldiers might join the pro-democracy activists and that, in turn, would be the beginning of the end of military-dominated rule in Myanmar. Consequently, in order to prevent a crack in the ranks, everything was done to keep at least the officer corps satisfied.

Beginning in 1989, the Tatmadaw spent more than a billion dollars on procuring new, more sophisticated military equipment. It came primarily from China but also from Singapore, Pakistan and Israel. Most of it, however, was materiel that Myanmar did not actually need, such as missile systems that would be of little use in counter-insurgency operations, huge tanks, armoured vehicles, naval patrol boats and various kinds of radar equipment. It was simply toys for the boys, and the troops also got new, smart uniforms. Before long, Myanmar's own defence industries began producing new infantry rifles to replace the old, heavy G-3, which was based on German designs.

Equally important was a decision to scrap the previous, unpopular system of constant rotations of regional commanders, which had been done in order to make sure that no such officer built up his own power base in a certain part of the country. And then came a series of ceasefire agreements between the military and a number of ethnic rebel armies. Those agreements, initiated by Khin Nyunt, worked as there was never any linkup between the ethnic rebels and the urban dissidents of 1988 that had any impact on the political situation in the country.

But, to be on the safe side, the size of the military was increased dramatically. The three services—the army, the air force and the navy—amounted to no more than 195,000 men before 1988. Nearly all of them belonged to the army; the air force as well as the navy were very small and, many would argue, almost insignificant. According

THE MILITARY

to the London-based International Institute for Strategic Studies and other international think-tanks, the army now has 507,000 men, the air force 23,000 and the navy 19,000, so altogether 549,000 in total.[47] Those think-tanks may have grossly overestimated the strength of the military because most units are undermanned and many troops may exist only in official reports from the field.

Be that as it may, it is undeniable that the strength of the armed forces in terms of manpower and equipment is way above that of the 1980s. But, because of the old ceasefire agreements, which lasted for nearly two decades, there is also a generation of troops with very limited fighting experience. They are, as a source said, better at parades showing off their new uniforms and guns than at combat. And then, the embrace of the market economy that followed the 1988 uprising gave the officers ample opportunities to earn vast amounts of money.

As one Myanmar source wrote on social media: 'the army officers are only interested in taking bribes and making business deals with the cronies, they don't want to fight battles anymore, they joined the army to get rich quickly'.[48] Or, as a retired Myanmar army officer once told this writer: 'luxury when I was in the army consisted of a badminton set and a bottle of army rum, and I was a colonel. Now even captains and lieutenants have more than one car, several sets of golf clubs, and at least two mistresses. And they don't have to fight.'[49]

That changed again when, in June 2011, the ceasefire with the KIA broke down. For the first time in more than a decade, major battles raged in an ethnic minority area—and the military performed extremely poorly. In the beginning, they sent in the infantry, which was inadequately trained and had limited fighting experience. Casualties were extremely heavy as the advancing troops were mowed down by KIA guerrillas. It became so bad that the military leadership had to withdraw its infantry and rely instead on its Russian-supplied helicopter gunships, attack aircraft and heavy artillery fired from bases far from the KIA's positions. According to credible reports from Yangon at the time, some officers paid bribes to avoid being sent to Kachin State to fight.[50] This was not the armed forces of the 1970s or the 1980s.

Then came another fierce war in Rakhine State as a new rebel force, the Arakan Army (AA), rose up in arms. Military deaths and wounded personnel numbered in the thousands, including some senior officers. And, again, the infantry's poor performance prompted the military to resort to air power, firing indiscriminately into villages where they thought the AA would be present, but to no avail. Today, the AA and its civilian wing run a de facto parallel government in Rakhine State.

The AA is closely allied with the Ta'ang National Liberation Army, a Palaung force, and the Myanmar National Democratic Alliance Army, which is made up of fighters from Kokang, an area in north-eastern Shan State dominated by ethnic Chinese. Judging from independent reports, those three armies, called the Brotherhood Alliance, have fought what appear to be numerous successful battles with the Tatmadaw. According to a November 2020 paper published by the United States Institute of Peace, 'Myanmar has not experienced this intensity of fighting in decades.'[51] Nor has the Myanmar army suffered such heavy casualties.

The 'new' Myanmar army is entirely different from the one founded by Aung San in the 1940s. Of the legendary Thirty Comrades, two—Bo La Yaung and Bo Taya—commanded the PVO rebellion. Three—Bo Zeya, Bo Ye Htut and Bo Yan Aung—joined the CPB when the communist insurrection broke out shortly after independence. Only Brig. Kyaw Zaw, Gen. Ne Win and Maj. Bo Bala remained in the army in the 1950s. Four of the others—Bo Let Ya, Bo Yan Naing, Bohmu Aung and Bo Setkya—rallied behind the right-wing resistance, which the ousted prime minister U Nu organised on the Thai border in the 1960s. And, in late 1976, as we have seen, Kyaw Zaw, once the most popular commander in the army who had been pushed out by Gen. Ne Win in 1956, went underground and joined the CPB.

Even the 4th Burma Rifles tradition now belongs to history. A new generation of army officers who worship Anawrahta, Bayinnaung and Alaungpaya has emerged, but, as any serious study of history would reveal, those kings, though they may have been excellent warriors and conquerors, were very bad state builders.

THE MILITARY

The empires they established were poorly organised and never lasted more than a couple of reigns under weaker successors. The kings lost their conquests because they established few administrative institutions—other than those responsible for tax collection—and depended solely on military might to control the people they had subjugated. That is the Myanmar military of today, and that is why it is never going to be able to establish a union consisting of the country's many ethnic groups, or even crush the post-coup resistance against its rule. Three medieval warrior kings cannot possibly serve as role models for a functioning, modern state.

3

THE ETHNIC JIGSAW

The military's decision to change the name of the country from 'Burma' to 'Myanmar', which was announced on 18 June 1989, caused a great deal of confusion. The military claimed that 'Burma' was a name given to the country by the British colonial power. 'Myanmar', on the other hand, was said to be a more indigenous name and, it was later claimed, it encompassed all the 135 'national races' of the country. In Burmese, however, the country has since independence in 1948 been called 'Myanmar Naing-Ngan', or 'the State of Myanmar' and, in more colloquial usage, 'Bama-Pyi', 'the Land of the Bama'.

The two names have been used interchangeably throughout history, and the national anthem, which was sung at official functions and in schools from 1948 to 1989, contained the lines *Gaba ma kyae, bama-pyi, do bo bwa a mwae sit mo chit myat no bae, ga ba ma kyae, bama-pyi, do bo bwa a mwae sit mo chit myat no bae*, or, in English 'Until the world crumbles, bama-pyi, the land of our ancestors, our true inheritance, the land we cherish, the land of our ancestors.'[1]

If 'Myanmar' meant all the different nationalities within the country's present borders, how could there be, according to the Myanmar Language Commission, a 'Myanmar language'?[2] Adding to the confusion was that the name *bama* was still retained after

1989 for the country's main ethnic group, the Bamars, or Burmans or Burmese in English.

The best explanation of the difference between *myanmar* (or more correctly *myanma*, since there is no 'r' sound in modern Burmese) and *bama* is found in the old *Hobson-Jobson* dictionary, which despite its rather unorthodox name remains a useful source of information: 'The name [Burma, Burmah] is taken from *Mran-ma*, the national name of the Burmese people, which they themselves generally pronounce *Bam-ma*, unless speaking formally and emphatically.'[3] Evidently, Burma and Myanmar mean exactly the same thing, and one name does not include any more ethnic groups than the other.

But the confusion is an old one and, when the Burmese nationalist movement, called the *Dohbama Asiayone*, was established in the 1930s, there was a debate among the young activists as to what name should be used for the country: the formal, old royal term *myanma* or the more colloquial *bama*, which the British had corrupted into 'Burma' and made the official name of their colony. The nationalists concluded:

> Since the *Dohbama* was set up, the movement always paid attention to the unity of all the nationalities of the country...and the *thakins* noted that *myanma naingngan*...meant only the part of the country where the Burmese lived. This was the name given by the Burmese kings to their country. But this is not correct usage. *Bama naingngan* is not the country where only the *myanma* people live. It is the country where different nationalities such as the Kachins, Karens, Kayahs, Chins, Pa-Os, Palaungs, Mons, Myanmars, Rakhines, Shans reside. Therefore, the nationalists did not use the term *myanma naingngan* or *myanmapyi*, but *bama naingngan* or *bamapyi*. All the nationalities who live in *bama naingngan* are called *bama*.[4]

Thus, the movement became the *Dohbama Asiayone* ('Our Burma Association') and not the *Dohmyanma Asiayone*. The slogans of the *Dohbama* were (in English translation): 'Bama-pyi is our country, bama-sar is our literature, bama-saka is our language, love our country, raise the standards of our literature, respect our language.'[5]

THE ETHNIC JIGSAW

Half a century later, the country's military decided that the opposite was true. All those contradictions reflect an inescapable fact that many Burmese rulers, and others, are still reluctant to acknowledge: there is no term in any language that covers both the majority Bamars (or Burmese) and the minority peoples, since no such entity existed before the arrival of the British in the nineteenth century. Burma, or Myanmar, as we know it with its present boundaries, is a colonial creation rife with internal contradictions and divisions.

Myanmar may not have as many as 135 'national races', but the country is nevertheless the home of a multitude of ethnic groups, and successive post-independence governments—as well as forces that for decades have resisted central authority—have all failed to create the shared sense of nationhood and belonging that everyone has been talking about since even before independence. And the figure '135' has more to do with numerology than reality, as the digits add up to nine, the military's lucky number, which also symbolises fulfilment and unity. The army was founded on 27 March 1945, and the military stepped in to reassert power after crushing the 1988 pro-democracy uprising on 18 September. The name change occurred on 18 June 1989, and the first election was held on 27 May 1990. Ceasefire talks between the military and some ethnic rebel armies began in Naypyitaw at 9am on 9 September 2015. From 1987 to 1989, Burma even had banknotes in denominations of 45 and 90 Kyats.

And then it is unclear what the military means by 'national race'. The concept of 135 (1 + 3 + 5 = 9) national races was first advanced in the early 1990s, but those precise ethnicities were not specifically identified at the time. Myanmar expert Martin Smith wrote in his 1994 study 'Ethnic Groups in Burma: Development, Democracy and Human Rights' that the then junta, the State Law and Order Restoration Council, mentioned '135 national races' but 'has produced no reliable data or list of names'.[6]

One of the earliest references to 135 national races was in an article written by an unnamed 'Tatmadaw officer' in the 7 August 1991 issue of the official organ *Working People's Daily*. 'The fact that there are 135 national races living in Myanmar…is a hindrance to the idea of drafting a constitution based on the "big concept",' the officer wrote. The seminal article's underlying, though not overly stated, premise was that all major ethnic groups should be split into smaller subgroups to avoid recognition of and negotiations with 'big races' such as the Shan, Karen, Kachin, Chin, Mon, Rakhine and Kayah (Karenni). Those groups have their own 'ethnic' states within the Union of Myanmar, but there was no difference in status between them and the ethnic Burman Divisions, which now are called Regions.

The first official list of the 135 national races was produced just prior to the 2014 election, but it does not, as some military spokesmen asserted at the time, date back to the British colonial era. The 1931 Census of India, the last census conducted during British rule and while Burma was still a province of British India, lists nineteen ethnic groups, including people of Indian and Chinese descent, plus 'others'.[7]

The 2014 list is a major undertaking of ingenuity. There are supposed to be a dozen different 'national races' in Kachin State, nine in Kayah State, eleven in Karen (now called Kayin) State, fifty-three in Chin State, thirty-three in Shan State, seven in Rakhine State, one in Mon State and nine separate Bamar groups. Ethnic lines are blurred in nearly all the classifications. The Shan State list, for instance, has a group called 'Tai Long' and another identified as 'Shan Gyi'. But Tai Long is Shan for 'big Shan' and Shan Gyi is Burmese for—'big Shan'.

In Kachin State, the Hkakhu is classified as a separate ethnic group, although it refers to people living 'up the river', or above the confluence of the Mali Hka and Nmai Hka Rivers, which form the Irrawaddy. Gauri is a clan rather than a separate 'race'. The list of fifty-three national races in Chin State is an actual compilation of various dialects spoken among the Chins. The rest of the racial list is similarly fanciful in its creation of separate races from coherent ethnic groups. And all of them are ostensibly 'Myanmars'.

But all this wrangling with names and terms is not just a matter of semantics. Apart from splitting up major ethnic nationalities into an abundance of smaller groups, the military has also, somewhat contradictorily, tried to create an entirely new, purportedly unifying 'Myanmar' identity.

THE ETHNIC JIGSAW

The Dutch academic Gustaaf Houtman calls this development the 'Myanmafication of Burma', and describes it as a move away from the original idea of a 'unity in diversity', and the establishment of a federation based on ethnic lines, which was agreed upon between independence hero Aung San and the leaders of the ethnic minorities in talks in the 1940s.[8] The military has now replaced that idea with their own interpretation of the meaning of the name 'Myanmar' and what it entails for the various peoples of the country.

It was not only the country that was given a new, official name, in 1989. There were name changes in the ethnic minority areas, especially in Shan State, as well. Pang Tara, Kengtung, Laihka, Hsenwi and Hsipaw, place names that have a meaning in Shan, were renamed Pindaya, Kyaington, Laycha, Theinli and Thibaw, which sound Burmese but have no meaning in any language. The spelling of names of Kachin, Karen and other non-Burmese personalities in official documentation follows the same pattern. It is obvious that 'Myanmafication' equals Burmanisation. And that is precisely what it is meant to be.

Even if the correct number of nationalities in Myanmar is closer to twenty than 135, the British still left behind an ethnically diverse country with artificial borders and where the peoples in the periphery have throughout history tended to perceive the Burmese kingdoms as hostile powers which have always tried to conquer them.

No authoritative history of the country's many ethnic nationalities has ever been written, but most historians accept the theory that the Burmans, or Burmese, migrated south from the Tibetan plateau and settled in the Irrawaddy plain between the ninth and eleventh centuries. The Burmese migrants were an agrarian people who established small, relatively self-sufficient villages but, in the beginning, no kingdoms or empires.

But some of their leaders became more powerful than others. Those kings began to expand their respective lands, and the first clash with non-Burmese neighbours was with the Mons, or Talaings, a people closely related to the Khmers of present-day Cambodia. The Mons had been living in the coastal areas in the south long before the arrival of the Burmese, and they were the first to come into direct contact with Indian civilisation, adopt Theravada Buddhism, develop a written script and adapt Indian law to their local needs.[9]

The Burmese, under the leadership of King Anawrahta, conquered the Mon kingdom in the south in 1067. More than thirty thousand Mon scholars, religious leaders, artisans and slaves were brought back to Anawrahta's capital Pagan (now Bagan). Under the influence of those subdued Mons, the hitherto rustic Burmese were uplifted socially and culturally, and Pagan grew into a grand city with thousands of pagodas. The Burmese also adopted Buddhism from the Mons and learned their alphabet, which was modified and used to write their own language.[10] The Mons gradually assimilated into their new environment and many of them became indistinguishable from other subjects.

Anawrahta established what became known in history as the First Burmese Empire, which, however, crumbled in the late thirteenth century because of pressure from the Mongol empire in the north, conflicts with the Shans in the east and, in the south, Mons who were resisting attempts to subjugate them. The First Burmese Empire subsequently broke up into a number of smaller kingdoms. The rulers of the most powerful of those, the Kingdom of Ava (now Inwa), tried to re-establish control over the territories which had been lost, but failed.

It was not until the 1486–1531 reign of King Minkyinyo of Toungoo that a new empire, known as the Second Burmese Empire, was established, although many scholars attribute that achievement to his more dynamic son Tabinshwehti. He reigned from 1531 to 1550 and consolidated and expanded his domains but was defeated when he tried to conquer the Siamese kingdom of Ayutthaya in the east. A period of unrest and rebellions among other conquered peoples followed, and Tabinshwehti was assassinated by Mon rebels in 1550.

Tabinshwehti's brother-in-law and successor Bayinnaung, who reigned from 1551 to 1581, captured Pegu from the Mons and made it his royal capital. The city prospered and Bayinnaung became the ruler of one of the largest empires in Southeast Asian history.

THE ETHNIC JIGSAW

It stretched as far east as modern-day Thailand and Laos, and from Shwebo in the north to Dawei in the south. But Bayinnaung's attempt to conquer the Arakan kingdom in the west failed and he died in 1581. Bayinnaung's weaker successors had to face uprisings in several parts of the realm, and the Second Burmese Empire gradually disintegrated. The Burmese were forced to withdraw from the Lan Na Kingdom in the north of today's Thailand, which had been a tributary state, while the Kingdom of Ayutthaya invaded Tenasserim (now Tanintharyi).

It was during this period that the Burmese first came into contact with Europeans. Tabinshwehti as well as Bayinnaung employed Portuguese mercenaries because they knew how to use artillery and muskets. Portuguese soldiers of fortune assisted those two kings as well as their successors in their wars, but some of them grew powerful and began to act independently. One was Felipe de Brito, who served as ruler of Arakan during the first successful Burmese invasion of that kingdom in 1599 and then gained control of the port of Syriam (now Thanlyin) opposite today's Yangon, where he tried to establish his own independent realm. De Brito initially enjoyed cordial relations with the Mons, who were prepared to recognise him as king of Syriam with full honours. But many Burmese as well as Mons in the region turned against him because of his pompous and self-important behaviour, which included the plunder of Buddhist pagodas and plans to convert his subjects to Christianity.[11] Syriam was occupied by the Burmese, and de Brito was executed by impalement in 1613. Most of his officers were also killed, while others were taken to the north, where they served in the king's army as musketeers, retained their Catholic beliefs and formed their own distinct community.[12]

What remained of the Toungoo Dynasty and its weakened Second Burmese Empire moved from Pegu to Ava in the north in 1634. It was not until 1752 that a new, strong-willed monarch appeared on the scene, and that was Alaungpaya, the third of the warrior-king role models for the Myanmar military. He was the first king of the Konbaung Dynasty and the founder of what became the Third Burmese Empire. Alaungpaya also moved the capital to his hometown, Moksobomyo, which he renamed Shwebo (literally

'Golden Chief'). He conquered land as far south as the town of Dagon, which he renamed Rangoon (now Yangon), meaning 'end of strife'. Pegu was conquered in 1757, and that marked the end of the last separate Mon kingdom. Alaungpaya's military expeditions took him as far west as Manipur in north-eastern India. But he failed to conquer Ayutthaya and died in 1760 as he and his forces were retreating into Tenasserim.

According to Myanmar scholar Donald Seekins: 'An exemplar of warlike Burman values, historians believe that Alaungpaya's reign marked the beginning of polarisation between the Burmans and the ethnic minorities, especially the rebellious Mons. Earlier kings, such as Bayinnaung, were great admirers of Mon culture. Lower Burma was largely depopulated by Alaungpaya's campaigns.'[13]

Alaungpaya was succeeded by his son Naungdawgyi, who spent most of his short reign, from 1760 to 1763, suppressing multiple rebellions across his kingdom. He was only twenty-nine when he died of illness. The next king, his brother Hsinbyushin, reigned until 1776 and was best known for his wars with China and Ayutthaya. In 1767, his forces even managed to occupy Ayutthaya, which was sacked and burned.

As usual after a conquest, a huge booty was carried back to the motherland. It consisted of gold and weaponry—and thousands of artisans, musicians and even members of the Siamese royal family. The captives were resettled in Ava, where traces of their artistic skills can be seen even today. The Kyauk Taw Kyi Temple, despite being built in conventional Burmese architectural style, features Ayutthaya-influenced mural paintings, which are believed to have been created by 'Yodia people', or artisans who were brought there in 1767.

The destruction of Ayutthaya made the Siamese move their capital to a place closer to the coast, where it could be more easily defended. The first location was Thonburi on the west banks of Chao Phraya, and then, in 1782, the capital was moved to Bangkok on the eastern side of the river. That became the seat of the Chakri Dynasty, the founders of modern Siam, which was renamed Thailand in 1939.

The Konbaung kings waged several other wars against their neighbours. In 1784–5, King Bodawpaya's troops conquered and subdued the Arakan kingdom. A huge Buddha statue, the Maha Muni ('Great Sage'), was brought to a temple near the present-day city of Mandalay, where it is still being kept today.

The fall of the Arakan kingdom was followed by a military expedition to Manipur in 1819. Burmese troops looted every house in sight and killed men, women and children. Thousands of others were marched off to Amarapura (Bodawpaya's new capital, before it was moved back to Ava in 1823) as slaves and were resettled in villages where many of their descendants remain. The Manipuris brought with them certain types of silk weaving that were considered the most exquisite in Burma. Descendants of those captives, known as *kate*, also became renowned astrologers.

In Manipur, the Burmese kept only as many local people as were needed to grow rice and produce food for their garrison. But the Manipuris fought back as well and, whenever possible, bands of armed men ambushed the occupying forces. The period from 1819 to 1826 is known in Manipuri history as *Chahi Taret Khuntakpa*, or 'the Seven Years of Devastation', and still evokes bitter memories.

The attempts to expand the Third Burmese Empire to the west put troops in direct contact with a more powerful force: the British in India. What is called the First Anglo-Burmese War lasted from 1824 to 1826 and marked the beginning of the end of Burmese independence. The Burmese were commanded by a skilled military officer named Maha Bandula, who had planned to subjugate not only the small kingdoms in today's north-eastern India but also British Bengal. That was a huge mistake. The British, with their superior firepower, pushed him back and came within sixty kilometres of Ava, threatening the new capital. In April 1825, Maha Bandula was killed in a battle at Danubyu in the Irrawaddy delta.

Bagyidaw, who had succeeded his grandfather Bodawpaya after his death in 1819, was forced to sign the Treaty of Yandabo on 24 February 1826. He had to cede Arakan and Tenasserim to the British—and recognise British dominance of Manipur and Assam. Bagyidaw had to pay a million-pound indemnity to the British and agree to the establishment of diplomatic relations between Ava and Calcutta (the then capital of British India). The Third

Burmese Empire was in decline and the British colonisation of Burma had begun. Arakan and Tenasserim came under rule from British India, and colonial administrators—and businessmen with a focus on extracting teak and exporting rice—arrived in those captured territories.

A series of legal and commercial disputes between the British and what was left of independent Burma led to a Second Anglo-Burmese War in 1852. Again, the Burmese were defeated and the British gained control over most of lower Burma, including Rangoon. The Burmese called it Yangon, but that was because of changes in the pronunciation of certain letters of the alphabet. The Burmese have two letters for the sound 'y': *ya gaut* and *ya palait*. But *ya gaut* was once an r and has remained so in the more archaic dialects spoken in Arakan and Tenasserim, from where the interpreters came. So, in English, it became 'Rangoon', not 'Yangon'.

The Third Burmese Empire was now landlocked, losing its trade ports. But it continued to prosper and became partly modernised under the dynamic King Mindon, who reigned from 1853 to 1878. In 1857, he founded a new capital at the foot of Mandalay Hill. Scholars were sent to France, Italy, the United States and Britain to study the industrial revolution that was taking place there. He improved the efficacy of the civil service, introduced a new system of tax collection and made efforts to professionalise the military. But he also had to face rebellion plotted by two of his own sons and escaped an assassination attempt.

One of Mindon's queens, Hsinbyumashin, came to dominate the last years of his reign, and she ordered all possible heirs to the throne to be killed so that her daughter Supayalat and son-in-law Thibaw would become the next king and queen. All potential heirs were slaughtered, and Hsinbyumashin got her way. Thibaw ascended the throne after Mindon's death in 1878, but it was actually Supayalat who ruled the country. She was also his half-sister, as both were children of Mindon but by different mothers. Thibaw had two more wives, Supayagyi and Supayalay, who were Supayalat's sisters and therefore also his half-sisters.

THE ETHNIC JIGSAW

Palatial intrigues and moral decay further weakened the kingdom, and it ceased to exist altogether after the Third Anglo-Burmese War in 1885. That began with a decision made by the government in Mandalay, the new capital of independent Burma, to impose a fine on the Bombay Burmah Trading Company for illegal extraction of teak from the forests around Toungoo. Lord Dufferin, the Viceroy of British India, sent an ultimatum to Thibaw, the king in Mandalay, demanding a settlement to the dispute, and that Britain would take over Burma's relations with foreign countries.

Thibaw refused, and his fate was sealed. On 14 November, British troops entered Mandalay, the last of Burma's royal capitals. Thibaw and two of his queens, Supayalat and Supayalay, were apprehended and sent into exile in India. The third queen, Supayagyi, and Hsinbyumashin, the mother of the three sisters, were also taken away, but to Tavoy in the south-east. Those humiliating events marked the rather inglorious end of the Third Burmese Empire, and Burma was made a province of British India.

Meanwhile, the French had extended their sphere of influence over Laos in the east. In between lay the wild and rugged Shan Hills with an abundance of principalities and local rulers. Sir Charles Crosthwaite, British Chief Commissioner of Burma from 1887 to 1890, described the situation in this manner:

> Looking at the character of the country lying between the Salween and the Mekong, it was certain to be the refuge of all the discontent and outlawry of Burma. Unless it was ruled by a government not only loyal and friendly to us, but thoroughly strong and efficient, this region would become a base for operations of every brigand leader and pretender where they might muster their followers and hatch their plots...To those responsible for the peace of Burma, such a prospect was not pleasant.[14]

To avoid the emergence of an uncontrollable buffer between the two colonial powers, the British extended their Burmese conquest to the Shan States, which were 'pacified' over the years 1885–90. Apart from preceding the French and keeping them at bay on the other side of Mekong, the British also wanted to control trade routes from Burma to China, which passed through the north-eastern border areas of the Shan-inhabited territory. In the final years of the nineteenth century, the British even surveyed the possibility of constructing a railway from Burma through the northern Shan States to Yunnan. Henry Rudolph Davies, the army officer who was in charge of the project, argued that 'the eventual object of any railway scheme now proposed must not be merely to encourage local trade across the Burma frontier, but the attainment of a through route from India to Ssu-ch'uan [Sichuan] and to Eastern India'.[15] The plan never materialised, mainly because parts of China were completely lawless and ruled by local warlords.

The conquest of Burma was complete, but the new colonial possession brought together peoples with nothing, or little, in common—or with a long history of conflict and hostility. Among them were the Karens, who had suffered more at the hands of the aggressive Burmese kings than any other people in the region. They were treated as inferiors and, unlike the Mons, discouraged from intermingling with the Burmese. During the time of the kings, the Karens who lived under direct rule were forced to provide corvée labour for their masters, and heavy taxes were imposed on them.[16] There were frequent raids into unadministered Karen territory by the politically better organised lowland Burmese. Many references are made in Karen folklore to hardship and suffering experienced during their history.

Before the arrival of the British, the Karens had no political organisation of their own, and most of them were not fully integrated into any governmental system. Karen historian San C. Po describes their situation as that:

> of a subject race in true Oriental fashion. They were treated as slaves, hence, they made their homes on the mountain-side or on tracts of land far away from the towns and larger villages occupied by the Burmans. High stockades surrounded those Karen villages, and sure death was the fate of all intruders.[17]

This situation was soon to change, and that change began, improbably enough, in Salem, Massachusetts. In 1810, the state's

THE ETHNIC JIGSAW

Congregationalists and Presbyterians decided to set up the first overseas American missionary society, the American Board of Commissioners for Foreign Missions, and, on 6 February 1812, its followers were called to a historical service in the huge barnlike Tabernacle Church in Salem. More than two thousand devoted Christians attended the event and six of them were set aside 'for the sake of Christ and the promotion of His Kingdom in some Asiatic Field'.[18] More than six thousand dollars, a huge amount of money at that time, was collected for the undertaking. Members also donated food, including cartloads of New England gingerbread, for the missionaries to eat during their voyage to 'some Asiatic field' of which they had no knowledge and, once there, would not know what to expect.

On 19 February, their ship, the *Caravan*, set sail from Salem harbour. Four months later, the missionaries reached Calcutta. Among them were Adoniram and Nancy Judson, a young newlywed couple. For reasons that are not entirely clear, the Judsons converted to Baptism while in India and decided to move to southern Burma. As soon as the Judsons arrived there—and to their great surprise—Karens came down in hordes from the hills to welcome them. Although the Judsons had not been aware of it, there were in Karen folklore obscure references to a 'white brother' with a 'holy book' and a god called 'Y'we':

> The Karen was the elder brother,
> And obtained all the words of God (Y'we),
> God formerly loved the Karen nation above all others,
> But because of their transgressions, He cursed them,
> And now they have no books.
> Yet He will again have mercy on them,
> And love them above all others.
>
> God departed with our younger brother,
> The white foreigner.
> He conducted God away to the West.
> God gave them power to cross waters and reach lands,
> And to have rulers from among themselves.

Then God went up to heaven,
But he made the white foreigners,
More skillful than any other nation.

When God had departed,
The Karens became slaves of the Burmans.
Became sons of the forest and children of poverty;
Were scattered everywhere.
The Burmans made them labour bitterly,
Till many dropped down dead in the jungle,
Or they twisted their arms behind them,
Beat them with stripes, and pounded them with the elbow,
Days without end.[19]

The origin of this astonishing song is uncertain, but the reference to a 'white brother' could indicate that the Karens had met Nestorian Christians in China while migrating south from Mongolia, which is believed to be their ancestral homeland. Whatever the reason, it made the Judsons' work much easier than they could ever have expected. The Judsons baptised thousands of Karens, and the Baptist church gained a solid foothold in the Karen hills.

For the first time in history, many Karens now had a chance to attend schools. The colonial power was not, as some historians believe, behind this development. On the contrary, the British viewed the activities of the missionaries with deep suspicion because they wanted all tribal territories, which were often located near sensitive border areas, to come under their administration rather than being controlled by dubious and unreliable spiritual organisations.

But the British did not miss the opportunity to take advantage of these recently converted minorities. Once educated and strengthened spiritually, the Karens did not hesitate to strike back at their traditional enemies in the plains. They willingly fought alongside the British against the Burmese in all three Anglo-Burmese wars. When Burma was made a province of British India, many Karens were recruited into the army and the colonial police.

THE ETHNIC JIGSAW

The promotion of 'His Kingdom' in 'some Asiatic field' gave the Karens a new life; a common creed instead of scattered beliefs in the power of spirits; a written language and their own literature. With this came self-esteem and ethnic pride. Significantly, one of the first institutes of higher learning in Burma was Judson College, which was founded in 1894.

At one time, Christian Karens numbered nearly a quarter of the student body at the University of Rangoon, while they were only a few per cent of the total population of Burma.[20] Colin Metcalfe Enriquez, a British army officer, commented on the Karen during British rule:

> Owing to the missionaries' activities, the Karens are often better educated than the Burmans…and they have been taught to cooperate and cultivate their racial individuality…their outside affections…are reserved for the British. They have no delusions of Home Rule. The more anti-British the Burmans become, the more passionately loyal are the Karens.[21]

The Karen took no part in the political activities of the Burmese, but a Karen National Association (KNA) was established as early as in 1881—the first political organisation in British India. The KNA was set up four years before the Indian National Congress, and more than twenty-five years before the Burmans formed the Young Men's Buddhist Association, their first political organisation. The KNA was dominated by Christian Karens although they never actually made up more than 15 per cent of the Karen population in Burma. And Christians have dominated their political movement ever since, primarily because their education has been superior to that of Buddhist and animist Karens.

Under the colonial regime, many Karens migrated from their hills in the east to the Irrawaddy delta, which was being opened for rice cultivation by the British. These lowland Karens became the most assimilated: many adopted Buddhism as well as Burmese customs and social habits. Even so, the Christians, mostly Baptists but including a fair number of Roman Catholics, were represented in major delta towns such as Bassein, Henzada and Myaungmya—and whether Christians or not, the Karens developed a new consciousness during the colonial era and were no longer willing to accept a subordinate position. The first demands for a separate Karen state were raised in 1928 by Sir San C. Po, one of the best educated Karens at the time: 'The Burmans have the whole country to themselves. Where have the Karens a place they can call their own?...a "Karen Country", how inspiring it sounds!'[22]

According to the 1931 Census of India, there were 1.37 million Karens in Burma, or nearly 8 per cent of the population at that time—a significant increase from earlier estimates. But the name 'Karen' actually includes a number of different tribes, of which the Sgaw by the end of colonial rule had become the largest and most widely dispersed. They were found all over the Irrawaddy delta, from the area around Prome down to the Arakan coast in the west and the hills along the Thai border in the east.

The other main tribe, the Pwo, lived almost exclusively along the seacoast from Arakan down to Mergui in Tenasserim Division, where they intermingled with the Mons. A third subgroup, the Bwe, were found in the vicinity of Toungoo and in the territory extending from the foothills east of that city into the Karenni states bordering Thailand. The Karennis (literally 'Red Karen'), now called Kayah, are yet another Karen subgroup, and so are the Kayan, or Padaung, who are known for their tradition of elongating the necks of the women with brass rings. The majority of Kayan are Roman Catholics with only a few Baptists and Buddhists among them. The Pa-Os, a Karen-related people who live mainly in southern Shan State but also in Thaton in central Burma, are predominantly Buddhist.

Besides the Karen tribes and subgroups, the Shans are the most numerous of Burma's many ethnic groups. They formed 7 per cent of the population in the 1930s and are not related to any other ethnic group in Burma. The word 'Shan' is actually a corruption of 'Siam' or 'Syam' and is the name given to them by the Burmese; the letter 'm' becomes a nasal 'n' as a final consonant in the Burmese language. The Shans call themselves 'Dtai' (sometimes spelled 'Tai') and they are related to the Thais, the Laotians, the Hkamti in Arunachal Pradesh and the Tai Dam ('Black Tai') of northern Vietnam. In southern and western Yunnan, they are known as Dai.

THE ETHNIC JIGSAW

The origin of the Tai peoples, as they are collectively called, is still a question of academic controversy, but the emerging consensus among scholars in many fields is that they most likely were among the highly diverse groups living in the monsoon regions south of the Yangtze River, especially in Guangxi and Guizhou provinces, before the expansion southwards of the Chinese empire in the second century BCE. In subsequent centuries, as China's southern border fluctuated with the ambitions and weaknesses of succeeding dynasties, some Tai groups were absorbed into the mainstream, while others achieved semi-independence under Chinese suzerainty. But many, perhaps most of them, emigrated south and westwards, where they set up independent principalities and kingdoms of their own.

The western group, those who were later referred to as the Shans, descended along the Salween River into the vast high plateau of north-eastern present-day Burma. They settled in the valleys between ridges on both sides of the river and established an abundance of principalities, varying in size and importance. The smallest, Namtok, measured thirty-five square kilometres and was inhabited by a few hundred peasants scattered in three tiny villages, while the largest, Kengtung, encompassed 32,000 square kilometres, roughly the same area as Belgium, and had a population of several hundred thousand.[23]

The thirty or so Shan States were never effectively united, but for a short while after the fall of the First Burmese Empire in the late thirteenth century, the Shans overran most of upper Burma and established their rule over the other ethnic groups. Burma scholar Josef Silverstein writes: 'The Shans were direct political rivals of the Burmans for control over the entire area from that period until 1604, when they ceased resisting and accepted indirect rule by the Burmans.'[24]

But despite increasing pressure from the Burmese kingdoms in the plains as well as Burmese military presence in some of the principalities, the Shan hereditary chiefs, or *saohpas* (*sawbwa* in Burmese), managed to retain a large degree of sovereignty. Neither Burma nor China was ever able to achieve effective conquest of the fiercely independent Shan princes and their states.[25] Like their Thai and Laotian cousins, the Shans are Theravada Buddhists with their own script, history and centuries-old literature.

The Shan people, and the numerous hill tribes who inhabit the mountains surrounding their valleys, are today found on all sides of the borders in this region: in Burma, Thailand, Laos, China and even in north-western Vietnam. There are also Shans in Kachin State, primarily in Bhamo, Waingmaw and Hopin, and in the valley around Putao (Hkamti Long) in the far north of the state, which was also once ruled by a local *saohpa*. In addition, there were two Shan states in north-western Burma: Singkaling Hkamti and Hsawnghsup (corrupted in Burmese to 'Thaungdut').[26]

Because the Shan States were protectorates and administered separately from Burma proper, the Shans were not affected by the Burmese nationalist movement, which grew strong in the 1920s and, especially, in the 1930s. Burmese influence was negligible and British presence was confined to a chief commissioner in the administrative centre of Taunggyi and a few political officers in the more important states. Administration and law enforcement were in the hands of the *saohpas*, who had their own armed police forces, civil servants, magistrates and judges.[27] In essence, *saohpas* enjoyed a status somewhat similar to that of the maharajahs and other rulers of the Indian princely states.

In 1922, the British created the Federated Shan States, and for the first time the Shan area gained a governing body common to all the principalities. The Federated Shan States' Council was established, comprising all the ruling princes and the British governor in Yangon. The council dealt with such common concerns as education, health, public works and construction. Peace and order were established in the area for the first time in many centuries. In addition to the hereditary *saohpas*, there were also *ngwegunhmus* ('tax collectors') and *myosas* (literally 'town eaters', or another kind of tax collector), who either inherited their titles or were appointed by the *saohpas* to oversee local administration in towns and villages.

But very little was done to exploit the rich natural resources of the area and uplift it economically. The major economic preoccupation of the British in Burma was to develop the lowlands into a granary and rice exporter for India. The colonial epoch meant peace and stability for the Shan States, but it was also a period of economic and political standstill. The situation was even more backward in the hills surrounding the Shan valleys. These highlands were inhabited by a variety of tribes, mostly of Tibeto-Burman stock—Kachins, Lahus, Lisus and Akhas—who were comparatively recent arrivals in the area.

The movement of Kachins from the mountains of southern China and eastern Tibet was still going on when the British entered the area in the early twentieth century. But there were also tribes that had been there at least as long as the Shans, if not since before them, such as the Mon-Khmer-speaking Palaungs and Was. The Palaungs, who lived mainly in Tawngpeng State in the north, developed into relatively prosperous tea-growers and adopted Buddhism and elements of Shan culture.

The Wa, on the other hand, were still head-hunters well into modern times. The wild hills they inhabited east of the Salween River, adjacent to the Chinese frontier, were never fully conquered by the British. According to British researcher G.E. Harvey:

> Throughout history the only administered areas on either side of the Burma-China frontier were the valleys and a few main routes. The hills were No Man's Land, even for the Chinese, and the Wa massif was especially terra incognita. Nobody ever went there and even the approaches were dreaded, the Salween and Mekong valleys being malaria-ridden. Chinese officers regarded the whole area as a penal station.[28]

It was not until 1937 that the British stationed two officers in the Wa hills to introduce some light administration.

But such conditions could not stop the missionaries. Vincent Young, whose family had been active among the Lahu in Kengtung, dared to venture into the Wa Hills in the 1930s to spread the gospel. He and his Wa converts romanised one of the major Wa dialects and compiled a translation of the Bible in 1939. He was also active among the Wa on the Chinese side of the border and founded a church and a missionary school in Menglian in Yunnan.[29] But most Wa remained animist while some living close to the

Shans adopted Buddhism, the Shan language and Shan customs. A few chiefs, among them the ruler of Möng Lun, even proclaimed themselves *saohpas*.

In the north-easternmost corner of the Shan States was another area over which there was virtually no central control: a district called Kokang, which was inhabited by ethnic Chinese of Yunnanese stock. Kokang's mountains are some of the most strikingly beautiful in Southeast Asia; shrouded with mile-high clouds during the rainy season, they strongly resemble traditional Chinese scroll paintings. But the magnificent landscape has always contrasted starkly with the austere life in its villages. The Kokang Chinese live at an altitude where not even dry paddy farming is practicable, and they have traditionally had to depend on various cash crops—tea, corn or opium—to buy rice from the more developed valleys.

The local opium trade was controlled by other Chinese groups, mostly immigrants from Yunnan. Many of these came from the Muslim, Panthay, minority of southern China, descendants of Kublai Khan's Arab and Tartar soldiers who settled in the Dali area of Western Yunnan and married local women.[30] The Panthays (called *hui* in China) remained a distinct community and, in 1855, they rose in rebellion against the emperor in Beijing. The fighting blocked Yunnan for nearly two decades, and it was eventually crushed with a heavy loss of life.

Tens of thousands of Yunnanese Muslims were butchered when Beijing reasserted control over the area, and many survivors migrated across the mountains into the north-eastern Shan States. Speaking the same dialect as the Kokang Chinese, they settled in the vicinity, mainly in the Hopang-Panglong area immediately south of Kokang proper.[31] Deprived of land to cultivate, the Panthays of Panglong became traders. Since their arrival there more than a century ago, they have been first-class muleteers and opium smugglers.[32] Yunnan, not Burma or the so-called Golden Triangle, was the main source of opium in East Asia at this time. But the cross-border trade in opium was significant, and illicit drugs from Yunnan found their way into Burma, Siam and beyond.

The Kachin in northernmost Burma did not historically have any literature of their own, and neither Burmese nor Chinese sources are much help when determining where they came from. The only clues come from oral tradition, and the traditional storytellers claim that they came from a place called Majoi Shingra Bum, or 'Naturally Flat Mountain'. Its exact location is unknown but is believed to be somewhere in Tibet, which would make sense, because all Kachin dialects belong to the Tibeto-Burman group of languages.

What can be said with certainty, however, is that they were a warlike tribe who over the centuries pushed south from their known homelands on the foothills of the Himalayas, driving the Shans and the Palaungs out of most of northern Burma. The Hukawng Valley in what is today western Kachin State was given its name during this ongoing conflict: *ju-kawng* in the Jingphaw Kachin dialect means 'cremation mounds', referring to the innumerable graves where bodies of the Shans killed by the Kachins were cremated. From the Hukawng Valley, they went on to capture old Shan areas such as Mogaung and Bhamo.

Just before the end of the nineteenth century, a Swedish-American Baptist missionary, Ola Hanson, arrived in the Kachin Hills. He was not the first Western missionary to the Kachins, but he was by far the most energetic. The Kachins, until then animists, were converted to Christianity faster than any other ethnic group in Burma. After Hanson had put their language into the Roman alphabet, the Bible was translated into Kachin, and they achieved a relatively high literacy rate. Baptist congregations were soon to be found all over the Kachin-inhabited areas in the far north, as well as in the Kachin-inhabited areas of northern Shan States.[33]

Akin to the Kachin were two other Tibeto-Burman tribes in the north-west: the Chins and the Nagas. The latter are also closely related to the Mizos (or Lushais, as they were called during the colonial era) of north-eastern India. Like the Kachins, the Chins were animists until the arrival of Baptist missionaries in the late nineteenth century. They transcribed the major Chin languages into written form as well, using the Roman alphabet. But the difference was that, whereas the Jinghpaw dialect became the lingua franca of the Kachin tribes, the Chins remained divided by more than forty, perhaps fifty, mutually unintelligible dialects.

Politically, the northern Chin tribes were ruled by hereditary chiefs and an aristocracy, while many of the southern Chins had a democratic type of organisation.[34] Each village was governed by a council which was elected to represent the main families or residential sections of the village. Contributing to the diversity and lack of ethnic cohesion in the Chin Hills was the fact that each village was usually autonomous.

Unlike the Kachins, who were never conquered by any Burman state, the Chins were forced to pay tribute to the kings in Mandalay. But there was never any love lost between the two peoples. According to Chin historian Vumsom:

> [The] Zo [i.e. the Chins] refer to [the] Burman as Kawl and to the country they inhabit as Kawlram, in a somewhat derogatory sense. Kawl means 'under' or 'below', therefore Kawl must have originally referred to the plain dwellers. [The] Zo profess low regard for Burmans and Burman social behaviour, but they envy the cleverness of the Burmans and their ability to take advantage of them in many ways...Zo people feel that they are in constant danger of exploitation by the Burmans, and therefore the term Kawl for the Burmans is associated with ill-bred, unstable, tricky and treacherous character.[35]

The British recognised the fighting abilities of the Kachins and the Chins at an early stage. Along with the Karens, these two ethnic groups came to make up the backbone of the colonial army. Only 1,893 of the soldiers were Burmese, compared to 2,797 Karens, 2,578 Indians, 1,258 Chins and 852 Kachins.[36]

The Nagas inhabited the remote mountain regions immediately to the north of the Chin Hills. Like the Chins, they spoke an abundance of local dialects, and were grouped into clans and independent village clusters. Henry Noel Cochran Stevenson, the Assistant Superintendent of the Burma Frontier Force, stated that there were approximately 75,000 Nagas in Burma in 1941, and that the greater portion of this number came under 'a gentle form of regular administration' only in 1940.[37]

While the Naga tribes on the Indian side of the border were converted into Christianity at about the same time as the Kachins

THE ETHNIC JIGSAW

and Chins of Burma, and obtained their own Roman script as well, the Burmese Nagas lived in isolation. There were no roads, no towns, only villages on hilltops surrounded by stockades. The Nagas were head-hunters and were feared by the plainspeople. Few ever dared to venture into their wild mountains, and whatever administration existed was exercised from a safe distance in Singkaling Hkamti by the Chindwin River on the plains below. Socially and politically, the Nagas were torn apart by tribal warfare. Not surprisingly, the Nagas felt no affinity to Burma; most probably, the vast majority of them had not until very recently ever heard of that country, let alone agreed to belong to it.[38]

To the south of the Chin and Naga Hills was a territory which sharply contrasted with this primitive wilderness: Arakan, once an independent kingdom. It is believed—nothing is certain in early Burmese history—that the Arakan coast was originally inhabited by Indians. In the tenth century, it was invaded by a people closely related to the Burmans, probably called Kanran, one of the earliest Tibeto-Burman tribes from eastern Tibet to enter present-day Myanmar.[39] The newcomers mixed with the original inhabitants and formed the kingdom of Arakan. The Arakanese language is an earlier, archaic form of Burmese, but the two languages are not always mutually intelligible.

The Arakan area was separated from Burma by a densely forested mountain range, which made it possible for the Arakanese to maintain their independence until the Burmese conquest in 1784–5. Contacts with the outside world had until then been mostly to the west, which, in turn, had brought Islam to the region. The first Muslims on the Arakan coast are believed to have been Moorish, Arab and Persian traders who arrived between the ninth and the fifteenth centuries. Some of them stayed and married local women, and their offspring became the forefathers of a people now known as Rohingya. They speak a version of the Chittagonian dialect of Bengali interspersed with words borrowed from Arakanese and Burmese.[40]

There is no evidence of friction between them and their Buddhist neighbours in the earlier days. Indeed, after 1430 the Arakanese kings, though Buddhists, even used Muslim titles in addition to their own names and issued medallions bearing the *kalima*, or Muslim confession of faith.[41] Persian was the court language until the Burmese invasion. The separate identity of the Arakanese was further enhanced by the early introduction of British education, newspapers and other cultural influences which entered the area from Bengal.

During the colonial era, Arakan also attracted thousands of seasonal labourers, especially from the Chittagong area of adjacent East Bengal. Many of them found it convenient to stay since there was already a large Muslim population who spoke almost the same language. At that time, there was no ill feeling towards those immigrants. Many Buddhist Arakanese, on their part, had over the centuries, and especially after the Burmese conquest of their kingdom in 1784, migrated to East Bengal, where they settled along the coast between Chittagong and Cox's Bazar. The Naaf River, the official boundary, united rather than separated the two British possessions.

The Mon, another people who once had their own kingdoms, were involved in the pro-independence movement, in which they cooperated with the Burmese while retaining their own customs and culture. In 1947, a Mon National Day was established to commemorate the founding of Hanthawaddy, the kingdom they established in 825 and which was conquered by the Burmese in 1757.[42]

Modern Burma emerged against this backdrop of ethnic confusion and centuries of mistrust: a Burman-dominated, central heartland on both sides of the Irrawaddy River, surrounded by a horse-shoe-shaped ring of mountain ranges inhabited by altogether more than a hundred different Tibeto-Burman, Mon-Khmer and Tai nationalities. But even inside this 'horseshoe', there were some important minorities: the Indians and the Chinese, who dominated trade and commerce in virtually every urban centre across the country. Indian influence dates back to the time of the Mon empires and kingdoms, when Buddhism entered Burma along with an alphabet based on South Indian script.

During the British era, thousands of people from the Indian subcontinent were brought in to work on the railways, in the postal services and the civil service, or to labour as coolies, stevedores, rickshaw-pullers, gardeners and watchmen. Many more were soldiers in the colonial army, among them Gurkhas from Nepal, whose descendants are still living in and around the old garrison town of Maymyo (now Pyin Oo Lwin) and in Kachin State. Others were encouraged to settle in the Irrawaddy delta, which became the new centre for Burmese agriculture and rice cultivation. Many Indians also went into business and, being more familiar with modern finance and commerce than the Burmans, soon came to control a disproportionately large share of the country's economy. Before the Second World War, nearly half of Yangon's population was of South Asian origin—Hindu, Muslim or Sikh.

The most detested of all immigrants from India were the moneylenders, the majority of whom were *chettiars*—a caste originating from the Madras area. The peasants, hard hit by the international rice market in 1930, and burdened by heavy taxes, were rapidly losing their land, chiefly to British banks but also to the *chettiars*. The nationalist movement that emerged during the colonial days campaigned not only against the British but even more fiercely against the *chettiars* and the Indians who worked for the British administration. Generally speaking, any person of South Asian origin was looked down upon and referred to as *kala*, a pejorative meaning 'foreigner' or 'Indian'.[43]

The Chinese community was less numerous and better off than those of Indian origin. They were mainly Cantonese- and Fujianese-speaking migrants who had come from Hong Kong, Penang and Singapore—or Calcutta, which once had a thriving Chinese community. There was also a smaller number whose mother tongue was Hakka, another distinct Chinese dialect.

The Chinese migrants lived almost exclusively in urban areas, and some of them became very wealthy. One of the best known of them was Aw Chu Kin, a Hakka herbalist who invented a balm he called *Ban Kin Yu*, or 'Ten Thousand Golden Oil'. To gain a greater appeal, the name was changed to Tiger Balm, and it sold well in Burma and was exported to China, Southeast Asia and Japan. Then, of course, there were the Chinese in Kokang, who were not migrants, and the Panthay, who ended up in the Shan States for entirely different reasons than the urban Chinese in Burma proper.

Such was the scene when the British began negotiating their withdrawal from Burma. The governor formed what was called a Frontier Areas Committee of Enquiry (FACOE) to ascertain the views and aspirations of the minority peoples living in the highlands surrounding the central plains. It was composed of Burmese politicians, minority representatives and British civil servants, and the hearings were conducted with representatives of the various hill peoples. Then, in March 1946, the first round of talks was held in Laihka in the Shan States. Thirty-four *saohpas* came to the meeting along with Stevenson representing the governor, U Nu from the Anti-Fascist People's Freedom League, two other Burmese politicians, and Dr Gordon Seagrave, who ran a hospital in Namkham in northern Shan State and who spoke non-politically on the medical needs.[44]

U Nu made a strong plea for the non-Burmese nationalities to unite with Burma proper, and he blamed the British for separating, for instance, the Kachins from the Burmese. Some Kachin elders, who had observed the talks in Laihka, refuted those claims:

> This we deny emphatically. What have the Burman people done toward the hill peoples to win their faith and love? Did not a section of the Burmese public, who while saying we all belong to the same race, blood and home call in the Japanese and cause the hill peoples to suffer? If therefore the Burmese want unity with the hill peoples, they must change.[45]

The Karens, who also fought against the Japanese and their Burmese nationalist allies during the Second World War, were not interested in negotiating their future with any Burmese politician. The Karenni saw no reason to take part in the talks at all, because they were already 'independent'. It was deemed impractical to invite the Nagas, whose area was too remote and almost inaccessible, and talks with the Wa before FACOE revealed a wide gap between their way of looking at life and the committee's perception of it.

When asked if they wanted to have any association with other people, the Wa representative Hkun Sai allegedly replied: 'We do not want to join anybody because in the past have been very independent.'⁴⁶ And they were not interested in having education, good housing and hospitals, because 'we are very wild people and don't appreciate all these things'.⁴⁷ David Rees-Williams, an English politician who visited Maymyo (Pyin Oo Lwin) at the time, recalled that the FACOE had had great difficulty getting any representative to come to the hearings. Those who did so came only 'after being bribed with substantial amounts of opium'. And when the Was were asked what constitutional reforms they desired, they replied: 'More opium'!⁴⁸

Despite the difficulties, a second conference was held in the Shan market town of Panglong in February 1947. This time, results were produced. On 12 February, Aung San and leaders of the Shans, Kachins and Chins signed the historic Panglong Agreement, a key document in post-independence relations between the hill peoples and the central Burmese authorities, and the day on which it was signed is still celebrated officially as Union Day. The wording is not very precise, but the agreement stated that 'full autonomy in internal administration of the Frontier Areas is accepted in principle' and 'citizens of the Frontier Areas shall enjoy rights and privileges which are regarded as fundamental in democratic countries'.⁴⁹

Moreover, Shan *saohpas* also asked for, and were granted, the right to secede from the proposed Union of Burma after a ten-year period of independence—that is, in 1958—should they be dissatisfied with the new federation. This right was also granted to the Karenni states and ensured under the first, 1947 constitution. The Panglong Agreement, as well as the constitution, further stipulated that a Kachin State be formed, but without the right to secede. The constitution, though not the Panglong Agreement, also outlined the provisions for the establishment of a Karen State, also without the right to secede.⁵⁰

Given the shaky foundations on which the Union of Burma was founded, and the assassination of Aung San and its most competent leaders on 19 July 1947, it is hardly surprising that its first, post-independence government could not keep the country together. The Karenni had even before Burma's independence proclaimed a 'local government', and as army mutineers and communists, from the mainstream Communist Party of Burma (CPB) as well as the Communist Party (Red Flag), were battling government forces, the Karen National Defence Organisation (KNDO) rose up in arms. On 31 January 1949, they managed to occupy Insein, immediately north of Yangon.

At the same time, a smaller Mon rebel army which was modelled on the KNDO and hence named the Mon National Defence Organisation, went underground with the Karens. A band of Pa-Os in the southern Shan States formed yet another rebel army, though its main enemy was not the central government but the Shan *saophas*. Their struggle was against feudalism, they said. Meanwhile, the *mujahids* had abandoned their plans to join Pakistan. In the early 1950s, they began to identify themselves as Rohingya and stated that their goal was the establishment of an autonomous area for their people in northern Arakan.[51]

The rebels received no foreign support and had to rely on taxes and whatever supplies they could collect for the local population. The first sign of any outside interest in their struggles came after a Burmese aircraft strayed across the border with Thailand in October 1953, and accidentally bombed a village, killing two people and injuring five. Traditional Thai fears of the Burmese, dating back to the destruction of Ayutthaya in 1767, were brought to life, and the Thai prime minister, Plaek Phibunsongkhram, publicly threatened to shoot down any aircraft that violated the country's sovereignty. Privately, however, he invited leaders of the Karen and Mon rebel armies to Bangkok for talks. They arrived in the Thai capital in March 1954.

For Thailand, to police the porous, 2,100-kilometre border with its historical enemy would have been a difficult and extremely costly business. Instead, Karen and Mon rebels were encouraged to serve as buffers. While the Thai army officers the Karen and Mon representatives met did not pledge any direct support, the rebels were allowed to set up camps along the frontier, their families were permitted to stay in Thailand, and they could buy arms and ammunition from middlemen acting on behalf of the Thai military.[52]

Thailand's policy of maintaining such border buffers prevailed for several decades. In the beginning, the Thais were interested only in ensuring security along the border and the rebels needed guns and other supplies. Following the collapse of the Burmese economy after the 1962 coup, this informal arrangement became economically lucrative as well. The Karen and the Mon rebels prospered from the tax they collected on black-market goods, while the trade, albeit illegal, contributed to the spectacular growth of the Thai economy in the 1960s and 1970s.

In the 1950s, dissent was also growing in the Shan States. The presence of Kuomintang (KMT) forces, and the government's relentless military campaigns to rebel the invaders, meant that the Shans had become squeezed between two forces, both of which were perceived as foreign. The KMT was conducting a reign of terror from its strongholds in the hills, while the government's soldiers were no better in their treatment of the village people in the Shan countryside.[53]

Ordinary Shans, for the first time since pre-colonial days, came in close contact with the Burmese, and the ethnic differences became more apparent. In the countryside, an unarticulated movement started to grow while Shan intellectuals in the cities founded semi-political organisations such as the Shan Student Association and a Shan Literary Society. But those groups as well as the Federal Movement led by the Yawnghwe *saohpa*, ex-president Sao Shwe Thaik, sought a peaceful solution within the framework of the federal, parliamentary system. They—and the central government—had not forgotten that the Shan States had the constitutional right to secede from the union, and that right would come into effect in 1958. *Noom Suk Harn*, which was set up in 1958 and fought for that goal, was not a major player, but, gradually, young Shans became even more nationalistic and began to doubt that the government would agree to hold a referendum on independence if the leaders of the Shans so demanded.

In 1959, the Shan *saohopas* formally renounced all their powers at a grand ceremony held at Taunggyi and attended by all the princes. What had been the de facto Shan States now became only Shan State (which the area was also actually referred to in the 1947 constitution), and the duties of the *saophas* were taken over by the elected Shan State government. The position of the *saophas* towards the fledgeling armed insurrection had been very awkward. They could not condemn the young rebels because they were their own people, but they could not support them either. Open confrontation with the central government might lead to a large-scale war in Shan State. There was also a certain amount of distrust between the *saophas* and some of the youngsters who, influenced by revolutionary ideas, were opposed to the old leaders, symbols of a feudal society they wanted to change.

The Kachins had got their own state, but it was poor and neglected. The Kachins had fought tenaciously against the Japanese, but, apart from a few jeeps for the state ministers, no other 'war reparations' from Tokyo even reached this remote tribal state. In early 1958, seven young Kachins met secretly at night near Inya Lake in Yangon. The meeting was organised by Zau Seng, a veteran of the Second World War, and attended by Phungshwi Zau Seng, a civil servant and university graduate. The other five present were young intellectuals—and they decided to follow the Karens and other ethnic minorities and take up arms against the government.

Other grievances, such as U Nu's decision in 1960 to make Buddhism the state religion, and an unpopular border agreement with China—under which some Kachin villages were handed over to the Chinese—hastened the movement from word into action. Two days after setting up the Kachin Independence Army on 5 February 1961, Zau Seng, his brother Zau Tu and eight other Kachins stormed the treasury in Lashio. They made away with 90,000 kyats in cash, which provided the financial basis for the rebellion they were about to launch. Zau Dan, a third brother, was with the KIA from the very beginning.

A renewed full-scale war across the frontier areas, which many had feared, became reality after the 1962 coup. Sao Shwe Thaik was dead, most of the other political and ethnic leaders were in prison, and Myanmar's federal democracy had been replaced by a military dictatorship that no one really wanted. It should have been possible to form a united front against General Ne Win and his coup makers, but self-interests—and China's decision to

THE ETHNIC JIGSAW

support the CPB in 1968—complicated matters, especially in Shan State, the ethnically most diverse state in the union which was now a union in name only. Overlapping territorial claims in northern Shan State pitted the Shans against the Kachins, and the Palaungs claimed areas there as well. The Pa-Os built up their own fiefdom in southern Shan State and, in the east, the Lahu also rose in rebellion.

The CPB, after its successful thrust into northern Shan State, had gone on to take over the Wa Hills and Kokang as well as areas north of Kengtung in eastern Shan State. The CPB also began to reach out to the ethnic resistance armies. In July 1976, the staunchly Christian KIA formed a military alliance with the CPB, and, on 16 January 1977, the SSA entered into a similar agreement with the communists. Smaller groups broke away from the Pa-O, Karenni and Kayan (Padaung) armies and joined forces with the communists.

Needless to say, the lure was access to the CPB's vast arsenal of Chinese-supplied weapons. The smaller groups could now defend and even expand their respective territories while the KIA managed to take over most of Kachin State and build up its own 'buffer state' with an administrative system, schools, hospitals and infrastructure. The central government soon controlled little more than major towns and the roads between them in Kachin State. The SSA, however, split because of disagreements over the alliance with the CPB. Several of the old leaders retired in Thailand—and those who agreed to go to party headquarters in Panghsang on the Chinese border returned with brand-new machine guns, grenade launchers and assault rifles.

The proliferation of groups, shifting alliances and the wealth that could be generated through the local opium trade threw Shan State into a cockpit of chaos and anarchy that only got worse over the years. The war in Shan State had devastated the local economy, and the KMT had encouraged farmers to grow opium as a substitute cash crop. In a surprisingly candid interview with a British newspaper in 1967, Duan Xiwen, a KMT general, said: 'Necessity knows no law…We have to continue to fight the evil of communism and to fight you must have an army, and an army must have guns, and to buy guns you must have money. In these mountains the only money is opium.'[54]

Tax on poppy farmers and opium convoys that passed through their areas of operation provided some income for the rebels, but their role in the trade was minor. A more important player was the Myanmar military, which, in the early 1960s, decided to jump on the opium bandwagon. There was not enough money in central coffers to sustain an effective counter-insurgency campaign, and the government was also tied up with political and economic problems closer to home. To fight the rebels, the military had in 1963 authorised the setting up of local, home guard armies called *Ka Kwe Ye* (KKY; 'defence')—and these militias were given the right to use all government-controlled roads and towns in Shan State for opium trafficking in exchange for combating the rebels. By trading in opium, the military hoped that the KKY home guards would be self-supporting. Lo Hsing-han, the commander of Kokang KKY, and Zhang Qifu alias Khun Sa of Loi Maw KKY were among those who became rich on the deal.

That, however, did not solve the problems the government had with counter-insurgency finance, and the situation was getting out of control. The KKY militias were disbanded in January 1973, but that led only to even more confusion. Lo Hsing-han went underground and teamed up with the SSA, which agreed to shelter him—if he pledged to sell all his opium to the US government. Adrian Cowell, a British documentary filmmaker who spent sixteen months with the SSA in 1972–3, helped the Shans draft a proposal to that effect to the US government. But just as Cowell was going to deliver it to the US embassy in Bangkok, Lo Hsing-han was arrested near the Shan border in northern Thailand—and extradited to Burma.

Lo was sentenced to death for 'rebellion against the state', a reference to his brief alliance with the SSA—but not for opium trafficking, in which he had official permission to engage. But he was never executed. Instead, he was released during a 1980 amnesty and given two million kyats (a lot of money at that time) by the government to build a military camp south-east of Lashio. Called the Salween Village, it became the base for a new home guard unit, this time under the government's new *pyi thu sit* (people's militia) program, which had been launched after the disbandment of the old KKY. The new agreement was effectively the same as the former accord between the military and the local militias: fight the rebels and gain, in return, access to government-controlled roads and towns for smuggling.[55]

The other prominent KKY commander, Zhang Qifu, was arrested in 1969 after a meeting with representatives of the Shan resistance. His men subsequently went underground and, on 16 April 1973, kidnapped two Russian doctors from a Soviet-built hospital in Taunggyi. It was not until August 1974 that the doctors were released, and then through Thailand. Zhang's men had told the Thais that the two doctors would be released unconditionally. But by strange coincidence Zhang was released on 7 September. What actually happened is hardly a secret: General Kriangsak Chamanan, the commander of the northern Thai forces, had been called in by Yangon to negotiate with Ronald Chang, Zhang's uncle, for an exchange of prisoners.[56]

Zhang rejoined his men in February 1976, moved to Ban Hin Taek in northern Thailand and adopted the Shan name Khun Sa. The former Loi Maw KKY was renamed the Shan United Army (SUA), ostensibly a rebel army fighting for the Shan cause. But Khun Sa's presence in Thailand became an embarrassment and, in January 1982, Thai forces forced him and the SUA out of Ban Hin Taek. However, the SUA simply moved to the south-west and established a new headquarters at Homöng across the border from the town of Mae Hong Son in Thailand, where Khun Sa stayed until he surrendered in January 1996 and moved to Yangon with a few of his mistresses. His more than 15,000-strong force, then called the Möng Tai Army, was subsequently dissolved. But Yawt Seik, one of Khun Sa's junior officers, remained on the Thai border, where he and his followers formed a new army.

It is not only the military government that has failed to unify the country. The rebels' own efforts to forge some kind of consensus among themselves have invariably been unsuccessful as well. There were a number of short-lived fronts in the 1950s involving various rebel armies. Some included the CPB but most of them did not. After the 1962 coup, ethnic groups formed the Nationalities Liberation Alliance, which was succeeded by the United Nationalities Front, the Nationalities United Front and the Revolutionary Nationalities Alliance. In 1975, yet another gathering of ethnic armies formed the Federal National Democratic Front, which a year later changed its name to the National Democratic Front (NDF), the longest-lasting of the pro-federal alliances. But the NDF remained a basically Thai-border-based entity. It always held its meetings at the Manerplaw headquarters of the Karen National Union (KNU) and its armed wing, the Karen National Liberation Army (KNLA), which could trace its origin to the KNDO.

In a separate development, U Nu was released from 'protective custody' in an army camp in October 1966 and, in April 1969, managed to leave the country under the pretext of going on a pilgrimage to India. U Nu made it to London, where he announced at a press conference the formation of an entirely new organisation called the Parliamentary Democracy Party (PDP). Its declared aim was to overthrow Ne Win's military government by force, and several prominent personalities rallied behind him and his party. Among them were several of the legendary Thirty Comrades, Brig.-Gen Henson Kya Doe, the Karen officer who had been dismissed from service when the Karen insurrection broke out, and Air Commodore Tommy Clift, a Anglo-Shan former chief of the air force. Karen rebel leader Mahn Ba Zan and Jimmy Yang (Yang Kyin-sein), a former MP from Kokang, also decided to work together with U Nu. Edward Law-Yone, the well-respected editor of the *Nation*, who had been arrested after the coup and then released in 1968, became the brain behind the scheme.

An informal headquarters for the resistance was set up in Bangkok, and military training was carried out in camps on the Thai-Burma border. The Karen and Mon ethnic armies also expressed their support, and they fought together with the Burmese under the umbrella of the National United Liberation Front (NULF), which at one stage claimed to have 50,000 fighters under its command.[57]

Although the West most probably found U Nu's and Law-Yone's political ideals more attractive than Ne Win's atavistic military dictatorship, the timing of the launch of the campaign could not have been more unfortunate. The CPB was advancing in northern and north-eastern Burma, and American and British security planners saw little viability in the attempt to offer a third alternative to Ne Win's regime and the communists. The CIA maintained through its agents in Thailand some contacts with U Nu and Law-Yone so as not to antagonise them. But no assistance of any consequence was forthcoming. Instead, Ne Win's government received clandestine military support from the United States because it, and not the group led by U Nu and Law-Yone, was seen as a bulwark against the spread of communism.[58]

U Nu went into exile in India in 1974 and the PDP had in 1973 become the People's Patriotic Party (PPP), led by Bo Let Ya, one of the Thirty Comrades. But political disagreements and a conflict over territory led to a conflict with the Karens. On 29 November 1978, Bo Let Ya was killed by the Karen rebels in a jungle hideout near the Thai border.

The final blow to the Burmese resistance came when the government in May 1980 announced a general amnesty for insurgents. According to official figues, a total of 2,189 rebels surrendered, while independent estimates put the figure at 300–400.[59] But among them were what remained of the PPP on the Thai border and U Nu, who returned from India. And Lo Hsing-han was not the only one who was released from jail—so was the Red Flag leader Thakin Soe, who had been apprehended in 1970, and several of his associates.

It was against this backdrop of unsuccessful alliances that renewed attempts were made to unify the resistance after the 1988 uprising. The first was the Democratic Alliance of Burma, which, like the old NULF, was supposed to bring together the Burmese resistance and the ethnic armies. But it—and the NDF—became defunct when the KIA began to negotiate a separate peace deal with the government in 1993, which was finalised in 1994.

The National Coalition Government of the Union of Burma, which was led by Aung San Suu Kyi's cousin Sein Win and other MPs elect from the National League for Democracy, was never a success. An expanded front called the National Council of the

Union of Burma, with KNU/KNLA leader Bo Mya as the official president, also soon faded into oblivion because the Burmese and the ethnic armed groups could never agree on any fundamental political issues.

When looking at the situation today, it is hard not to feel a sense of déjà vu. It has all happened time and again before. Ousted politicians have formed a National Unity Government, a broader front known as the National Unity Consultative Council, and it has its own armed units called the People's Defence Forces. But what is fundamentally different today is the scale of the fighting and, most importantly, the role that China has come to play after the collapse of its main ally, the once powerful CPB. With that has come an entirely new Chinese strategy for dealing with the armed resistance as well as general opposition. And, it is often forgotten, China also has a long history of involvement with whoever is in power in the capital, first Yangon and now Naypyitaw.

4

THE CHINA FACTOR

Burma and China established diplomatic relations on 8 June 1950, less than a year after Mao Zedong, standing before a huge crowd in Beijing's Tiananmen Square, proclaimed the People's Republic and hailed the communist victory over Chiang Kai-shek's nationalist Chinese Kuomintang, the KMT. Judging from official Chinese declarations and speeches, that was the beginning of a friendship which has over the decades been nothing but close and cordial. In January 2020, for instance, the Chinese Ministry of Foreign Affairs stated in a press release:

> Since the two countries established diplomatic relations seventy years ago, China-Myanmar relations have enjoyed constant development on the basis of mutual respect, mutual trust and mutual assistance, and have set an example of harmonious co-existence and win-win cooperation between big and small countries. The Chinese side adheres to non-interference in Myanmar's internal affairs and supports Myanmar in safeguarding national dignity and legitimate rights and interests.[1]

All that is, of course, utter nonsense. In fact, no country has interfered in Myanmar politics and internal conflicts as much as China, and it began with giving cadres from the Communist Party of Burma (CPB) and the Kachin warriors led by Naw Seng shelter in Sichuan and Guizhou respectively in the early 1950s. That, in turn, developed in the late 1960s into full support for a communist insurrection aimed at overthrowing the government in Yangon. Chinese-supplied weapons pounded government garrisons all over northern, north-eastern and eastern Shan State, as well as parts of Kachin State. Tens of thousands of government soldiers died in that war, and while that is seldom mentioned in public fora, army officers have not forgotten what China was responsible for throughout the 1970s and 1980s.

Today, and thanks to China's peculiar foreign policy of differentiating between 'government-to-government' and 'party-to-party' relations—a peculiar concept in a country which has only one political party, which controls the government—Beijing maintains links with the Myanmar military as well as the country's ethnic armed organisations. And both sides are benefiting from the supply of military hardware from China. Myanmar is also totally dependent on China for foreign trade and, of utmost importance, for diplomatic protection in the United Nations whenever Western powers have tried to get the Security Council to impose sanctions on successive military regimes.

In the years immediately after Burma's independence and the imposition of communist rule in China, relations were troubled by a disputed and largely un-demarcated border, illegal immigration by vast numbers of Chinese labourers, businessmen and even farmers in search of greener pastures, and smuggling. Relations became even more uncertain when KMT forces retreated into Burma's north-eastern hill areas following their defeat in the Chinese civil war. There was a definite possibility of a war involving Chinese communist forces crossing the border into Burma. But the Sino-Burmese relations that developed from this initial possibility of a wider conflict provide a good example of how a small, comparatively weak country worked to preserve its independence and neutrality in dealing with the largest and then most powerful nation in Asia.

Regardless, the U Nu government made its point, and on 22 April 1954, China and Burma for the first time signed a bilateral trade agreement. On 28–9 June, Chinese Premier Zhou Enlai visited Yangon and held talks with U Nu. A joint Sino-Burmese declaration was signed by the two leaders on 29 June, endorsing the 'Five Principles of Peaceful Co-existence': mutual respect for each other's territorial integrity and sovereignty, non-aggression, non-interference in each other's internal affairs, equal and mutual benefits, and peaceful coexistence.[2]

Even though this policy was labelled *pauk-phaw*, a term denoting a close, almost fraternal relationship, Yangon adopted a neutral stand on foreign policy, with the ultimate aim of preventing China from interfering in its internal affairs. The *pauk-phaw* concept relied on a deeply asymmetrical 'friendship' between China—a huge and often threatening regional superpower—and Burma, a much smaller country on its periphery.

Although the basically Maoist CPB was one of the major rebel forces during the first years of independence, Beijing then refrained from supporting its armed struggle inside Burma.[3] But the military strongly suspected that China had a hand in a peace initiative launched by veteran nationalist leader Thakin Kodaw Hmaing in the mid-1950s. He had travelled to China, Mongolia, Hungary and the Soviet Union in 1953 and, in 1954, he was awarded the Stalin Peace Prize by the Supreme Soviet Presidium in Moscow. There was no evidence of that, but it meant that the military refused to enter into any talks with the CPB. The ethnic Chinese community in Yangon was overwhelmingly business-oriented, but there was also among them—and separate from the CPB—a communist cell with the pretentious name 'the Provisional Committee of the Special Division, Burma, Branch of the South Seas Communist Party'. It had links with the Chinese-dominated communist parties in Malaya and Singapore and, most likely, also with the Chinese embassy in Yangon.[4]

The main bilateral issue to settle was the disputed Sino-Burmese border, which U Nu discussed in detail during a September 1956 visit to China. He returned with a tentative plan for a settlement that called for Chinese recognition of Burmese sovereignty over the so-called Namwan Assigned Tract in exchange for ceding to China three villages in Kachin State: Hpimaw, Gawlum and Kangfang.[5] China also pledged to recognise Burmese claims on the remainder of the 2,129-kilometre-long frontier.[6]

111

U Nu's concessions provoked protests from both Burmese politicians and ethnic groups such as the Kachin, who rose up in rebellion as a direct result of the border talks with China. However, negotiations continued for nearly four years until an initial agreement was eventually signed on 28 January 1960. More agreements were announced when Zhou Enlai visited Yangon in April and, on 1 October, a final boundary treaty between China and Burma was signed in Beijing.[7]

In addition to the three Kachin villages (153 square kilometres), the Panhung-Panglao area of the northern Wa Hills (189 square kilometres) was also ceded to China. In return, the Namwan area (220 square kilometres), which for all practical purposes was part of Burma anyway, formally became Burmese territory. More importantly, though, China did renounce all its claims to areas in northern Kachin State. Until that time, Chinese maps had shown the border to be just north of the Kachin State capital of Myitkyina and Taiwanese (or Republic of China) maps still show the border at that point, since Taipei has never recognised any agreements signed between the communist government in Beijing and other nations.[8]

The deal was not unfair by international standards, but rumours soon spread across Kachin State to the effect that vast tracts of Kachin territory had been ceded to China. Even today, it is not unusual for many Kachins to point across the border at a piece of land and claim that it was given to China by Yangon. The failure of the central government to clarify the nature of the border agreement was at the root of misunderstandings which, together with the decision to make Buddhism the state religion, were soon to drive hundreds of young Kachins underground.

With the border finally demarcated, Burma launched a new offensive against the KMT forces in north-eastern Burma the following year. This time, thousands of troops of the Chinese Communist Party's People's Liberation Army also crossed the border into Burma near the town of Mong Yang north of Kengtung in eastern Shan State, where the KMT maintained a major base. Mong Pa Liao, another KMT base near Burma's border with Laos, was also attacked in a campaign that was clearly coordinated with the Burmese military. It is reasonable to assume that this was part of the new friendship agreements between China and Burma as well, although it has never been admitted officially.[9]

It is generally assumed that Sino-Burmese relations took a turn for the worse in June 1967, when anti-Chinese riots broke out in Yangon. The fervour of the Cultural Revolution influenced the Chinese community in the Burmese capital and many young Sino-Burmese began wearing red Mao badges. This violated an official Burmese regulation banning the display of such political symbols in public, and the young 'Red Guards' were ordered to take off their badges. When some of them resisted, anti-Chinese riots broke out. Chinese shops and homes were ransacked and looted, and many Sino-Burmese were killed. A mob even attacked the Chinese embassy in Yangon before the situation was brought under control.

The role of the authorities in this affair was a matter of dispute: the Chinatown riots came at a time when there were acute shortages of rice and basic food supplies in Yangon. According to eyewitnesses, the police did not interfere with the killings and the looting until the Chinese embassy was attacked. It is widely believed that Burma's military government encouraged the riots in order to deflect attention from the country's internal problems at that time.[10]

But the 1967 incident was actually little more than a convenient excuse for the Chinese to intervene directly in Burma's internal affairs. A new era in Sino-Burmese relations had begun in 1962 when General Ne Win seized power. The military takeover had upset the regional stability that existed by virtue of Burma's weak but neutral democratic government. Furthermore, China had long been wary of the ambitious and unpredictable general. Six important events took place immediately after the coup. The first was that the CPB exiles in China were for the first time allowed to print propaganda leaflets and other material in Beijing. On 1 August 1962, Beijing- and Sichuan-based exiles published a document titled 'Some Facts about Ne Win's Military Government', denouncing the new regime.[11]

But the most urgent task for the CPB exiles in China was to find a way to contact units in the old base area in the Pegu Yoma, where the once strong communist army was crumbling. There had been no links between them and the exiles in China since the latter had trekked to Yunnan in the early 1950s. By a strange twist of historical events, it was Ne Win's military regime that unwittingly provided an opportunity for the CPB exiles in China to re-establish these links, the second important event.

Probably hoping that the insurgents would give up when faced with the massive force of the military government, the Ne Win regime called for peace talks after about a year in power. On 14 July 1963, representatives of the military government sat down with delegates from the CPB, Thakin Soe's 'Red Flags', the Karen, Mon, Shan, Kachin ethnic rebel armies and some smaller groups. They had all been promised free and safe passage to and from the peace parley, regardless of the outcome.

The colourful Thakin Soe probably attracted the most attention when he arrived accompanied by a team of attractive young girls in khaki uniforms. He placed a portrait of Joseph Stalin in front of him on the negotiating table and then began attacking the 'revisionism' of Soviet leader Nikita Khrushchev and the 'opportunism' of Mao Zedong's China. Not surprisingly, Thakin Soe was soon excluded from the talks.

The Chinese may or may not have been involved behind the scenes during the peace talks in the 1950s, but this time they were. Twenty-nine veterans from the main CPB who were exiled in China also arrived in Yangon, purportedly to participate in the peace talks. Among the 'Beijing Returnees', as they came to be known, were veterans such as *yebaw* ('Comrade') Aung Gyi, Thakin Bo and Bo Zeya, one of the Thirty Comrades—and the veteran Thakin Ba Thein Tin, who did not actually participate in the talks but seized the opportunity to visit the Pegu Yoma, bringing with him radio transmitters and other equipment from China.[12] Until then, the exiles in China had had no means of communicating with their comrades in the Pegu Yoma. The peace talks had, inadvertently, made that possible and the poorly armed fighters in the Pegu Yoma were also told that massive aid from China would be forthcoming. There was no reason to surrender.

According to CPB documents, the government demanded that the communists should concentrate all their troops and

THE CHINA FACTOR

party members inside an area stipulated by the authorities, inform local authorities if there were any remaining guerrillas or cadres elsewhere, stop all organisational activities of the party and cease fundraising.[13] The intransigence of the military regime was a blessing in disguise for the CPB. The talks broke down in November and the various insurgents returned to their respective jungle camps. Thakin Ba Thein Tin and another CPB cadre returned to Beijing, while the other twenty-seven returnees stayed in the Pegu Yoma, where they assumed de facto leadership of the party at home. And a radio link had now been established between the exiles in China and the cadres in the Pegu Yoma. Everyone was getting ready for the grand plan which was going to be put into action a few years later.

The third major event that had an impact on China's designs for Burma came in the aftermath of the Sino-Soviet split in the international communist movement, which took place in the early 1960s. In November 1963, some CPB cadres who had been studying in Moscow were expelled from the Soviet Union and flown to Beijing. To direct the work in China, a 'leading group of five' was set up in Beijing shortly after Thakin Ba Thein Tin's return from the failed peace talks in Yangon. This group, which became the nucleus of the new leadership of the CPB that emerged during the 1960s, was led by Thakin Ba Thein Tin.

The fourth undertaking was to conduct a survey of possible infiltration routes from Yunnan into north-eastern Burma. In late 1963, San Thu, one of the Moscow returnees, was put in charge of a team which did exactly that. During this period, China built a network of asphalted highways, leading from Kunming to various points along the borders with Burma and with Laos, where another communist movement was active.

The fifth thing that happened, even before the peace talks were held, was a meeting between Naw Seng and his men and Thakin Ba Thein Tin. The Kachins were told that the time had come to go back to Burma to fight and, eager to leave their people's commune in Guizhuo, they were elated. The sixth event, part of the plan, was taken care of by the Chinese embassy in Yangon. Intelligence officers based in the capital arranged for ethnic Chinese communists from Yangon and some small towns in the Irrawaddy delta to travel to an old CPB base area along the Shweli River in northern Shan State, from where they later went on to the north-eastern base area when it was set up after the push across the Sino-Burmese border in 1968.

Kang Sheng, at the time China's intelligence chief and the mastermind behind the formation of a 'new' CPB, had grander plans. During the Indochina Wars in the 1960s and 1970s, the Americans talked about what they called 'the domino theory'; if communism was not stopped in Vietnam, Laos and Cambodia, it would spread to the rest of Southeast Asia and perhaps even beyond.

That theory may have been correct, but for Kang and Mao as well, the North Vietnamese leadership and the National Liberation Front in the south were too close to the Soviet Union to be trusted. Instead, Burma would be the gateway through which revolution would spread across the region. Once the CPB had taken over Burma or most of it, Chinese weapons would flow down to fraternal, Maoist-leaning parties in Thailand, Malaysia and Indonesia. In the end, communism would emerge victoriously throughout the region. The plan, absurd as it may seem, also included a linkup with the Communist Party of Australia (Marxist-Leninist), a tiny group of pro-Beijing Australian radicals.[14]

There was never any way the grandiose plan was going to work, and it was buried along with Kang when he died on 16 December 1975. His death went almost unnoticed in the official Chinese media and his name has been erased from most official history books. Kang's brutality was well known and the ferocity of his purges in China had made him few friends even among senior party cadres. Questions have even been raised about his mental state. While ordinary opium smokers who refused treatment were executed after the Chinese revolution, Kang continued to enjoy the drug inside his well-protected offices and was known by some fellow party leaders as 'the Old Opium Pipe'.[15]

As Mao grew old and infirm, a serious power struggle broke out within the Communist Party of China (CPC). In April 1976, when China's radical left reasserted itself and ousted the more pragmatic Deng Xiaoping, the CPB, unlike other communist parties in the region, spoke out loudly in favour of the hard-line Maoists. On the fifty-fifth anniversary of the founding of the CPC in June 1976, the CPB offered the following congratulatory message:

> The revisionist clique with which Deng was linked headed by [former and ousted president] Liu Shaoqi has been defeated...The movement to repulse the Right deviationist attempt at reversing correct verdicts, and the decision of the Central Committee of the CPC on measures taken against rightist chieftain Deng Xiaoping, are in full accord with Marxism-Leninism, Mao Zedong thought.[16]

In a second message mourning the death of Mao on 9 September, the CPB stated:

> Guided by Chairman Mao Zedong's proletarian revolutionary line, the Chinese people seized great victories in the socialist revolution and socialist construction in the Great Proletarian Cultural Revolution, in criticizing Liu Shaoqi's counter-revolutionary revisionist line, in criticizing Lin Biao and Confucius and in criticizing Deng Xiaoping and repulsing the Right deviationist attempt at reversing correct verdicts and consolidating the dictatorship of the proletariat, thus, consolidating the People's Republic of China—the reliable bulwark of the world proletarian revolution.[17]

The CPB had reason to re-evaluate the reliability of that bulwark in 1977 when Deng began his return to power in Beijing. The CPB, which once had branded its own 'revisionists', *yebaw* Htay—who led the delegation to the 1963 peace parley—and party theoretician Hamendranath Ghoshal as 'Burma's Deng Xiaoping' and 'Burma's Liu Shaoqi' respectively, became silent. Htay and Ghoshal were two of the founders of the CPB and they had been executed during a series of bloody internal purges led by the Beijing returnees in the late 1960s. The *Beijing Review* and other official Chinese publications, which had previously published battle views and CPB documents, stopped printing anything about the 'revolutionary struggle in Burma'.

The CPB was mentioned in the *Beijing Review* for the last time in November 1976, when Thakin Ba Thein Tin, chairman since

1975, and his vice chairman Thakin Pe Tint were received by the new CPC chairman, Hua Guofeng, in Beijing.[18] No details about the meeting were disclosed, but it is plausible to assume that the two CPB leaders wanted to ensure continued Chinese support for their party and army in the post-Mao era. But Hua was soon to fall into disgrace as Deng managed to defeat his enemies and emerge as the final winner of the power struggle.

The Burmese military quickly and shrewdly exploited the CPB's rift with Beijing by lending its good offices to China in Cambodia as Beijing shifted its focus to Vietnam's designs on its Indochinese neighbour. In November 1977, Ne Win became the first foreign head of state to visit Phnom Penh after the Khmer Rouge takeover in April 1975. The Chinese were no doubt behind the unusual visit, hoping to draw the Khmer Rouge out of its diplomatic isolation. Ne Win played along, for his part hoping that Beijing would further reduce its support for the CPB. He was not disappointed. In 1978, the CPB's entire China-based central office, including the People's Voice of Burma broadcasting station, was forced to move to Panghsang on the Yunnan frontier. The Chinese 'volunteers', who had fought alongside the CPB since 1968, were also recalled.

In September 1979, Burma left the Non-Aligned Movement—which it had helped form in the 1950s—at its Havana summit to protest against Cuba assuming the chairmanship and its decision not to let the Khmer Rouge represent Cambodia. President San Yu, who was Burma's delegate, said in a report to parliament after the Havana meeting: 'Every nation has the inalienable right to freely choose its political, economic, social and cultural system without interference in any form by another state...Burma strictly stands for the solution of problems by peaceful means rather than resorting to threats or use of force.'[19] San Yu's remarks were made with a vague reference to Vietnam's December 1978–January 1979 invasion of Cambodia, but they were also interpreted as a signal to Beijing that Rangoon disapproved of its continued support for the CPB, however limited it had become.

The 1970s became a decade of gradual rapprochement between Yangon and Beijing and, at the same time, there was a virtual standstill in the previously extremely heavy fighting between government forces and the CPB. Following Ne Win's trip to Cambodia via China, Deng Xiaoping had at the end of January 1978 paid a politically important visit to Yangon. Diplomatic relations on the ambassadorial level between China and Burma had been restored in 1970, but it was not until Deng's visit that the hitherto strained relationship between the two countries could be described as reasonably normal. Aid to the CPB was downgraded, but not completely cut off—all in line with the policy of differentiating between government-to-government and party-to-party relations.

Relations between Rangoon and Beijing were nevertheless improving noticeably. Burmese prime minister Maung Maung Kha visited China from 9 to 13 July 1979 and signed an agreement on economic and technical cooperation. Ne Win returned to China in October 1980 and again in May 1985. China's President Li Xiannian visited Rangoon in March 1985. Meanwhile, the CPB forces in Burma's north-east were becoming increasingly irrelevant and anachronistic. They neither advanced nor were defeated by the Burmese army.

A new facet of the CPB was also becoming important for the group. In their base area, a lucrative, cross-border contraband trade was starting to become economically significant. When the Chinese in the late 1970s decided that the CPB had to become 'self-sufficient', illicit cross-border trade became its main source of income and the orthodox Burmese Maoists morphed into freewheeling capitalists. Chinese consumer goods—textiles, plastic products, cigarettes, beer, bicycles, petrol and household utensils—were exchanged for Burmese timber, minerals, precious stones and jade. The CPB survived by taxing this increasingly lucrative, but still illegal, cross-border trade. This became the foundation for an entirely new kind of relationship between China and Burma, both at the central level and along the border.

A seemingly insignificant event in the midst of the political turmoil that engulfed Burma during the summer of 1988 turned out to be an extremely important watershed in Sino-Burmese relations. On 6 August 1988, as mass demonstrations shook Yangon and other cities and towns almost daily and only two days before a general strike crippled the entire country, most observers were probably amused to read in the official media in Yangon that China and Burma had signed an agreement, allowing official cross-border trade to take place between the two countries. While the rest of the world was watching what they thought were the last days of the old regime, Beijing was betting on its continued ability to play a double game that leveraged both its historic and cultural ties to cross-border ethnic rebels and its neutral approach to engagement with whatever government was in power in Yangon.

The Chinese had expressed their intentions, almost unnoticed, in an article in the *Beijing Review* as early as 2 September 1985. Titled 'Opening to the Southwest: An Expert Opinion', this article by the former Vice Minister of Communications Pan Qi outlined the possibilities of finding an outlet for trade from China, through Burma, to the Indian Ocean.[20] Pan mentioned the railheads of Myitkyina and Lashio in north-eastern Burma as possible conduits for the export of Chinese goods but refrained from saying that all relevant border areas were not under central Burmese government control.

At that time, nearly the entire Sino-Burmese frontier was actually controlled by the CPB and other non-state armed groups who had ties—political, ethnic or both—to China. Following the 1960 border agreement, a joint Sino-Burmese team had marked the frontier with border stones that literally covered the full length of the common border. After these had crumbled more than two decades later, new stones were erected in 1985 in accordance with a new agreement. But this time, the border stones, the location of which the Chinese had decided, were conveniently located in open paddy fields and glades in the jungle, far from major rebel bases along the frontier.

By early 1987, the Burmese government had managed to recapture a few CPB strongholds along the frontier, including the booming border town of Panghsai, where the fabled Burma Road crosses into China. At the same time, the Chinese, whose policies had changed dramatically since the Cultural Revolution, began to penetrate the Burmese market through an extensive economic intelligence reporting system within Burma. This network monitored the availability of domestically manufactured Burmese products, as well as the nature and volume of illegal trade from other neighbouring countries such as Thailand, Malaysia, Singapore and India. China could then respond to the market conditions by producing goods in its state sector factories. More than 2,000 carefully selected items were reported to be flooding the Burmese market. Chinese-made consumer goods were not only made deliberately cheaper than those from other neighbouring countries but were also less expensive than local Burmese products.[21]

The crushing of the August–September 1988 pro-democracy uprising and the March–April 1989 mutiny became two milestones in China's new designs for expanding its influence in the region. This time, Burma was going to become a gateway for exports of consumer goods, not revolution. Deng was in many ways the opposite of Kang on the political spectrum and times had changed. But Burma remained of utmost strategic importance to China.

In the wake of the Yangon massacre of 1988, and the Tiananmen Square massacre in June 1989, it was hardly surprising that the two isolated, internationally condemned neighbours would move closer to each other in the following years. This new, very special relationship between Burma and China was first articulated by Burma's powerful intelligence chief Khin Nyunt, then a lieutenant-general, in an address to a group of Chinese engineers working on a project in Rangoon: 'We sympathise with the People's Republic of China as disturbances similar to those in Burma last year [i.e. 1988] broke out in the People's Republic of China [in May–June 1989].'[22]

The importance of relations between these two bloodstained authoritarian regimes increased after a twelve-day visit to China in October 1989 by a twenty-four-member military team from Burma. Gen. Than Shwe led the team, which also included Khin Nyunt, the director of procurement Brig.-Gen. David Abel and the chiefs of the air force and navy. The visit resulted in a massive arms deal: China pledged to deliver US$1.4 billion worth of military hardware to Burma, including a squadron of F-7 jet fighters (the Chinese version of the Soviet MiG-21), at least four Hainan-class naval patrol boats, about 100 light tanks and armoured personnel carriers, anti-aircraft guns, rockets, a substantial quantity of small arms and ammunition, and radio equipment for military use.[23]

By the early 1990s, military-ruled Burma had become China's principal political and military ally in Southeast Asia. Chinese arms pouring across the border into Burma were crucial to the survival of the extremely unpopular junta in Yangon. After the signing of the border-trade agreement in August 1988, Burma became China's chief foreign market for cheap consumer goods, and China became the major importer of Burmese timber, forestry products, minerals, sea food and agricultural produce. At the time, World Bank analysts estimated that nearly US$1.5 billion worth of goods were exchanged along the Burma-China frontier, not including a flourishing trade in narcotics from the Burmese sector of the Golden Triangle.

In addition to trade, China soon became involved in upgrading the country's badly maintained roads and railways, as Pan Qi had suggested in 1985. By late 1991, Chinese experts were working on a series of infrastructure projects in Myanmar. That same year, Chinese military advisers arrived and were the first foreign military personnel to be stationed there since the 1950s. Burma, now Myanmar, was indeed becoming a Chinese client state. What the CPB failed to achieve for the Chinese on the battlefield was accomplished by shrewd diplomacy and flourishing bilateral trade.

The role China may have played behind the scenes in the 1989 CPB mutiny is a matter of conjecture. There is no doubt that it was a genuine uprising by mainly ethnic Wa soldiers who were tired of fighting and dying for an ideology which did not mean anything to them. By the time it broke out, the Chinese had signed several trade agreements with the Burmese authorities. Chinese pressure on the CPB to reconsider its old policies had also become more persistent. Already in 1981, as Deng was beginning to put his first pro-market reforms into practice, the Chinese had offered asylum to party leaders and high-ranking cadres. This offer included a modest government pension—250 renminbi a month for a politburo member, 200 renminbi for a member of the central committee, 180 renminbi for any other leading cadre and 100 renminbi for ordinary party members—and a house with a plot of land.

However, this was on condition that the retired CPB cadres refrained from political activity of any kind in China. The old guard, especially the Sichuan veterans who had lived in China during the Cultural Revolution and been close to Mao, saw the offer as treachery, although they did not, at first, criticise China's new policies openly. The offer was repeated in 1985 and again in 1988. Some of the younger low-ranking CPB cadres accepted the chance to give up and retire in China. The senior members simply ignored it.[24]

Then, in early 1989, the Chinese once again approached the CPB and tried to persuade the leadership to give up. A crisis meeting was convened at Panghsang on 20 February, and for the first time Thakin Ba Thein Tin lashed out against the Chinese. In an address to the secret meeting, he referred to 'misunderstandings in our relations with a sister party. Even if there are differences between us, we have to coexist and adhere to the principles of non-interference in each other's affairs. This is the same as in 1981, 1985 and 1988. We have no desire to become revisionists.'[25]

The minutes of the secret meeting were leaked, and this may have encouraged disgruntled local commanders to rise up against the old leadership. A major reason it did not happen earlier was that the ordinary soldiers and their officers were uncertain of China's reaction to such a move. After all, the CPB leaders still went to China every now and then, and they were always picked up at the border by Chinese officials in limousines.[26]

After the February meeting, it is plausible to assume that the Chinese gave some local commanders the green light to rise up against the outdated and anachronistic leadership of the CPB. The mutiny was supposed to be launched in the Wa area, but it broke out prematurely in Kokang in March 1989. The reason could well have been that the Chinese had closer fraternal relations with the ethnic Chinese in Kokang than with the potentially more unruly Wa, who rebelled in April.

Whatever the case, more than 300 party members and their families were first trucked through China north to Pangwa in the area in Kachin State which had been controlled by the CPB. Some remained there while most of them were later moved to Kunming. Thakin Ba Thein Tin, who had once been a personal friend of Mao and the other top leaders of the CPC, ended up sitting on the back of one of those trucks, but was later provided with a more dignified retirement home in Changsha in Hunan province. He died there in 1995.

The distinction between 'government-to-government' and 'party-to-party' relations could soon be seen even when it came to trade. Jiegao near the town of Ruili in Yunnan and opposite Muse in Myanmar became the gateway for official trade, with hundreds of trucks crossing the border every day and in both directions. But China also desired to have a solid foothold inside Myanmar, and that came by way of the United Wa State Army (UWSA) and the other three ethnic groups that emerged from the collapse of the CPB in 1989: the Myanmar National Democratic Alliance Army (MNDAA) in Kokang, the National Democratic Alliance Army-Eastern Shan State (NDAA-ESS) in the hills north of Kengtung, and the New Democratic Army-Kachin (NDA-K), which controlled Pangwa and other places adjacent to the Chinese border in eastern Kachin State. And all of them entered into informal—not signed—ceasefire agreements with the Myanmar military.

The Chinese had had a long-standing relationship with the leaders of those four groups dating back to their CPB days and it would have been foolish from a strategic point of view to ignore them. The UWSA, by far the strongest of the ex-CPB groups, has a political wing as well, the United Wa State Party (UWSP), and party-to-party relations with it enabled the Was to acquire weapons from China at the same time as Beijing maintained cordial relations with the central government.

Over the years, transfers of Chinese weapons to the UWSA have included HN-5A Man-Portable Air Defence Systems, or MANPADS, heavy machine guns, automatic rifles, mortars, artillery, armoured fighting vehicles and other sophisticated military equipment. Among the most recent deliveries are FN-6 MANPADS, 105mm recoilless guns, 122mm howitzers, 107mm surface-to-surface free-flights missiles, Xinxing ('New Star') wheeled armoured personnel carriers and even Chinese-made Unmanned Combat Aerial Vehicles, or weaponised drones.[27] This is not the kind of equipment that could be supplied by some local Chinese army commander in Yunnan. The deliveries were almost certainly directed from the highest level in Beijing, and to disguise the origin often shipped into the UWSA's area via Laos.[28]

The exact number of soldiers is not known but there is no doubt that the UWSA is stronger and much better equipped than the CPB ever was. A fair estimate of the troop strength would be between 20,000 and 30,000 men equipped with new Chinese weapons and dressed in smart uniforms, not the baggy, old-fashioned clothes the fighters in the CPB had worn. Given the fact that the UWSA had had a ceasefire agreement with the government since 1989, the average age of the soldier was also much higher than in the CPB's erstwhile army. Towards the end the latter was made up of forcibly recruited teenagers because the majority of able-bodied men in the CPB-controlled area had been killed in the wars while many of the survivors were cripples. The UWSA's troops are well trained, and discipline is much better than it was among the young fighters in the old CPB's army.

And relations with the Chinese military are perhaps even closer than they were during the CPB era. In 2007, advisers from the PLA provided training in the use of 122mm howitzers and 130mm field guns in the Lu Fang mountain range west of Panghsang. The UWSA's artillery regiment had been equipped with those weapons along with 12.7mm and 14.5mm anti-aircraft guns. Soldiers were mobilised to dig a complex of underground command centres near Panghsang, clearly intended for protection against aerial attacks by the Myanmar air force in the event of hostilities breaking out.

Chinese support for the UWSA also serves a very specific purpose. When Aung Min, then a minister in the Burmese president's office, visited Monywa, a town north-west of Mandalay, in November 2012 to meet local people protesting a controversial Chinese-backed copper mining project in the area, he openly admitted: 'We are afraid of China…we don't dare to have a row with [them]. If they feel annoyed with the shutdown of their projects and resume their support to the communists, the economy in the border areas would backslide. So you'd better think seriously.'[29]

By 'the communists' he clearly meant the UWSA and its allies. And he was right. It may not be in China's interest to see fighting and unrest along its south-western border, which could lead to a massive influx of refugees into China. That happened in 2015 when the MNDAA broke its ceasefire agreement with the junta and attacked Myanmar army positions in Kokang. It led to a massive counteroffensive, and 40,000–50,000 people sought refuge across the border in Yunnan. China intervened, and the conflict came to a standstill which lasted until the Three Brotherhood Alliance—the MNDAA, the Palaung Ta'ang National Liberation Army and the Arakan Army—launched Operation 1027, in October 2023. And this time as well, China has been able to negotiate on-and-off ceasefires.

While the UWSA declared its 'neutrality' in the present conflict, it has supplied the Three Brotherhood Alliance arms and ammunition, and that is also part of the arrangement with China's security services. A strong UWSA that shares its Chinese-made arsenal with other ethnic armies serves as the stick in Beijing's relationship with Myanmar. Diplomacy and promises of aid to the central authorities come under 'government-to-government relations', or the carrot. That fictitious division of duties comes in handy whenever fighting erupts in Myanmar's frontier areas. The Chinese can show that they, and only they, are able to help the Myanmar government solve its internal ethnic problems.

And it is through the UWSP/UWSA that China carries out its informal, 'party-to-party', trade relations. It is beyond doubt that the UWSA for more than two decades was heavily involved in the production and sale of illicit narcotics, but today it appears that the Wa administration earn more from mining than from the trade in heroin and methamphetamine. After agreeing to a ceasefire deal with the Myanmar military, the UWSA was awarded lucrative business concessions, including permission to trade in jade from the Hpakant mines in Kachin State. Jade mining has for years provided the Kachin Independence Army

(KIA) with substantial revenue, and the Kachins now had to compete with the Was.[30]

Before long, however, tin mining, and in the UWSA's own territory, became more important than drugs and jade. According to a research paper published in *Resources Policy* in December 2015, a newly established tin-mining operation in a UWSA-controlled area had risen from being a minor player in the global tin industry 'to the status of the World's third largest tin producing country'.[31] The mines, located at Man Maw in the northern Wa Hills, produced an estimated 30,000 tons in 2014, 'making it one of the largest tin mining sites in the world...[and because] the Wa territory has no tin smelting capacity of its own...everything mined in Man Maw appears to be destined for China'.[32] In recent years, rare earth mining has become an equally, if not more, important source of income.

China may have changed economically and politically since the days of Mao and Kang, but Myanmar has not lost its importance as a gateway to the outside world. And it is not only about the extraction of minerals—and timber—and orchestrated 'peace-making', but the China-Myanmar Economic Corridor (CMEC), as it is called, provides China with geostrategic advantages as well. Bypassing the contested waters of the South China Sea and the congested Strait of Malacca, it gives China direct access to the Indian Ocean for not only exports but also imports. Myanmar's strategic importance to Beijing cannot be overestimated—and that is why China wants to construct railways for high-speed trains from Yunnan to a projected deep-sea port at Kyaukphyu in Rakhine State. Pipelines for the importation of oil and gas along the same route have already been built. Henry Rudolph Davies's dream of a railway connecting Burma, now Myanmar, with China finally seems about to be materialised—but with the Chinese, not the British, in the driving seat.

More than 60 per cent of the world's oil shipments pass through the Indian Ocean, from the Middle East's oil fields to China, Japan and other strong economies in the region, as does 70 per cent of all container traffic to and from the Asian industrial countries and the rest of the world. While traffic across the Atlantic has diminished and that which crosses the Pacific is static, trade across the Indian Ocean is increasing. Pirates are active in parts of the ocean, especially around the Horn of Africa in the west and next to the Strait of Malacca in the east. Terrorists and rogue nations such as Iran have also been shipping arms to various conflict zones in the region. Since war broke out between Israel and Islamic militants in Gaza in October 2023, extremist groups in Yemen have been bombarding the entrance to the Red Sea, forcing a virtual closure of the Suez Canal. All this has prompted tighter regional cooperation between the United States, Australia, India and Japan, as well as the United Kingdom and European powers. Myanmar has found itself in the middle of this imbroglio—and China is doing its utmost to preserve its influence over the country in order to secure its long-term interests.

China's revolutionary days may have passed into history, but Myanmar has always—during and after Mao and Kang—been wary of threats posed by its northern neighbour. And that was why Aung Kyaw Hla as early as 2004 wrote his thesis with suggestions for alternative policies towards the outside world. Thein Sein during his presidency from 2011 to 2016 succeeded in his and the military's efforts to lessen dependence on Beijing, and China's leaders were most probably unpleasantly surprised when his government announced, on 30 September 2011, that a China-sponsored, US$3.6 billion hydroelectric power mega-project at Myitsone in the far north had been suspended.[33] By this time, there were other signals as well that Beijing could no longer ignore regarding its loss of influence, including a budding relationship between Myanmar and the United States, which became even stronger and more cordial when Aung San Suu Kyi served as state counsellor in the years before the coup.

All that changed after the 2021 coup. The West condemned the takeover and sanctions were reimposed on leading figures and companies connected with the military. China, on the other hand, called for all parties in Myanmar to 'resolve their differences', and the official Xinhua News Agency on the day of the coup described the military replacing elected ministers as a 'major cabinet reshuffle'.[34] Hundreds of angry demonstrators gathered outside the Chinese embassy in Yangon, shouting slogans and carrying placards with text in English and Chinese saying: 'Support Myanmar, Don't support dictators.'[35]

But the coup-makers were pleased and probably felt they had no choice but, once again, to turn to China for help and support.[36] And China has had to secure the future of the CMEC, no matter who is in power in Naypyiyaw—while at the same time keeping close links with various opposition forces.

Relations with the SAC-installed government are maintained through China's ambassador to Yangon (where most embassies are located) and special envoys who come to Myanmar to help negotiate ceasefire deals between the military and various resistance forces. But since the coup, China has yet to extend an invitation to Min Aung Hlaing to visit China. While maintaining a certain distance from the junta in Naypyitaw so as not to be totally discredited in the eyes of the Myanmar public, China along with Russia vetoed a United Nations Security Council resolution drafted by Britain which expressed concern at the violence and serious humanitarian situation in the country.[37]

All these developments have not gone unnoticed in China's regional rival India, which also has a long, often troubled relationship with Myanmar. Well aware of the role the Indian community played during the colonial era as a layer between the colonial power and the local population, the Indians have always posted Southeast Asian-looking people from the north-eastern states at the embassy in Yangon. Two of them, Ralengnao 'Bob' Khathing, a Naga from Manipur, and George Gilbert Swell, a tribal Khasi from Meghalaya, were ambassadors and although they were skilled diplomats in their own right, their presence in Yangon served as a reminder of India's ethnic diversity.

The main issue in bilateral relations for many years was the demarcation of the 1,643-kilometre-long border between the two countries, an issue which is also rooted in the legacies of colonialism and, therefore, fraught with misunderstandings and mixed-up versions of history. One misunderstanding concerns the Kabaw Valley, a highland area in western Sagaing Region opposite the Indian state of Manipur. It is a widespread belief among people in Manipur that it rightfully belongs to them. According to the popular Manipuri website *E-Pao*:

> There are now so many questions in the minds of the people of the state of Manipur as to why, how and on what pretext, such a vast expanse of land known as Kabo [Kabaw] Valley was given away to the Burmese by the then Prime Minister of India, Jawaharlal Nehru.[38]

This, according to *E-Pao*, happened 'on 13 January 1954' and it was done 'without the consent of the people of Manipur'.[39]

Even Brahma Chellaney, a prominent and otherwise well-respected Indian commentator, presented in an article for the *Asian Age* on 7 April 2007 an equally twisted version of the history of the Kabaw Valley. The alleged handover, Chellaney stated, took place a year earlier: 'A sore point in Manipur remains the way Nehru unilaterally accepted Burmese sovereignty over the 18,000-square-kilometre Kabaw Valley in 1953.'[40]

A third version was presented on the Manipuri blog *exmeitei* on 28 November 2018: 'In 1952, India's first Prime Minister Jawaharlal Nehru completely gifted the Kabaw valley to the Myanmar government as a token of peace without the consent of natives living there nor the Ninghthouja dynasty [Meitei royal family].'[41]

In reality, however, no such handover occurred in 1952, 1953 or 1954. In pre-colonial days, the Kabaw Valley changed hands between Manipuri and ancient Burmese rulers before finally becoming part of the then Burmese kingdom on 9 January 1834. The border, with the Kabaw Valley on the Burmese side, was known as the Pemberton Line after Boileau Pemberton, the British commissioner who negotiated the deal. On 25 January 1834, another agreement was signed which stipulated that the king of Manipur would be compensated for the loss of the valley. No map from the colonial era or later would show the Kabaw Valley as part of Manipur. The validity of colonial agreements and how they came about can always be questioned, but the fact remains that the Kabaw Valley has been within the boundaries of Burma—and now

Myanmar—for nearly 190 years. Nehru never handed over the Kabaw Valley or any other part of India to Burma.

On 10 March 1967, India and Burma signed the first agreement that delineated the entire common border. According to a 15 May 1968 study of the issue by the US State Department's Bureau of Intelligence and Research: 'Numerous earlier treaties and acts have affected the alignment of portions of the boundary and form much of the basis of the new act.'[42] In other words, no major changes were made to what had been referred to as the 'the traditional line'. The precise location of the border that was being formalised at the time the agreemnent was signed was unclear in some places, so only some minor adjustments were made and new border stones were erected.

The only problem, which remains a thorny issue in Indo-Myanmar as well as Sino-Myanmar relations, is the demarcation of the border between Myanmar and the north-eastern corner of the Indian state of Arunachal Pradesh. China lays claim to most of Arunachal Pradesh, calling it 'South Tibet', and that includes the area at the border between China's claim and the line of actual control that separates India from China. In 1962, the two countries fought a bitter war over control of what today is known as Arunachal Pradesh, and some of the fiercest battles took place near Walong in that particular part of the Indian-administered territory. The 1968 US study stated: 'Chinese claims to Indian territory in the North East Frontier Agency [now Arunachal Pradesh], however, have cast a shadow on the location of the northern terminus of the Burma-India border.'[43]

Therefore, it is not unusual to see differing figures for the total length of the border between India and Myanmar, but it is an issue that is never discussed when Burmese and Chinese officials meet because it would force Myanmar to take sides in the border dispute. If Naypyitaw recognised the entire length of its border with India, the Chinese would protest and argue that the northernmost stretch of the border is with their 'South Tibet'. A new, more aggressive view was presented by Zhou Bo, a retired Chinese army colonel, in an interview with the BBC on 9 March 2023: 'The entire Arunachal Pradesh [state], which we call southern Tibet, has been illegally occupied by India—it's non-negotiable.'[44] China has never before claimed 'the entire Arunachal Pradesh' as theirs, and if that is official policy, it would put Myanmar in an even more precarious situation in its relations with India as well as China.

Myanmar also has a maritime border with India which runs through the Andaman Sea and separates Myanmar's Coco Islands—Great and Little Coco—from the Indian union territory of the Andaman and Nicobar Islands. And once again, some Indian writers seem to believe that there is a territorial issue here that involves India and Myanmar. Nehru, some analysts assert, transferred the Cocos to then Burma in the 1950s, and, in the 1990s, they were supposedly leased to China, which, allegedly, operates 'electronic intelligence and maritime reconnaissance facilities' on the islands.[45]

The controversy—and speculation—began in the early 1990s, when the military launched a programme to upgrade its navy and naval facilities. The prestigious defence journal *Jane's Defence Weekly* reported on 29 January 1994 that technicians from China were present on Great Coco installing Chinese-supplied equipment.[46] That revelation led to wild, often exaggerated coverage of the issue, especially in the Indian media. Then came a report in the now-defunct Hong Kong-based weekly the *Far Eastern Economic Review* on 30 January 1997, of an unpublicised visit to Beijing by General Maung Aye, the vice chairman of the junta at the time, in October the year before. A deal had been finalised under which China would 'train 300 Myanmar air force and navy officers in flying skills, naval duties, and the gathering of intelligence in coastal areas'.[47] In contrast to those cautious and rather carefully worded reports, some analysts began to publish wild and exaggerated versions of what was happening in Myanmar.

Australian Myanmar scholar Andrew Selth wrote in a detailed and very comprehensive study, 'Burma's Coco Islands: Rumours and Realities in the Indian Ocean' in November 2008 that the British colonial authorities in Calcutta transferred jurisdiction from private entrepreneurs on the Coco Islands, which at that time had little more than a lighthouse on them, to British Burma in 1882.[48] Burma became a province of India in 1886, but that did not change the status of the islands. When Burma was separated from India in 1937 and became a separate colony, the Coco Islands remained Burmese territory. They never changed hands.

During the military Caretaker Government that ruled the country from 1958 to 1960, political prisoners were sent to Great Coco and, in February 1969, an attempt was made to establish a penal colony based on Indonesia's Buru Island concept, where the convicts would be both isolated and self-sufficient. Most of the convicts on Buru Island in Indonesia as well as Great Coco were members of communist or other leftist organisations. But while Buru Island became the involuntary home for thousands of convicts, only about 200 were sent to Great Coco—and they went on one hunger strike after another.[49]

After quite a few of them died, the plan was abandoned in December 1971 and the remaining prisoners were sent back to the mainland. Remnants of the old prison camp can be seen near the entrance to the causeway at the southern end of Great Coco. But India never 'transferred' the islands to Myanmar, they were not 'leased' to China and there has never been any Chinese base there, only a Myanmar naval base, which was upgraded with Chinese assistance. In the 1990s, the Chinese also helped the Myanmar navy modernise and improve the performance of naval bases on the mainland.

Then came a report, published in March 2023 by the London-based policy institute Chatham House, which sparked a renewed, heated debate about the geostrategic role of the Cocos.[50] The report contained satellite images of what appeared to be new military installations on the island, but all that could be said for certain—judging from the photographs gathered by Maxar Technologies, a private, US-based company that specialises in satellite imagery—is that the 1,300-metre runway on Great Coco's airport has been extended to 2,300 metres. It has also been widened and new hangars have been built. A large new pier is visible as well as a causeway connecting a cleared area on the southern tip of Great Coco with a smaller, uninhabited islet a short distance off the coast. South of the runway is a radar station, construction of which began in 2014 and was completed two years later. According to Maxar: 'Photographed in January 2023, the green dome covers the radar system to keep it protected from both the environment… and counter-surveillance efforts.'[51]

What Maxar and Chatham House appear to have overlooked is relatively new construction on the uninhabited, densely forested Little Coco: a huge building in the middle of the island with two nearby helipads, and a road connecting that place with the coast. Similar projects can also be seen on Preparis, a small island in the waters between Great Coco and the Myanmar mainland. Even there, military-style buildings and two helipads away from the coast can be seen. As with the two Cocos, Preparis is strictly off-limits to civilians.

On 10 April 2023, the foreign ministry in Beijing dismissed the reports of a Chinese-run spy post on Great Coco as 'complete nonsense'.[52] Major-General Zaw Min Tun, spokesman for Myanmar's ruling junta, called them 'absurd'.[53] But those statements are unlikely to allay fears of substantial Chinese military or intelligence involvement in a very sensitive maritime area.

According to classified documents from the Myanmar military's Department of Procurement, the armed forces did in the early 1990s take delivery of four unspecified radars for the navy and 12 JLP40 and JLG43 radars, presumably for the air force and the army.[54] But those radars seem to have been meant for navigation and height finding rather than surveillance, and fit into the pattern of the paranoia of the generals in power.

After the military had crushed the August–September 1988 pro-democracy uprising, the United States not only condemned the carnage but also deployed naval ships in the Bay of Bengal, a move that made the generals believe that they were there to invade and help topple the junta that had seized power in Yangon on 18 September 1988. In reality, the ships had been dispatched to, if necessary, help evacuate American citizens.

But the generals were never convinced and, therefore, they have been busy strengthening Myanmar's coastal and air defences ever since. When General Thura Shwe Mann paid a secret visit to North Korea in November 2008, a radar factory was among the facilities he and his delegation went to see. Details about the trip and photos were leaked and show that the visitors from Myanmar also gave a PowerPoint presentation about radars while they were in Pyongyang.[55] The images indicate that Thura Shwe Mann and his men wanted them installed along the coast, around the old capital Yangon and the newly built capital of Naypyitaw, again reflecting paranoid fears of a foreign invasion.

There is hardly any doubt that the radars and other equipment that were installed on Great Coco in the 1990s and that which has been delivered more recently come from China. But the question is what use the Chinese would have for a 'ground station' on an island in the Bay of Bengal. Buildings and other installations that can be gleaned from Google Earth images appear to be too small for advanced operations such as monitoring missile tests on India's east coast, and that appears to be what the Indians fear the most.

China's advanced satellites and its Yuan Wang tracking ships would be far more useful for such intelligence gathering. Those ships have powerful satellite and missile tracking and surveillance capabilities, and they are regularly deployed to three major oceans: the Western Pacific, the South Pacific and the Indian Ocean. They are officially classified as non-military research vessels which support, track and control missions of China's Shenzhou spacecraft and spaceflight programs. They are nevertheless operated by the People's Liberation Army Strategic Support Force, which is responsible for space, cyber and electronic warfare. In short, they are spy ships packed with all sorts of communication and surveillance gear.

In November 2022, one of those ships, the *Yuan Wang 6*, entered the Indian Ocean, only three months after its sister ship *Yuan Wang 5* had docked at Hambantota, a port in Sri Lanka that was built with financial support from China and is now managed by a Chinese firm through a ninety-nine-year lease agreement. The August mission by *Yuan Wang 5* was widely publicised in India, where the news sites said the government was concerned about 'the possibility of the ship's tracking systems attempting to snoop on Indian installations while on its way to Sri Lanka'.[56]

A more plausible explanation for China's involvement in the upgrading of Myanmar's naval bases in the 1990s and possibly even now is that it should be seen as a goodwill gesture that would help Beijing secure and perhaps even expand its influence in the country. The radars that China delivered in the 1990s may not have been that sophisticated, but that is not to say that old and new installations on the Coco Islands cannot be used for limited signals intelligence gathering from which the Chinese could benefit. But the Myanmar military's motivations behind the projects, no matter how far-fetched it may seem, remain fear and paranoia.

The Chinese probably view the issue more realistically, and with other considerations in mind. They want to establish a presence in the Indian Ocean in order to protect the CMEC and other, similar, initiatives in the region. The voyages of the *YuanWang* spy ships are one aspect of that; frequent visits to the Indian Ocean by Chinese submarines are another. In 2017, China also established its first overseas military base in Djibouti on the Horn of Africa and the gateway to the Red Sea and the Suez Canal.

China's presence in the Indian Ocean is a new development that could lead to conflicts with other powers in the region. India considers the Indian Ocean 'its lake', and its powerful navy patrols it from numerous bases on the country's coasts—and from the Andamans near the Coco Islands. Myanmar has once again found itself at the centre of a regional conflict over which its ruling generals have little or no influence.

Closer to home, India has had to grapple with cross-border insurgencies. In the mid-1950s, a rebellion broke out among Naga tribesmen in the hills on India's eastern border. Being a predominantly Christian tribe of Mongol stock, they did not feel that they belonged to India and demanded independence. Not surprisingly, they received support from India's arch-enemy Pakistan and training facilities were provided in what was then East Pakistan, now Bangladesh. But more significantly, much more aid came from China. From 1967 to 1976, nearly 1,000 Naga rebels trekked from north-east India through northern Myanmar to China, where they received military training. They were sent back to India equipped with assault rifles, light machine guns, rocket launchers and other modern Chinese weapons. The Nagas were escorted by troops from the KIA, which, in return for their services, kept some of the Chinese weapons.[57]

THE CHINA FACTOR

Various other insurgent groups in India's north-eastern states also sought Chinese assistance. In the early 1970s, about 200 Mizo rebels—a tribe then fighting for self-determination in what is now the state of Mizoram—were also trained in China. A smaller group of rebels from the majority Meitei population in Manipur made it to Tibet, where they received political and military training. In the 1980s, rebels from the state of Assam attempted to reach China through northern Myanmar, but ended up staying in areas controlled by the KIA—which trained some of them in guerrilla warfare.

It was clear the rebellions in India's north-east were not solely an internal affair and that Myanmar, the land in the middle of the two regional powers, would inevitably be drawn in. This became even more evident in the 1970s, when the Indian army managed to drive the Naga rebels out of their bases on the Indian side of the border. They regrouped in the rugged Naga Hills of the northern Sagaing Region. There, beyond the reach of the Indian army, they could launch cross-border raids into India.

Hundreds of rebels from north-eastern India are still based in hideouts in the mountains north of Singkaling Hkamti in Sagaing Region. And Myanmar's military, preoccupied with ethnic rebellions elsewhere in the country, has paid little attention to these insurgencies. Among them is the United Liberation Front of Asom [Assam] (ULFA), which advocates independence for Assam. Although the Assamese do not look different from the majority of other Indians and their language is related to Bengali, they trace their origin to the Ahom kingdom, which was established in the Brahmaputra valley in 1228 by Sukaphaa, a Shan warrior.[58]

The ULFA insurgency reached its peak in the 1990s, after which successive Indian Army campaigns forced even this group to seek shelter on the Myanmar side of the border. It has been further weakened by splits and surrenders, but a significant number of Assamese militants can still be found in the hills of northern Sagaing. The ULFA commander, Paresh Baruah, spends most of his time in and around Ruili in Yunnan, which is where some Manipuri and Naga rebels have found sanctuary as well. China's security services appear to reason that if India can shelter one of its main enemies, the Dalai Lama, then rebels from India's north-east are welcome to stay in Yunnan. Another, perhaps more important, reason is that they are useful intelligence assets and can report on Indian army movements in the north-east.

New Delhi, of course, wants to see peace established along its entire border with Myanmar so it can implement its Look East, now Act East Policy, which is aimed at linking India with the booming economies of Southeast Asia. Historically, independent India had maintained cordial relations with Yangon. Nehru and U Nu shared a common worldview and it was not forgotten that 'the Rangoon Government' survived because of massive support from India.

Relations between the two countries were not the same after the 1962 coup and the subsequent expulsion of hundreds of thousands of ethnic Indians that followed in the wake of the introduction of the 'Burmese Way to Socialism' and the nationalisation of private property.[59] But even so, New Delhi maintained formal relations with Yangon until the 1988 uprising. The prime minister at the time, Rajiv Gandhi, came out in open support of the movement for democracy and the stated policy that India would give shelter to genuine refugees.

Supporting the pro-democracy forces is thought to have been India's way of countering China's influence in Burma/Myanmar. However, around 1993 India began to re-evaluate its strategy out of concern that its policies had achieved little except to push Myanmar closer to Beijing. The result was a dramatic policy shift aimed at improving relations with Yangon. In January 2000, the then Indian army chief, General Ved Prakash Malik, paid a two-day visit to Burma, which was followed up with a visit by then army chief General Maung Aye, to the north-east Indian city of Shillong. The unusual nature of this visit by a foreign leader to a provincial capital was accentuated by the arrival of a group of senior Indian officials from Trade, Energy, Defence, Home and Foreign Affairs ministries to hold talks with the general. In the aftermath of these meetings, India began to provide material support to Myanmar troops along the common border. In November that year, the

THE CHINA FACTOR

Indian government felt confident enough about bilateral relations to invite Maung Aye to New Delhi as head of a delegation that also included several other high-ranking junta members and cabinet ministers. In February 2001, Jaswant Singh, then Indian foreign minister, visited Yangon to discuss avenues for closer cooperation.

Mystery surrounds the involvement of the Indian right-wing Hindu organisation Rashtriya Swayamsevak Sangh (RSS) in the efforts to improve bilateral relations. The RSS first came to Burma in the 1940s to provide services for the country's ethnic Indian minority, but it lay dormant after the 1962 coup and the departure of Indians from Yangon and other cities. Now, a renewed effort to build up a Yangon branch of the RSS was made, apparently with the blessings of Maung Aye. The RSS (which in Myanmar is called the Sanatana Dharma Swayamsevak Sangh) managed to convince some generals that Hinduism and Buddhism are 'branches of the same tree'. Parallel to this development, the Indian government, which is composed of the Hindu nationalist Bharatiya Janata Party and its allies, invited Maung Aye and other generals to visit Bodh Gaya, Nalanda and other historic Buddhist sites in India, underscoring the argument heard in New Delhi at the time that the best guard against atheist China is culture.[60]

It remains to be seen how New Delhi will balance its security concerns with its economic priorities—and how it will counter China, which is back in Myanmar with a vengeance after the 2021 coup. But it is the China factor that for the foreseeable future will most probably dictate India's policy towards Myanmar. India, however, is unlikely to replace China as Myanmar's main foreign ally. China has already made itself economically, politically and diplomatically indispensable to Myanmar's generals. India's Act East policy will remain a minor undertaking compared to the CMEC and all that it entails.

Washington's Myanmar policy must also be seen in the context of China's designs for Southeast Asia and beyond. There has also been an issue with United States agencies having different priorities, where one agency may not even be aware of what another is doing. That was the case with the CIA's support for the the 'secret' Kuomintang (KMT) operation in the Shan States in the early 1950s. The US ambassador to Yangon at the time, David McKendree Key, resigned in disgust when he found out about the CIA's covert activities in the border areas.[61]

It was all part of a plan worked out by CIA operatives during the 1950–3 Korean War, where United Nations forces with the US Army at the forefront fought against China-supported North Korea. The CIA's involvement with the KMT was part of a secret programme worked out by Claire Chennault, who had served as KMT leader Chiang Kai-shek's main adviser for many years, and, in the early 1950s, headed the so-called 'China Lobby' in Washington. His own airline, Civil Air Transport, had from the very beginning been responsible for air drops of arms and ammunition to the KMT in the Shan States. He later admitted publicly that a plan existed to launch a broader war against China—and using Burma as a springboard:

> It is reported—and I have reason to believe it is true—that the Nationalist [KMT] Government offered three full divisions...of troops to fight in Korea, but the great opportunity was not putting the Nationalists in Korea. It was a double envelopment operation. With the United Nations forces in Korea and the Nationalist Chinese in southern areas...the Communists would have been caught in a giant pincers...this was a great opportunity—not to put the Nationalist Chinese in Korea, but let them fight in the south.[62]

Later, as the KMT had not made any significant headway in those endeavours, and the military led by Ne Win had come to be seen as the only force that was strong enough to halt any communist advance into Southeast Asia, the CIA turned to him for support, which, again, was done clandestinely without informing any other US government agencies. It was under that scheme that Tin U, who later became head of intelligence, was invited to attend a CIA-operated training programme on Saipan in the Pacific.[63] And the Americans did send some weapons to assist the army in its war against the CPB.

But it was all fairly low-key and the Ne Win government made a point of keeping contacts between officials in the administration and foreign diplomats, especially Western ones, at an absolute

THE CHINA FACTOR

minimum. Burton Levin, US ambassador to Yangon before, during and for some time after the 1988 uprising, said in a speech at the Asia Society in New York on 29 November 1988:

> We had no meaningful contact with any element of the Burmese government. They had a designated group of foreign ministry types who would come to our dinners and talk about golf and tennis, the weather and what fruits were in season...During my first three months in Burma, my backhand improved immensely, and I even took up the game of golf, which I had thought was just a waste of time. But I had time to waste.[64]

In August and September 1988, the traditional, Western image of 'the Golden Land' collapsed like the fragile house of cards it had always been. Western diplomats were outraged and felt almost personally betrayed by the very same government officials and army officers they had befriended. Now they had sent their troops to gun down unarmed demonstrators, sometimes in full view of the embassies in central Yangon.

Western sanctions followed, but those were not the cause of Myanmar's economic—and strategic—fall into the hands of the Chinese, as many foreign observers have argued. However, Western policies certainly made it easier for China to implement its designs for Myanmar. This, in return, caused some in the West to criticise a policy of isolating Myanmar and 'handing it over to China'. These concerns were outlined as early as June 1997 in a *Los Angeles Times* article by Marvin Ott, an American security expert and former CIA analyst: 'Washington can and should remain outspokenly critical of abuses in Myanmar. But there are security and other national interests to be served...it is time to think seriously about alternatives.'[65]

But the turn took some doing. Between 2000 and 2008, the George W. Bush administration's bipartisan Myanmar policy not only maintained sanctions put in place by Congress during the previous Bill Clinton administration but added new ones in an attempt to support Myanmar's democratic forces. In the wake of the 2007 Saffron Revolution's popular uprising and the regime's disastrous response to Cyclone Nargis in 2008, the Bush administration did seek to take advantage of additional space to support civil society on the ground by expanding humanitarian assistance and other programmes inside the country, but overall, it maintained a hard line against the regime's leadership.

The revelation in the early 2000s that Myanmar and North Korea had established a strategic partnership helped to tip the balance in Washington.[66] North Korea reportedly was providing Burma with tunnelling expertise, heavy weapons, radar and air defence systems, and—it is alleged by Western and Asian intelligence agencies—even missile-related technology. Some leading foreign policy voices, such as then senator Jim Webb, began arguing that it was high time to shift tracks and start to engage the Myanmar leadership, which seemed bent on clinging on to power no matter the consequences. When the Barack Obama administration came into office in January 2009 on a platform of reversing Bush-era foreign policy, many saw an opening for a change on Myanmar as well.

The November 2010 elections in Burma, flawed as they were, paved the way for the United States and other Western countries to begin the process of détente. The leadership of the United States as well as Myanmar viewed pulling the country from its uncomfortable Chinese embrace and close relationship with North Korea as a key element of this new era. Visits to Myanmar by secretary of state Hillary Clinton in 2011 and Obama in 2012 were followed in May 2013 with a visit to Washington by Thein Sein, the first Myanmar head of state to visit the United States since Ne Win in 1966. By the time Aung San Suu Kyi arrived in Washington for a September 2016 visit as State Counsellor, relations between Washington and Naypyitaw had been almost completely normalised. On the occasion of her visit, she and Obama announced the lifting of all remaining economic sanctions.

The 2021 coup put an end to all that. Relations are back to how they were after the 1988 massacres. But if anything is going to change that, it would be the China factor. For, after all, regional security concerns always take precedence over issues like democracy and human rights.

5

THE POLITICIANS

The warrior kings, and their brutal and often costly military adventures, represent only one side of the history of Myanmar. The other is a solid intellectual and creative tradition. The yearly cycle in any Burmese village traditionally includes a number of *pwes*, usually translated into English as 'fairs', but they are actually much more than that. Every *pwe* worth mentioning includes a theatrical performance and there are few people in the world who are so fond of culture and drama as the Burmese. Sir James George Scott, a Scotsman who wrote about Burma under the pseudonym Shway Yoe in the nineteenth century, aptly said that 'probably there is no man, otherwise than a cripple, in the country who has not at some period of his life been himself an actor, either in the drama or in a marionette show: if not in either of these, certainly in a chorus dance'.[1]

Burma has always had a high literacy rate and education has been a source of national pride since pre-colonial days. At a young age, every Burmese boy was sent to a local monastery to learn to read, write and memorise Buddhist chants and Pali formulas used in pagoda worship. For girls, education was less universal but even so, the census for British Burma in 1872 stated that 'female education was a fact in Burma before Oxford was founded'.[2] Most women in pre-colonial Burma could read and write and, according to an 1827 report from Ava (Inwa), they 'entered with the greatest warmth into the news and politics of the day'.[3]

The long and strong tradition of widespread literacy was further enhanced with the introduction of British-style education during the colonial era. Needless to say, the colonial authorities were mainly interested in procuring a stratum of English-speaking civil servants for the administration and skilled clerks for foreign-owned companies, but the inevitable result was also an abundance of bookshops and newspapers. The introduction of the printing press, originally by the missionaries to print translations of the Bible and hymn books, revolutionised the spread of all kinds of reading material. Prior to that, the literature consisted of mostly religious texts carved on stones or inscribed on palm leaves. The movie industry flourished too, and cinemas sprung up all over the country. The highly creative Burmese psyche also became increasingly politicised, which led to an active independence movement.

In contrast to the popular image of Buddhist monks as men aloof from worldly affairs who devote themselves almost entirely to tranquil meditation in monasteries, Burma's monks have played an important role in political and social movements since the struggle for independence. Following the British conquest of Mandalay in 1885 and the removal of King Thibaw from his palace, Buddhist monks, dressed in their crimson robes, led bands of armed rebels against the colonial power. As Donald Eugene Smith wrote in his study *Religion and Politics in Burma*, 'in the anti-colonial struggle, the *pongyis* [monks] were the first nationalists'.[4]

Smith describes how, in pre-colonial Burma, the king was the promoter and protector of the Buddhist faith, the Burmese language was strongly influenced by Pali, the canonical language of Buddhism, and the monks were teachers of the youth in virtually every village. Education, the yearly cycle of festivals, merit-making, the monks' retreat during the rainy season, the ordination of young boys to become novices—and almost any other communal activity in rural Burma—centred around the monastery and the nearby pagoda. In the capital, wherever it was located, the kings and their monks preserved the political order of the nation.

THE POLITICIANS

But the central role of the Buddhist *Sangha* (order of monks) was eroded under colonial rule. There was no place for the old-style *pongyi* in the new, Western-influenced social hierarchy:

> His [the monk's] educational function was assumed by other agencies, an unknown foreign language prevented him from understanding what was going on, and Westernised Burmese laymen increasingly regarded him as irrelevant to modern life. Of all sections of Burmese society, the *pongyis* had the strongest reason for hating the British and became almost uncompromisingly nationalists [sic].[5]

Although the colonial power made no deliberate effort to disrupt the Buddhist religion in Burma, political and religious authority was separated. As Czech scholar Jan Becka writes, 'The British government departed from the cosmic prototypes with which the traditional Burmese government, the king and the court, had linked the social order and the state.'[6] Many Burmese perceived this as the beginning of the decline of the traditional Buddhist *Sangha* as a powerful institution:

> Initially, the antipathy towards the British administration stemmed from the fact that it was a non-Buddhist authority and this argument was even more important than foreign domination. It was within this context that Buddhism began to play an important role as a symbol of subject Burmese nationality and as a factor in the nationalist movement in Burma, particularly in the period prior to the 1930s.[7]

At the same time, many Western-educated Burmese realised that it would be futile to oppose the colonial power with the 'traditional' response to the new order that the British had brought in and that there was no way the old Buddhist, Burmese kingdom would be revived.[8] But even to these 'modern Burmese', Buddhism was important and, in 1906, a group of laymen organised the Young Men's Buddhist Association (YMBA). It was modelled on the YMBA in Ceylon (now Sri Lanka), which had been set up in 1898 by C.S. Dissanayake, a convert from Roman Catholicism, who, in turn, had modelled his organisation on the international Young Men's Christian Association.

The Burmese YMBA strived to preserve the country's Buddhist heritage in the modern world. In the beginning, it was not a political organisation, although it fought issues such as the segregation of the railways, which provided compartments only for Europeans. Its members concentrated mainly on religious, social, and cultural issues and activities. All that, however, changed when many ordinary Burmese began to show their anger at the practice of Westerners in Burma wearing their shoes inside pagoda premises. Buddhists always remove their footwear before entering a pagoda or other holy place, but the British apparently thought they were above such taboos. To Buddhist Burmese, it seemed their traditional values were under attack.

People turned to the YMBA—still the only nationalist organisation at the time—and, in 1916, a meeting was held in the Jubilee Hall in Yangon. A statement was sent to the colonial authorities demanding that the customary rule against the use of footwear in the pagodas should be made into law. The British ignored the request, and the 'shoe issue' became the first major source of public anger to galvanise almost the entire Burmese nation against the colonial rulers. In 1919, a group of Europeans wearing shoes at the Eindawya Pagoda in Mandalay was attacked by angry monks. Four monks were arrested and brought to court for the assault. Their leader, U Kettaya, was convicted of 'attempted murder' and sentenced to life imprisonment.[9]

The 'shoe issue' became a point of convergence for both modernists and traditionalists to challenge British rule, and to do so in a way that supported the dignity of Buddhism and recognised its central importance to Burmese life. The movement gradually gained momentum. The next challenge to the colonial authorities came in December 1920, when hundreds of young urban intellectuals launched a strike against a proposed law that would provide Burma with its first resident university, replacing the two colleges that had previously been subordinate to the University of Calcutta.

Students and other nationalists had reservations about the bill, including matriculation requirements and tuition costs, but Lieutenant-Governor Sir Reginald Craddock turned a deaf ear to

THE POLITICIANS

the protests. Five hundred out of a total of six hundred students in Yangon began to strike against the colonial authorities. This was followed by strikes by high school students in Yangon, Mandalay and other towns. The students camped at the foot of the Shwedagon Pagoda, Burma's holiest shrine, showing the importance of Buddhism to political movements, even one addressing an issue such as education reform. Much later, one of the student activists, U Le Pe Win, reminisced:

> These propaganda campaigns as well as constant contacts made by our comrade boycotters with members of the Buddhist Bhikkhu Sangha everywhere throughout the length and breadth of our country brought about peculiarly prompt political awakening amongst the monks of both upper and lower Burma and even in the Mon area, Arakan, and Shan States. Very soon afterwards, by the beginning of the year 1922, a little over two years after we had launched our University Boycott, *pongyi* political parties, known in Pali and also popularly, as Sangha Sammeggi, sprang up, sprayingly, like mushrooms.[10]

Out of the YMBA grew the General Council of Buddhist Associations, a broader nationalist organisation. In 1920, it became the General Council of Burmese Associations (GCBA), which sought to widen support for the movement even further beyond the relatively Westernised leadership of previous organisations. The GCBA cooperated closely with the General Council of Sangha Sammeggi, which brought together radical monks, subsequently known as 'political pongyis'.

At the same time, a prominent monk from the Arakan region had returned from India. He was born as Paw Tun Aung, but became known under his monastic name, U Ottama. In India, he had been close to the Indian National Congress and Mahatma Gandhi, and he had also visited Japan, France and Egypt. In a Gandhian way, he transformed a basically political issue—nationalism and independence for Burma—into a religious one which appealed even to those who had not received a British education. A fiery speaker and agitator, U Ottama attracted a large following of mainly Buddhist monks, who, in turn, organised demonstrations and meetings for the general public. The British government responded fiercely, bringing in the military police to break up such gatherings.

U Ottama's activities led to the emergence of an anti-colonial movement that propagated a combination of nationalism, Buddhism and, in its later stages, socialism. This mix of political and religious beliefs was adhered to in varying degrees by most nationalist politicians in colonial Burma, and little changed in this regard after the country's independence in 1948. U Ottama, faithful to his Gandhian ideals, did not advocate the use of violence in the anti-colonial struggle. Nevertheless, during the 1920s, there were several violent incidents involving militant monks agitating against colonial rule.

U Ottama was arrested in 1921 for one of his nationalist speeches, the first monk in British Burma to be imprisoned specifically for speaking out against the colonial authorities. His offense was to call upon Sir Reginald Henry Craddock, the lieutenant-governor, to return to Britain. From 1921 to 1927, U Ottama spent more time in prison than outside. In the 1930s, he was imprisoned again and, to protest his detention, went on a hunger strike. The British ignored U Ottama's non-violent protest against colonial rule, and he died in prison in 1939.

U Ottama was the first of many monks in Burma who stood up against the colonial power. He is considered by many to be the father of the country's independence movement. His old monastery in Sittwe in what is now Rakhine State, the Shwe Zedi, continues to be an important focal point for political and anti-government activities. The monks' movement of August and September 2007 began with a march by monks from the Shwe Zedi monastery to the prison in Sittwe demanding the release of an imprisoned activist.

The second most important nationalist monk in the 1920s was U Wisara, who was also imprisoned several times for delivering anti-colonial speeches. He died in jail in 1929 after being on hunger strike for 163 days. U Ottama as well as U Wisara became an inspiration to activists involved in the independence movement.

In the 1930s, an ex-monk and former member of the GCBA called Saya San deviated from the non-violent struggle of the 1920s

THE POLITICIANS

and staged an armed rebellion against colonial rule. His followers, known as *Galons* after a powerful bird in Hindu mythology (*garuda* in Sanskrit), believed that their tattoos and amulets would make them invulnerable to British bullets. The rebellion was eventually crushed, though its impact was tremendous. Saya San was the traditional *minlaung* (pretender) to the throne, a figure that often emerges in Burma in times of crisis.[11]

Saya San wanted a return to the old Buddhist kingdom of pre-British days, but the young nationalists, who by then were organising themselves at Rangoon University, did not miss the point that most of his followers were young monks and impoverished farmers, and the Saya San rebellion had clearly demonstrated their political potential.

When the Burmese nationalists formed an organisation known as the *Dohbama Asiayone* in the early 1930s, its ideology was basically secular Marxism. Aung San himself emphasised that it was 'the only non-racial, non-religious, and impersonal movement that has ever existed in Burma'.[12] But, even so, Buddhism was always close to the hearts of many nationalists, before and after independence. U Ba Swe, the leader of the Burma Socialist Party (not to be confused with the Burma Socialist Programme Party) in the early 1950s, wrote in his pamphlet *The Burmese Revolution* that 'Marxist theory is not antagonistic to Buddhist philosophy. The two are, frankly speaking, not merely similar. In fact, they are the same in concept.'[13] In another pamphlet, Ba Yin, an education minister in independent Burma, took this theme a step further: 'Marx must directly or indirectly have been influenced by...Buddha.'[14]

Many members of the *Dohbama*, despite the supposedly secular policies of the organisation, also asserted that socialism would free people from poverty, thus enabling them to build monasteries and do charitable work. An advocate of that view was the old nationalist Thakin Kodaw Hmaing, the patron of the *Dohbama*. A former monk turned socialist, he steered Burma's left-wing movement in a uniquely Burmese direction. In the 1930s, Thakin Kodaw Hmaing declared that independence for Burma under socialist rule meant 'nirvana-within-this-world'.[15] The *Dohbama* flag had a white circle with a red hammer and sickle in it superimposed on its yellow, green and red stripes.

But Thakin Kodaw Hmaing was also a royalist. As a ten-year-old monastery pupil, he had been in the morning crowd that saw King Thibaw being led away in British captivity in 1885. And when Queen Supayalat, after the death of Thibaw in India in 1916, was allowed to return to Burma in 1919, Thakin Kodaw Hmaing became her closest adviser. This peculiar synthesis of Buddhism, left-wing nationalism—and a longing for the old days of the Burmese kingdoms—came to characterise the movement that eventually turned into an armed struggle against the British, and was then supported by the Imperial Japanese Army.

Nonetheless, some of the young nationalists did not hesitate to criticise the *Sangha*. In 1935, a satirical novel called *Tet Pongyi* ('The Modern Monk') by Thein Pe Myint, a leftist intellectual who later joined the Communist Party of Burma (CPB), denounced the traditional monastic hierarchy and even attacked breaches of discipline and highlighted acts of immorality among the Buddhist clergy, including sexual misconduct.[16] The book shocked many devout Buddhists, and Thein Pe Myint received death threats. *Tet Pongyi* was eventually banned by the government and the author was forced to make a public apology to the *Sangha*.

In the centre of this was the young and charismatic Aung San, who was born as Htein Lin in Natmauk, a small town in the central dry zone, on Saturday 13 February 1915.[17] His father, U Pha, was, as Aung San Suu Kyi described him in one of her writings, 'of solid farming stock, unworldly, of a somewhat taciturn nature and so sparing of words that he had no success in his profession as a pleader (advocate) in spite of a brilliant scholastic record'.[18] Aung San's mother, Daw Su, was 'an intelligent woman of considerable energy and spirit whose uncle U Min Yaung had led one of the earliest resistance groups against the British until he was captured and beheaded'.[19]

A Burmese child's name must begin with one of certain letters belonging to that particular day, and it is commonly believed that the day of birth will influence his or her character. Those who are born on a Saturday, have names beginning with N and aspirated

THE POLITICIANS

and non-aspirated T or D, and are believed to be hot-tempered and quarrelsome.[20] This belief may seem like superstition to most non-Burmese, but is it so strong that it moulds an individual's personality as he or she grows up. Htein Lin was the youngest of six children and once described himself as 'a sickly, unwashed, gluttonous, thoroughly unprepossessing child' who was so late beginning to speak that his family feared he might be dumb.[21]

But the seemingly awkward young boy turned out to be exceptionally bright—and quarrelsome as well. He won scholarships and prizes and took an arts degree at Rangoon University with English literature, modern history and political science. He also read law for a time, and it was during his student days that he became Thakin Aung San ('victory' + 'rare' or 'unusual'.) He served as editor of a student magazine called *Oway*, which, in 1936, published an article titled 'Hell Hound at Large'. It was a scathing attack on a British university official, and the authorities demanded the name of the author. Aung San refused on grounds that it would be against journalistic ethics, and he was expelled from the university.[22] The dispute led to a massive student strike that shook the colonial authorities. The official in question was forced to retire—and many older, Burmese politicians became aware of student power.

Then, on 20 December 1938, during a third wave of protests by the students, the movement suffered its first casualty. Aung Kyaw, a young student, was hit on the head by a baton-wielding mounted policeman and died. He was posthumously conferred the title Bo (military leader), and there is a street in downtown Yangon named after him, Bo Aung Kyaw Street. Even today, 20 December, is remembered as Bo Aung Kyaw Day. From this and other events in 1938, there was no way back. Nothing could stop the independence movement.

Aung San's rather controversial politics have been the topic of many debates, and it is no secret that he was the first secretary general of the CPB. While in Japan, he is supposed to have authored an outright fascist essay titled 'Blue Print for Burma' in which he argued that 'what we want is a strong state administration as exemplified in Germany and Italy. There shall be only one nation, one state, one party, one leader. There shall be no parlimentary [sic] opposition, no nonsense of individualism. Every one must submit to the state which is supreme over the individual.'[23]

However, the authenticity of that essay has been questioned by the anthropologist Gustaaf Houtman, who presents the view that 'the document is uncharacteristic when looked at in the context of Aung San's other writings'.[24] Kei Nemoto, a Japanese Burma scholar, 'found no claim that Aung San himself composed the Blue Print, only that he wrote a plan down'.[25] It could well have been a document written by Aung San's Japanese minders, and then attributed to him.

Whatever the case, when Aung San and his comrades had switched sides and he, on 15 May 1945, met Field Marshal William Smith, the British officer stated that 'the greatest impression he made on me was one of honesty. He was not free with glib assurances and he hesitated to commit himself, but I had the idea that if he agreed to something he would keep his word.'[26] That was also Lord Louis Mountbatten's impression of Aung San, and the reason why the British government—despite opposition from people like Winston Churchill, who wanted Aung San tried for high treason because of his alliance with the Japanese—decided to make a deal with him.

It is also evident that Aung San did listen to the grievances of the ethnic minorities and their demands, which resulted in the signing of the Panglong Agreement on 12 February 1947. Had he not been assassinated on 19 July of that year, Burma would not have been plunged into civil war after independence, the argument goes. But given the complexity of Burma's centuries-old ethnic conflicts, that is debatable, to say the least. The Karens, who had had to endure numerous atrocities perpetrated by Aung San's nationalist friends during the Japanese occupation, did not sign the Panglong Agreement. They wanted independence and would have fought any government in power in Yangon. And although the CPB was led by Aung San's brother-in-law Thakin Than Tun (his wife Daw Khin Gyi and Daw Khin Kyi, who married Aung San, were sisters), such relationships meant little in the turbulent years of the late 1940s.

THE POLITICIANS

The Kachins did sign the Panglong Agreement but, like the Karens, they and the Burmese nationalists had been on opposite sides during the war. Many Kachins dreamed of an independent Kachinland, and there were those among the Shans who thought they would be better off joining their Thai cousins. The Karennis continued to insist that they had always been independent. And then there were peoples like the Nagas and the Was who had never been under any central authority.

How would Aung San have handled all that? We can only speculate, but the challenge of trying to keep Burma together now fell on U Nu, the country's first prime minister. U Nu was seven years older than Aung San and also Saturday-born, hence the title of his autobiography: *Saturday's Son*.[27] U Nu, or Maung Nu and Thakin Nu in younger days, came from Wakema in the Irrawaddy delta. His parents, U San Tun and Daw Saw Khin, ran a store selling fabrics in the local market and were reasonably well off. As a high school student, Maung Nu took part in the 1920 students' strike and later entered university, where he continued to be active in nationalist politics. He was expelled together with Aung San in 1936 over the 'Hell Hound at Large' article, joined the *Dohbama Asiayone* and became Thakin Nu.

In 1937, U Nu co-founded with Thakin Than Tun the *Naga Ni* ('Red Dragon') book club, which introduced Marxist and other anti-colonial literature to Burma. But after independence, they ended up on opposite sides of the battle front: Thakin Than Tun an armed revolutionary and chairman of the CPB and U Nu as prime minister and a devout Buddhist who often mixed politics and religion.

Unlike Aung San, U Nu never had any military background. He first became foreign minister and then minister of information in the puppet government which the Japanese allowed the nationalists to form after 'independence' had been declared in August 1943. Like most of the other nationalists, he joined the Anti-Fascist People's Freedom League (AFPFL) when they broke with the Japanese. After the assassination of Aung San, he became its leader and signed an independence agreement, known as the Nu-Attlee Treaty, with the British Prime Minister Clement Attlee in October 1947.

THE GOLDEN LAND ABLAZE

It is hard to assess U Nu's time as prime minister, from 1948 to 1956, 1957 to 1958 and from the 1960 election to the 1962 coup, but he was a well-respected statesman who led the country through its first, difficult years of independence and also kept a high profile internationally. He took part in the Bandung Conference in Indonesia in 1955 and is regarded as one of the founders of the Non-Aligned Movement. He was close to India's prime minister Jawaharlal Nehru, but also managed to keep diplomatically correct relations with China. He paid visits to the Soviet Union and the West.

During Burma's experiment with democracy, there were also other prominent politicians. The best known were Kyaw Nyein, a lawyer and anti-colonial activist, who after independence served as home minister; foreign minister and deputy prime minister, U Raschid, a Muslim born in Allahabad, India, and former chairman of the All-Burma Federation of Student Unions, who held several ministerial posts in the 1950s; U Nu's secretary U Thant, who was appointed Burmese ambassador to the United Nations in 1957 and, from 1961 to 1971, served as its third general secretary, the first Asian to hold that post. And then, of course, there were politicians from the ethnic minorities such as the Shan Sao Shwe Thaik, and Saw Ba U Gyi, who led the Karens into rebellion in 1949, and the CPB chairman, Thakin Than Tun, who was a Mon.

U Nu's time as prime minister is often seen as the Golden Era of the Golden Land, and compared to what came after 1962, it is not surprising that many—Burmese as well as outsiders—feel that way. But it was also a time of lawlessness in many parts of the country, and that not only because of the insurgencies and counterinsurgency campaigns carried out by ill-disciplined soldiers. As Mary Callahan describes in her essay about criminality in the 1950s, the private militias did not disappear altogether when the government had regained control over most of Burma 'but instead multiplied in the chaos that characterised the physically devastated and politically mobilised country'.[28] Callahan quotes an army planning memo which states that 'the people are living in constant fear of being robbed and killed any day. The farmers have been unable to plough their fields, the traders have not been able to move about freely for trading purposes.'[29]

The media, however, remained strong, free and independent, and became an important pressure group to which U Nu was extremely sensitive. Throughout the 1950s, the parliament was dominated by the AFPFL, and in the absence of any real opposition, the press functioned as a public watchdog, especially through frequent interviews with the prime minister. At the time, India would be the only country in the region with a press that could rival Burma's in outspokenness and professionalism.

But Burma's long history of a lively press actually began as early as 1836, when the first printed newspaper, the English-language *Maulmain Chronicle*, appeared in Moulmein (now Mawlamyine) in the British-held south-east. It was followed on 5 January 1853 by the *Rangoon Chronicle*. The longest-lasting paper, the colonial *Rangoon Gazette*, was founded in 1861 and survived until the Japanese occupation in 1942.

The first Burmese-language newspaper, *Yadana-bon Nay-pyi-taw*—with the heading *Mandalay Gazette* in English on the masthead—was started by King Mindon in Mandalay in independent Burma in 1874 as the official organ of his kingdom. King Mindon also owned the Burmese-language *Burma Herald*, which was published in Yangon and founded to counter the pro-colonial views of other newspapers in British Burma. Even though those newspapers were owned by the king, he did not decide what they should and should not publish. At an official meeting at the palace in Mandalay, King Mindon introduced what was Southeast Asia's first press-freedom law:

> If I do wrong, write about me. If the queens do wrong, write about them. If my sons and daughters do wrong, write about them. If the judges and mayors do wrong, write about them. No one shall take action against journalists for writing the truth. They shall go in and out of the palace freely.[30]

The text of the law was published on the front page of *Yadana-bon Nay-pyi-taw*.

After the whole of Burma had become a British colony, the independent press lent support to the nationalist movement. Among the most outspoken newspapers were the Burmese-language *Thuriya* ('the Sun'), which was founded in 1911 and later taken over by the rightist politician (and the one who ordered Aung San's assassination) U Saw, and *Myanma Alin* with *The New Light of Burma* in English on the masthead. The *Myanma Alin* was set up in 1914 and for many years managed by U Tin, who became a minister in independent Burma's first government. There was also the *Liberty*, the *Modern Burma*, the *Bandoola Journal*, the *Observer*, the *New Burma*, the *Free Burma* and the *Rangoon Mail* in English.[31] *Kyemon* ('the Mirror'), founded in 1957 by veteran journalist U Thaung, was the first daily newspaper in Asia to be printed on an offset press.[32]

In the late 1940s, Burma had altogether thirty-nine newspapers: twenty-one in Burmese, seven in English, five in Chinese, two in Hindi and one each in Gujarati, Urdu, Tamil and Telugu. By political affiliation, there were three types of newspapers: pro-government, opposition leaning to the right and opposition leaning to the left. Edward Law-Yone's the *Nation* was often critical of the government, even though he, the editor, and U Nu were close friends. And then there were magazines and periodicals in ethnic minority languages like Shan, Kachin and Karen.[33]

All that came to an end after the coup. In 1966, it was announced that private newspapers were to be banned, and printing, Ne Win's Revolutionary Council announced, must henceforth be done only in Burmese or in English. The Burmese public had to be content with the dreary *Lokhta Pyithu Nezin* (the *Working People's Daily* in English) and a few other dailies, which were equally uninformative and lacking in substance.

U Nu's relationship with Ne Win was never particularly close and certainly not friendly, but the civil war made him dependent on the army chief, who, however, acted independently and did not always take orders from the elected government. The 1962 coup may have come as a surprise, or even a shock, to U Nu and other democratically elected politicians, but the takeover was not totally unexpected. U Nu had been warned by Sao Kya Hseng, the

THE POLITICIANS

saohpa of Hsipaw, who not long before the coup had urged him 'to control the military'.[34] U Nu reportedly replied, 'I will, believe me, I will', and then went to a nearby pagoda to offer his prayers.

In his autobiography, U Nu does not delve into what happened during his four years in 'protective custody' in an army camp, but it is reasonable to assume that he was treated quite well. In December 1968, Ne Win even made U Nu a member of a thirty-three-man Internal Unity Advisory Board which was tasked with providing suggestions for internal unity and political change. U Nu did submit a report recommending a return to parliamentary democracy—which, not surprisingly, was ignored by Ne Win.

U Nu's role in the anti-Ne Win resistance in the late 1960s and early 1970s was actually quite minor. In the beginning, the resistance was run almost entirely by the former newspaper man Edward Law-Yone, who was imprisoned after the coup and later went into exile in Thailand, and then by Bo Let Ya, one of the Thirty Comrades. U Nu retired in a section of the old royal palace in Bhopal, India, where Nehru allowed him to stay until he returned home during the 1980 amnesty.

U Nu played no role in politics after his return to Yangon—not until the 1988 uprising, when he, on 9 September, went public saying that he was still the legitimate prime minister of Burma. One of his sons, U Aung, became active in exile politics after the military intervention and the formation of the State Law and Order Restoration Council (SLORC) on 18 September. U Nu remained under house arrest when elections were held in May 1990 and was not released until 23 April 1992. But despite being one of the country's best-known politicians, the party he had founded during the 1988 uprising, the Democracy and Peace Party, failed to win a single seat in 1990. But when he died of natural causes in Yangon on 15 February 1995 at the age of eighty-seven, a huge crowd gathered for his funeral. He was not, after all, forgotten.

During the month from 24 August 1988—when the military withdrew from the streets and stayed in the background, regrouping and getting ready to strike back—until the SLORC assumed power on 18 September, Burma did enjoy a brief period of freedom. The traditional creativeness of the Burmese psyche flourished again after twenty-six years of silence. By the end of August, Yangon alone had almost forty independent newspapers and magazines, full of political commentaries, biting satires and witty cartoons ridiculing the military elite and the ruling Burma Socialist Programme Party. Even the official newspapers, including the *Working People's Daily* and the *Guardian*, began publishing outspoken political articles and pages full of pictures from the demonstrations.

The new, lively newspapers, some daily and others intermittent, had fanciful names such as *The Light of Dawn*, *The Liberation Daily*, *Scoop*, *New Victory* and *The Newsletter*. Some were hand-written and photocopied or mimeographed while others had access to professional printing presses, often free of charge since their owners wanted to show that they also supported the movement for democracy. The authorities seemed to tolerate this—but, significantly, the state-run radio and the government television station remained unchanged. Their employees protested and their demands for the same rights as the journalists working for the print media were dismissed. The military needed to maintain control over the radio so they could announce the takeover, which for weeks had been planned to take place on their supposedly lucky day, 18 September (1 + 8 = 9).

U Nu may not have had much to say in 1988 that would appeal to the general public, but the uprising gave rise to a new generation of politicians. The foremost of them was Aung San Suu Kyi. She was born on 19 June 1945 and, for those interested in astrology, it was a Tuesday, and a Tuesday-born child is destined to be honest. She was only two years old when her father was assassinated and cannot have any direct memories of him. Aung San Suu Kyi grew up with her mother Khin Kyi and, like many children from other elite families, she attended the Methodist English High School, the most prestigious and strictest in Yangon.

Aung San Suu Kyi had two older brothers, Aung San Oo and Aung San Lin. A younger sister, Aung San Chit, was only a few days old when she died on 26 September 1946, the same day as Aung San became a member of the Governor's Executive Council. Aung San Suu Kyi never got on with Aung San Oo, but was very close to Aung San Lin, who, tragically, fell into a pond in the grounds of the family's home in Yangon and drowned. He was only eight years old when he died, and the family was stricken with grief.

In 1950, when Aung San Suu Kyi (or Suu Kyi for short) had turned fifteen, Khin Kyi was appointed Burma's ambassador to India. She followed her mother to New Delhi and continued her studies, first at a local high school and then at Lady Shri Ram College. She was always top of her class and especially good at languages. Aung San Oo went to Britain to study engineering and never returned to Asia except on occasional visits. He later settled in San Diego, California.

It was during her formative, teenage years in India that she acquired her lasting admiration for the principles of nonviolence embodied in the life and philosophy of Mahatma Gandhi. Buddhist monks from Burma, Thailand and Cambodia were frequent guests at Khin Kyi's residence in New Delhi. Nehru, who was prime minister at that time, had been an acquaintance of Aung San, so it was not surprising that Suu Kyi made friends with his grandsons, Rajiv and Sanjay Gandhi.[35]

Suu Kyi left for Britain in 1964 to further her studies at St Hugh's College in Oxford and earned a BA in philosophy, politics and economics. After graduating, she went to work under U Thant at the United Nations Secretariat in New York. Her four years in the United States, from 1967 to 1971, coincided with the height of the Vietnam war and the upheavals that followed the assassination of Martin Luther King Jr. Her main intellectual inspiration during this time seems to have come from the civil rights movement and she found in Martin Luther King's speeches similarities with the ideals of Mahatma Gandhi, with which she was already keenly familiar.

In 1972, Suu Kyi married Michael Aris, a British Tibetologist whom she had met through the Gore-Booth family. Sir Paul, later Lord Gore-Booth, had been British ambassador to Yangon, and High Commissioner to India. He acted as guardian to Suu Kyi when she was at Oxford, and he worked for the Foreign Office in London. Michael Aris had been employed since 1967 as a private tutor to the royal family of Bhutan, and Suu Kyi had gone to see him there when she was still working for the UN in New York. It was in Bhutan that they became engaged. They rode on horseback and trekked in the Himalayan kingdom's spectacular mountains and green valleys. But Suu Kyi was acutely aware of the fact that she was Aung San's daughter, and before they were married, she wrote to Michael:

> I only ask one thing, that should my people need me, you would help me do my duty by them. Would you mind very much should such a situation arise? How probable it is I do not know, but the possibility is there. Sometimes I am beset by fears that circumstances might tear us apart just when we are so happy in each other that separation would be a torment. And yet such fears are so futile and inconsequential: if we love and cherish each other as much as we can while we can, I am sure love and compassion will triumph in the end.[36]

The wedding took place at the Gore-Booth's family home in London and consisted of a simple Burmese-style ceremony (there are no 'Buddhist weddings', as some people have suggested; a marriage is the beginning of a sexual relationship, and monks cannot oversee and bless such liaisons). After they were married, Michael continued tutoring the royal family in Bhutan while Suu Kyi worked as a research officer in the foreign ministry in Thimphu. Bhutan had joined the UN in September 1971 and needed someone who could advise them on how to make the best of their membership.

Back in London in 1973, their first son was born. He was given an English name, Alexander, but has a Burmese name as well: Myint San Aung. A second son, Kim, was born in 1977. He has a Burmese name as well: Htein Lin, the original name of his famous grandfather. They lived in Oxford, where Michael was involved in academic work while Suu Kyi was taking care of the sons. But by the beginning of the 1980s, Suu Kyi decided to go back to academic life. The outcome was a monograph on her father which was published in 1984 in the Leaders of Asia Series by the University of Queensland Press in Australia.[37]

THE POLITICIANS

The following year, she was invited by the University of Kyoto in Japan to be a visiting scholar at its Centre for Southeast Asian Studies. While there, she studied material about Burma from the Second World War, especially documents relating to her father and the Thirty Comrades. From Kyoto, she continued to Shimla, India, where she and Michael did research at the Indian Institute of Advance Study. That was when she wrote *Burma and India: Some Aspects of Intellectual Life Under Colonialism*, which, however, was not published until 1990.[38]

Then came the day when her life—and the lives of her husband and sons—changed forever. On 31 March 1988, the telephone rang in their home in Park Town in Oxford. Her mother Khin Kyi had suffered a stroke. Suu Kyi immediately went to Yangon to look after her. For nearly four months, Suu Kyi tended Khin Kyi in hospital, residing there herself. She had just managed to bring Khin Kyi to the family home on University Avenue when Michael and the boys arrived in late June. But then, the political situation in Burma exploded with Ne Win's resignation and subsequent events.

While the uprising was gathering force, she had stayed neutral, but after the August massacre, pressure for her to take an active role in resolving the crisis was growing. Tens of thousands of protesters had carried portraits of her father in demonstrations all over the country. For the protesters, Aung San symbolised all that Burma was not but should be: free, democratic and prosperous.

After the military had gunned down thousands of demonstrators on 8–10 August, the movement needed a leader, a voice that everyone could rally behind. Maung Thaw Ka, a former naval officer, U Win Tin, a well-known writer, and U Moe Thu, a film director, went to see her. They knew she was in town because they had seen her picture in the paper, laying a wreath on her father's grave on Martyrs Day, 19 July. They were not sure, however, that she could speak Burmese. She had been abroad for many years and, in her native country, few outside the immediate family knew her.

But it was worth a try, and the three intellectuals ventured over to her house on University Avenue. It soon became clear to them that her spoken Burmese was excellent. But she was not interested. She had come back only to nurse her ailing mother, she said. The trio persisted and paid a second visit to University Avenue. This time she agreed. She realised that, as her father's daughter, she could not remain silent when the country was in upheaval.

On 24 August, she stood on a makeshift platform outside Yangon General Hospital, made a brief speech and announced that a rally would be held at the Shwe Dagon. A photograph taken at the time shows her with a microphone in hand, some curious nurses looking out through a window in the hospital—and a tall man in a striped shirt and with a slightly bent back standing behind her. That was Maung Thaw Ka. Beside her was a young woman, the famous film actress Khin Thida Htun.

At sundown the following day, crowds began streaming to the open field at the foot of the Shwe Dagon. Some had brought their bed rolls and entire families squatted in circles around their evening meals. By mid-morning of 26 August, several hundred thousand people of all ages, and all national and social groups in Burmese society, had come together for what would be the biggest rally during the 1988 movement for democracy.

The mood was festive, but there were several bomb scares before the actual meeting began. Students and Buddhist monks were taking care of security and formed human chains around the stage where Suu Kyi was to address the crowd. A huge portrait of Aung San had been placed above the stage alongside a Second World War resistance flag. Loudspeakers were directed towards the ground outside the pagoda complex. It was jam-packed and even the roads leading up to the meeting place were full of people.

Eventually she arrived. Her car had to stop outside the meeting ground since there were so many people, and she walked the remaining stretch up to the stage amidst deafening applause and cheers. Htun Wai, a well-known film actor, introduced 'Aung San Suu Kyi, the daughter of Aung San' and told the crowd to sit down and listen to her. It was her first major political speech, and she was present at this historical time almost by accident. Yet she was confident, slipping easily into the heritage of her politician father. She moved from an initial message of democracy through unity to a more personal note:

> A number of people are saying that since I've spent most of my life abroad and am married to a foreigner, I could not be familiar with the ramifications of this country's politics. I wish to speak very frankly and openly. It's true that I've lived abroad. It's also true that I'm married to a foreigner. But these facts have never, and will never, interfere with or lessen my love and devotion for my country by any measure or degree. People have been saying that I know nothing of Burmese politics. The trouble is I know too much. My family knows better than any how devious Burmese politics can be and how much my father had to suffer on this account.[39]

Hundreds of thousands of people cheered and applauded. The roar reached its crescendo when she concluded: 'The present crisis is the concern of the entire nation. I could not, as my father's daughter, remain indifferent to all that was going on. This national crisis could, in fact, be called the second struggle for independence.'[40]

The uprising now had a leader who commanded admiration and popular support. But even Suu Kyi could not control the hordes of people who went after and captured real and suspected agents of the dreaded Military Intelligence Service. Some of them were beheaded in public. Nothing could contain the anger people felt after the indiscriminate killings in August, or the hatred towards Ne Win's regime and its secret police.

The founding of the National League for Democracy (NLD) on 27 September 1988 was an attempt to organise the democratic forces under one leadership—and to prepare for the elections that the State Law and Order Restoration Council (SLORC), the junta that had assumed power on 18 September, had after all promised to hold once 'law and order' had been restored. And the NLD was much more than Suu Kyi. Lawyers, university lecturers, medical personnel, writers and assorted intellectuals flocked to the new party. Among the best known of the writers were Win Tin and Maung Thaw Ka, who became members of the NLD's first central committee. The former naval officer Maung Thaw Ka was a Muslim, but that was not an issue at the time. Daw Mying Myint Khin, a female lawyer, kept in touch with international human rights organisations. Another prominent lawyer, U Ko Yu, had a background as a student activist in the early 1950s and was once a Red Flag communist. Tin U, the former army chief, brought with him many people with a military background. Thura, a popular comedian and film actor who is better known by his nickname 'Zagarnar' ('forceps', or 'tweezer'), also rose to prominence in the movement for democracy.

The first chairman of the NLD was Aung Gyi, a retired brigadier-general who had been a member of the 1962 Revolutionary Council but had later fallen out with Ne Win's austere pseudo-socialist policies. Aung Gyi was imprisoned from 1965 to 1968 and again from 1973 to 1974. In 1988, he wrote a series of open letters to Ne Win, criticising his policies and suggesting reforms. Those letters played an important role in the movement for democracy, and he was arrested on 26 July 1988. He was released on 25 August when the military decided to stay in the background and wait for the chaos they needed to justify the 18 September takeover.

But Aung Gyi began complaining about what he alleged was many former communists in the NLD leadership. That might have been true, but there were not many older Burmese intellectuals at that time who did not have a past as leftists. Aung Gyi and a few of his followers broke with the NLD in December and formed their own party, the Union National Democracy Party (UNDP). But Aung Gyi and his comrades failed to understand that the NLD was more of a mass movement than a properly organised political party, which was demonstrated in the May 1990 election, where the old order stood against the desire for a better future. Only one candidate from the UNDP was elected, and Aung Gyi did not return to politics.

Suu Kyi's mother Khin Kyi died on 27 December 1988, and the military could not prevent thousands of people from taking part in the funeral procession. But that was the last of the mass manifestations in the streets of Yangon. Suu Kyi, however, began to travel around the country, attracting huge crowds wherever she went. The military felt they had to deal with this renewed potential threat against its rule. On 20 July 1989, armoured cars rolled into Yangon once again, but this time not to shoot people. The entire leadership of the NLD and other activists were rounded up. Suu Kyi was placed under house arrest in her home on University Avenue, but all the others were carted off in handcuffs to Insein Jail. Many were beaten by military intelligence interrogators, and some died after torture.

Maung Thaw Ka was treated especially badly. He was sentenced to twenty years' imprisonment with hard labour. His 'crime' was that he had tried to 'split the armed forces', the judge said. Maung Thaw Ka had written a letter to his old friends in the navy asking for their support and urging them not to take part in the killings of unarmed demonstrators. The fact that he was a Muslim could also have been a reason why he received 'special treatment' while in prison. He was beaten severely and died on the concrete floor in his cell on 11 June 1991.

James 'Leo' Leander Nichols, a Eurasian businessman and friend of Aung San Suu Kyi who had served as honorary consul for Norway, Denmark, Finland and Switzerland, was arrested in May 1996 and sentenced to three years with hard labour for 'the illegal possession of two fax machines'.[41] His actual 'crime' was that he had allowed Aung San Suu Kyi, who was then for a brief period released from her house arrest, to use one of his fax machines to send articles to *Mainichi Daily* in Japan. Nichols was beaten while in custody and died in prison on 22 June, less than two months after his arrest.

With the NLD decapitated—and more than a hundred new parties which had been registered with the military authorities— the SLORC probably did not expect the outcome of the election to be as clear as it became. They probably even thought that the National Unity Party (NUP), the successor to the Burma Socialist Programme Party, through the mass organisations it had created during 1962–88, still enjoyed popular support.

Even some foreign scholars underestimated the desire of the people to see real change. Robert Taylor, whose writings were seen by his critics as pro-Ne Win and pro-military, wrote in *Current History* a few months before the election: 'Many observers feel [the NUP] will do well in the election.'[42] The argument was that the

NLD may be strong in cities and towns, but in the countryside, people would vote for 'the devil they know'.

That was only one of many misjudgements of the situation which foreign commentators made. The next was that the NLD's election victory was so overwhelming that the SLORC would have to accept it.[43] But instead, the military hit back with a sledgehammer and the NLD was decapitated for a second time. The second-rung leadership, which had taken over after the 1989 arrests and managed to lead the party to its election victory, was arrested.

The new central figure was Kyi Maung, a former army officer who had attended military training in Britain and staff college at Fort Leavenworth, Kansas. He had also been a member of the 1962 Revolutionary Council but resigned in 1963. His downfall highlighted the fear of retribution on the part of the military, and why they could not let the NLD form a government or even draft a new constitution. The fear of retribution was so strong that when, after the 1990 election, Kyi Maung, acting head of the NLD, said in an interview with the now defunct Hong Kong magazine *Asiaweek* that 'here in Burma we do not need any Nuremberg-style tribunals', he was promptly arrested.[44] The very mention of Nuremberg scared the generals.

It would be several years before the movement for democracy could gain momentum and even when it did—as in the 2007 'Saffron Revolution' and sporadic demonstrations whenever it was possible to protest—the military always managed to reassert power. Diplomatic campaigns by the National Coalition Government of the Union of Burma (NCGUB) and the armed struggle carried out by the All-Burma Students Democratic Front (ABSDF) may have ended in failure. But there was one sector of society that not only survived multiple crackdowns, it gave people inside the country hope and came to influence international opinion as well: the media.

Based in exile, young activists began publishing newsletters and, when digital media became available, websites. There was no mistaking which side the exiled media was on, but what they produced turned out to be surprisingly professional. The Thailand-based *Irrawaddy* began as an irregular newsletter, then became a monthly printed journal, and eventually a website with a digital TV link. A group of activists in India formed *Mizzima*, which disseminated news and analyses in print and online. After Suu Kyi had been awarded the Nobel Peace Prize in 1991, the Democratic Voice of Burma (DVB) began broadcasting programming from Norway. On 28 May 2005, DVB began transmitting television broadcasts over satellite and became immensely popular. Like *The Irrawaddy* and *Mizzima*, it had a network of contributors throughout the country. They worked under extremely difficult circumstances and under constant threat of being discovered and arrested. But, thanks to modern technology, they managed to do the job. Some of them were arrested, though, and were beaten and tortured by the dreaded secret police.

Meanwhile, the military maintained strict control of the media inside Myanmar, but the name *Working People's Daily* had become obsolete and belonged to the past. The old newspaper man U Tin could never had expected that the name of his paper, *Myanma Alin*, which was closed by the military government in 1969, would in April 1993 be the new name for the *Loktha Pyithu Nezin* and the *Working People's Daily*. Those now became *Myanma Alin* and the *New Light of Myanmar* and even added 'Established in 1914' at the top of the front page, although they had nothing to do with the old, now banned, newspaper.

The exiled media was able to return to Myanmar after Thein Sein became president in 2011 and the country enjoyed a period of relative openness. The decade before the 2021 coup saw the return of active political parties, an abundance of non-governmental organisations—and new media houses in Yangon. In 2012, Myanmar had sixteen daily newspapers and many more weeklies and monthlies. Not all of them survived, but that was not because they were banned. Myanmar had few agencies that could handle nationwide distribution, and getting enough advertising to cover costs was a constant problem. Even so, many, especially young people, still wanted to work with various kinds of media and privately run journalism schools sprung up in Yangon and Mandalay.

THE GOLDEN LAND ABLAZE

Aung San Suu Kyi, who had been under house arrest for almost fifteen of the twenty-one years from 1989 to 2010, once again came to the fore of the pro-democracy movement. Wherever she appeared, tens of thousands of people of all ages showed up to listen to her speeches, or just to line the roads and cheer along the route of her motorcade. Big-screen televisions, expensive sound systems and other paraphernalia at her rallies were clear indications of support from sections of the private business community, which for years had had links exclusively with the military establishment. The outcome of the 2015 election, therefore, must have come as a surprise only for the military. But they lived and still live in secluded communities, isolated from the public at large.

Internationally, she became a celebrity. She travelled to Europe, India, Thailand, Japan, the United States, Canada and Australia, and was met with utmost respect everywhere she went. But then came the Rohingya crisis. In August and September 2017, hundreds of thousands of Rohingyas fled across the border to Bangladesh, evicted by the military in the wake of attacks on police stations and army outposts in Rakhine State which had been carried out by the Arakan Rohingya Salvation Army (ARSA), a new group of Islamic radicals. Photos and television footage of poor, starving people arriving in Bangladesh on foot or by boat spread across the world, and the Myanmar army was accused of carrying out a genocide against the Rohingyas.

In November 2019, Gambia, a small Muslim nation in West Africa, with the support of the fifty-seven-member Organisation of Islamic Cooperation, brought the case to the International Court of Justice in The Hague. Myanmar was to be tried under the UN's 1948 Convention on the Prevention and Punishment of the Crime of Genocide—and the outside world was astonished to see that Suu Kyi and a team of NLD-affiliated colleagues went to The Hague to dispute the charges.

On 12 December, Suu Kyi spoke for thirty minutes, highlighting attacks carried out by the militant ARSA, and adding 'please bear in mind this complex situation and the challenge to sovereignty and security in our country when you are assessing the intent of those who attempted to deal with the rebellion. Surely, under the circumstances, genocidal intent cannot be the only hypothesis.'[45]

Many in the outside world were outraged. She had until then been seen as a beacon for human rights, a principled activist who gave up her freedom to challenge military rule in her home country and who received in 1991 the Nobel Peace Prize while still under house arrest, then hailed as 'an outstanding example of the power of the powerless'. And now she seemed to be defending the military. She was stripped of numerous awards she had received during her struggle for democracy. Even before her appearance in The Hague, Amnesty International had taken away its highest honour, the Ambassador of Conscience Award, which she had received in 2009. Now, she was accused of a 'shameful betrayal of all the values she once stood for'.[46] She had not spoken out against the military's violent campaign against the Rohingyas in 2017.

Edinburgh, Oxford, Glasgow, Newcastle, London, Dundee, Paris, Galway and Dublin revoked their Freedom of the City awards. She lost her honorary Canadian citizenship, the European Parliament's Sakharov Prize and the Elie Wiesel Award from the United States Holocaust Memorial Museum, as well as two honorary degrees from universities in Ontario, Canada and her honorary membership in the British trade union Unison. Attempts were even made to revoke her Nobel Peace Prize, but that cannot, according to the rules of the Nobel Peace Prize Committee, be done. Aung San Suu Kyi, the freedom fighter, became 'the democracy icon who fell from grace'.[47]

The reaction in Myanmar, however, was entirely different. Thousands of supporters greeted her on her return while social media was full of praise for her performance before the International Court of Justice. She and the civil servants she brought to The Hague, not the generals who were accused of genocide, had stood up for the country. And the military were certainly not pleased with what she said in The Hague. Unlike many in the outside world, they did not get the impression that she had defended them.

Suu Kyi had stated in her speech that:

under its 2008 Constitution, Myanmar has a military justice system. Criminal cases against soldiers or officers for possible war crimes committed in Rakhine must be investigated and prosecuted by that system [and] there will be…courts-martial if further incriminating evidence is brought by the Independent Commission of Enquiry…an independent special investigation procedure established…by the President of Myanmar, chaired by a former Deputy Foreign Minister from the Philippines, with three other members, including a former Under-Secretary-General of the United Nations from Japan.[48]

The fact that she mentioned war crimes and courts-martial was enough for the military to react as they did in 1990, when Kyi Maung happened to mention more or less in passing something about the Nuremberg trials. In a remarkable muscle-flexing exercise on the evening of 12 December, armoured vehicles and soldiers with guns showed up in the streets of central Yangon. The military said the mobilisation was a mere rehearsal for an upcoming Myanmar Navy anniversary but did not explain why armoured vehicles and soldiers from the infantry, not the navy, were in the streets. Hardly by coincidence, the display of force was done on the same day as Suu Kyi made her presentation in The Hague.[49] It is plausible to assume that her performance in The Hague, and what she said, was one of the reasons why the military decided to assume total power in February 2021. Civilians are not supposed to interfere in military matters.

Now, Suu Kyi is not under house arrest but is kept in solitary confinement in a prison in Naypyitaw with extremely limited ability to communicate with the outside world. She was initially sentenced to thirty-three years in prison on nineteen charges, including corruption. In August 2023, her sentence was reduced to twenty-seven years after she was pardoned for five cases. Her son Kim is one of the few who has managed to get a message to her. In January 2024, he received a handwritten letter from her, the first since she was taken away by the military in 2021. In an interview with Voice of America on 10 February 2024, Kim said she thanked him for sending her a care package. But Suu Kyi also mentioned that she is still suffering from ongoing health problems.

'Her teeth are bad,' Kim said, 'which makes eating very difficult at times, and she has osteoporosis, which is ongoing even though she is generally well.'[50] And, on 19 June 2024, she turned seventy-nine.

The outside, mainly Western world may have turned its back on Suu Kyi, but she remains immensely popular inside the country. According to a March 2024 opinion poll carried out by the Blue Shirt Initiative, a private undertaking, four out of five respondents expressed trust in her while less than 10 per cent indicated distrust.[51] And 72 per cent had no confidence in the SAC and the government it appointed in 2021, making it the most detested regime the country has had since independence. By contrast, 65 per cent responded that they had 'quite a lot of confidence' or 'a great deal of confidence' in the National Unity Government (NUG).[52]

Suu Kyi and president Win Myint were not the only ones who were arrested after the coup. The NLD was decapitated for a third time, but those who managed to escape are now rallying behind the NUG. Among them are spokespersons who have some international acclaim. One of them is the NUG's acting foreign minister, Zin Mar Aung. Born in 1976, she took part in the 1988 uprising. Ten years later, she was arrested for reading a poem and a statement calling on the military government to respect the results of the 1990 elections. She spent eleven years in prison, nearly nine years of which was in solitary confinement. In 2015, she was elected to the parliament on an NLD ticket and kept her seat after the 2020 election. She is known for having created a cultural impact studies group to spread the idea that Asian culture and democracy are compatible, as well as a self-help association for female ex-political prisoners and, later, the Yangon School of Political Science.[53]

Another 'new generation politician' is Aung Myo Min, NUG minister for human rights. As a young student during the 1988 uprising, he had led fellow activists at demonstrations in Mudon in Mon State. He joined the ABSDF on the Thai border after the crackdown, and later managed to go to the United States, where he continued his studies at Columbia University in New York. Aung Myo Min is best known for being one of Myanmar's first openly gay politicians and, as such, in 2000 he founded the Human Rights Education Institute of Burma, which was later renamed Equality Myanmar. He has received seven international awards for the work he has done for human and LGBT rights in his country and abroad.

Aung Myo Min returned to Myanmar in 2012 and became a prominent speaker at meetings and seminars. He managed to flee after the 2021 coup and now, despite serious health problems, tours the world defending peace, democracy and human rights. In 2023, he received a gold medal from the Sydney Peace Foundation for Human Rights, a non-profit organisation associated with the University of Sydney, Australia.

It is obvious that the NUG has become more influential and high-profile than the erstwhile NCGUB. It has also certainly been much more innovative. In May 2022, the NUG announced it had raised US$42 million from fundraising activities abroad. Money came from a number of initiatives, including the sale of treasury bonds, an online lottery and the sale of military-linked land and properties. The NUG has also launched NUGPay, a parallel digital currency system.[54] No foreign government has recognised the NUG, but it maintains representative offices in the United States, Britain, France, the Czech Republic, Norway, Australia, South Korea and Japan.

On the battlefield, however, the armed resistance has won unprecedented and for many unexpected successes, but continues to be fragmented without any central military command. After Min Aung Hlaing staged his politically, economically and socially disastrous coup in February 2021, the feudal, warrior-king mentality of crush-and-subdue has become an even stronger guiding principle than it has ever been before. Ancient history seems to be repeating itself in other ways as well. An unnamed Englishman wrote *c*.1750 about an uprising in the province of Pegu against the Court of Ava:

> People are chusing to live among the Wild Beasts, than be at the Mercy of the cruel and tyrannical Government, which at present has a King, without any experience, and intirely ruled by Ministers, without any other knowledge but a bare private

THE POLITICIANS

Interest, which makes the Country in general wish for change, because every petty Governor of Towns or Cities, if he can but satisfy the Minister at Court, can at his pleasure oppress the people under him, without any fear of punishment, which has caused the Revolt of the richest and largest Province of this Kingdom [Pegu], who for this last 10 years has baffled all attempts that have been made by all the King's forces to bring them again under Subjection; having at present no hopes to accomplish it, being quite disheartened by their continual losses, which are wholly owing to the bad Government all over the Kingdom.[55]

Although this was written in the eighteenth century and Ava (Inwa) was sacked in 1752 by ethnic Mon rebels, the account strikingly resembles today's Myanmar. Little has changed since the days of the old warrior-kings. The only differences are that the current revolt is not confined to 'the richest and largest province' but nationwide, and now there are 'hopes to accomplish' the overthrow of the present despotic order. But the manipulative skills and the strength of the formidable adversary they are facing on the battlefield should not be underestimated.

And it is not the first time the Burmese (and now Myanmar) army has had to fight for its survival. This happened during the first years after independence when it controlled little more than Yangon, and when in the late 1960s and early 1970s the CPB unleashed its massive, Chinese-supplied firepower on government positions and provided several of the ethnic armies with guns of a kind they had never had before. On both occasions, the army managed to subdue the resistance and reassert control. And hold on to power.

6

MYANMAR TODAY—AND TOMORROW

On 27 October 2023, the same day the Brotherhood Alliance issued a statement announcing Operation 1027, their military operation 'aimed at eradicating the military dictatorship that the entire Myanmar population is united in opposing', the National Unity Government's (NUG) Ministry of Defence stated that they would 'join forces with the Brotherhood Alliance in Operation 1027. We will actively engage in the required operations to collaborate effectively in their endeavours.'[1] The NUG's rather ambiguous statement seems to imply that Operation 1027 was not their initiative. It most likely was not, and it could hardly have been a coincidence that fighting erupted shortly after China had begun a crackdown on the scam centres operating from sanctuaries near or in more or less the same areas as the heaviest fighting took place.

Now, the problem has been dealt with, and the Chinese must be very pleased with the outcome of the Brotherhood Alliance's campaign. But it would be too simplistic to look at Operation 1027 as a Chinese conspiracy, or to underestimate the anti-junta sentiments and determination of the Brotherhood Alliance, the allied Kachin Independence Army (KIA) and local People's Defence Forces (PDF) to fight for what they believe in. Resistance is everywhere, in the ethnic minority-inhabited frontier areas as well as in central Myanmar, and it is homegrown and genuine. But the importance of the China factor should not be overlooked. The SAC is universally hated and large parts of the country are ablaze, and that has also provided China with a golden opportunity to intervene more directly in Myanmar's domestic affairs. China, the only country with a foot in every camp, has once again managed to act as peacemaker. Several ceasefire agreements have been reached in northern Shan State and, in April 2024 in Rakhine State as well. But those have been short-lived and there seems to be no end in sight for the most intense civil war Myanmar has experienced since the years immediately following independence in 1948.

Beijing's long-term objectives remain the same: to exploit Myanmar's natural resources and, most importantly, to secure the so-called China-Myanmar Economic Corridor (CMEC) which gives it strategic access to the Indian Ocean. To achieve those goals, China has always played all sides in Myanmar's internal conflicts and it is therefore not, it should be remembered, in China's interest to see the emergence of a strong, peaceful, democratic and federal Myanmar. As long as Myanmar is weak, China can play official games of being a 'friendly neighbour' and 'peacemaker' and, at the same time, use a carrot-and-stick approach with whatever government is in power: trade coupled with investment on the one hand and indirect support for the ethnic armies on the other. If Myanmar ever became exactly that—strong, peaceful, democratic and federal—China would be the first to lose. The leverage China has today inside Myanmar would be gone. But then China does not want to see the situation get totally out of hand either, because that would mean serious instability in the frontier areas and, most likely, an unwanted flood of refugees across its border.

Apart from China, the only other major country that has close relations with the SAC is Russia, a new player to be reckoned with on the Myanmar chessboard. The friendly relationship that has been established in recent times between the militaries of the two countries was clearly shown when a group of Russian and Myanmar officers met for a party in Yangon on 31 January 2021. The mood was festive and the vodka flowed freely. They were celebrating the opening of a military high-tech multimedia complex in which the children of Min Aung Hlaing have a financial interest. But they also toasted the coup that was going to be launched in the morning. The troublesome civilians who had raised questions about arms purchases from Russia and tried to interfere in military affairs in other ways would be dealt with once and for all.[2]

In June, Min Aung Hlaing, who was on a visit to Moscow, told Russia's defence minister Sergei Shoigu that, 'thanks to Russia, our army has become one of the strongest in the region'.[3] A year later, foreign minister Sergey Lavrov visited Naypyitaw and said that his government was 'in solidarity with the efforts aimed at stabilising the situation in the country', thus using the same expression as the SAC does to justify its attempts to crush the resistance.[4] Thus, Russia has been blunter and far less diplomatic in its relations with the coup-makers than China, which is playing its cards much more carefully.

Cooperation between Russia and Myanmar began in the 1990s, when the Myanmar military sought to diversify its sources of procurement in the hope of lessening its dependence on China. Boycotts and sanctions had made it impossible to acquire military hardware from the West, so the ruling generals turned to Russia. They knew that Moscow would not be concerned about human rights violations and the suppression of pro-democracy movements, and, consequently, Myanmar became a lucrative market for the Russian war industry.

Russia sold its first consignment of four MiG-29 jet fighters to Myanmar in 2001. That sale was followed by another ten MiGs in 2002. In 2006, the state-owned Russian Aircraft Corporation MiG, now restructured as the United Aircraft Corporation, opened an office in Yangon. The Myanmar Air Force has also acquired at least nine Russian-made Mi-35 Hind helicopter gunships, as well as twelve Mi-17 transport helicopters.[5] The Hinds, used during an offensive against the KIA in 2012–13 and in Kokang in 2015, are now in use all over the country against the various forces opposing the rule of the SAC.

Russia has also sold heavy machine guns and rocket launchers to Myanmar and, before the Russians launched a full-scale military operation against Ukraine in February 2022, Russian-made tanks and armoured personnel carriers were obtained through arms dealers in Kyiv. Not surprisingly, the SAC came out in support of Russia's invasion. In an interview with the Burmese language service of Voice of America shortly after the invasion, SAC spokesperson General Zaw Min Tun cited the reasons for the junta's stand on the issue: 'Number one is that Russia has to consolidate its sovereignty. I think this is the right thing to do. Number two is to show the world that Russia is a world power.'[6]

Moreover, the Myanmar military has sent personnel to training facilities in Russia, including the Omsk Armor Engineering Institute, the Air Force Engineering Academy in Moscow, the Nizhniy Novgorod Command Academy and the Kazan Military Command Academy.[7] Others have been serving as cadets with the Russian Air Force. Probably as many as 5,000 Myanmar officers, soldiers and scientists have studied in Russia since the early 1990s, more than from any other Southeast Asian country.

Furthermore, in 2007 Russia signed an agreement to build a nuclear research reactor in Myanmar, but construction has yet to be started and may not ever materialise.[8] But the plan was revived in February 2023 when Min Aung Hlaing met with Alexey Evgenievich Likhachev, director general of the Russian State Atomic Energy Corporation, or Rosatom, somewhere near Yangon to inaugurate what was called a 'nuclear power information centre'.[9] It was described in the media as a step toward developing atomic power to fill energy shortages in Myanmar.

As another sign of the growing friendship between the two militaries, Russian officers have been guests of honour at Myanmar's Armed Forces Day celebrations in Naypyitaw. Among the most prominent is deputy defence minister Alexander Vasilyevich Fomin, who, on 27 March 2021, attended the event dressed in his full colonel-general attire.[10] Fomin was back in Naypyitaw in March 2024, and then ostensibly to visit religious sites in the new capital.[11]

Min Aung Hlaing and other military leaders may not yet be welcome in China, but they have paid numerous visits to Russia. Min Aung Hlaing was there only a few months after the coup, and Ko Ko, the SAC-appointed head of its election committee, went to Moscow in March 2024 to observe the presidential election. While in the Russian capital, he met Central Election Commission chairwoman Ella Pamfilova and, rather ominously, they reportedly 'discussed bilateral cooperation in electoral processes'.[12]

On the soft power side, the Russian language is being taught at Yangon University of Foreign Languages and there is a Russian cultural centre in the old capital as well. There may not be many people in Myanmar who are eager to study Russian, but Moscow's schemes for closer links with Myanmar's military leadership were helped when the West turned its backs on Myanmar in the wake of the forced exodus of hundreds of thousands of Muslim Rohingyas in 2017. Russia and China have in their capacity as permanent members of the UN Security Council consistently used their veto powers to block any attempts to take action against the iron-fisted rule of the Myanmar generals.

While Beijing has vital strategic interests in Myanmar, distant Russia is more concerned about making money. But Moscow's involvement in Myanmar cannot be explained solely in that context. The erstwhile Soviet Union was once a major power in Asia and also a bitter enemy of not only the United States but also China, which saw the leaders in Moscow as 'revisionists' and 'traitors' to the communist cause. The Soviet Union had a close alliance with India and pro-Moscow regimes were in power in Vietnam, Laos and, after the Vietnamese intervention in 1978–9, also Cambodia. North Korea was neutral in the rivalry between the world's two most powerful communist nations.

All of that disappeared after the collapse of the Soviet Union in 1991 and the beginning of Boris Yeltsin's chaotic rule in Russia, which then became a separate country. It needed the firmer hand of his successor Vladimir Putin to restore some of the old glory, and the Chinese have become allies in their common cause against the United States and its power in the Indo-Pacific region. Russian influence over its old allies has vanished, but Myanmar has become a willing new partner in Moscow's plans for playing a greater role in regional affairs.

Myanmar's relations with Moscow have had many ups and downs since independence in 1948. There was no shortage of leftists in Myanmar in the 1950s, but neither of the two communist parties at the time was leaning towards the Soviet Union. From his jungle camp in the Arakan Yoma, Thakin Soe, the fiery leader of the Communist Party (Red Flag), denounced the new Soviet chief Nikita Khrushchev for condemning Stalin at the 1956 congress of the Communist Party of the Soviet Union. The other, much stronger Communist Party of Burma (CPB) remained Maoist and, in line with Beijing's policies, denounced the leaders of the Soviet Union as 'revisionists'.

Reflecting the limits of Soviet influence in Myanmar in the 1950s, Aleksandr Kaznacheev, a Soviet diplomat who defected in the summer of 1959 to the West from his posting in Yangon and later wrote a book titled *Inside a Soviet Embassy*, stated that Moscow's policy at the time was guided by 'a desire...not to annoy the Chinese by too much active penetration in Burma'.[13] Kaznacheev also mentions an odd character called U Ba Tin (no relation to CPB theoretician *yebaw* Ba Tin alias Hamendranath Ghoshal) as 'our man' in the country. U Ba Tin was a popular lawyer, a devout leftist—and a romantic poet. Shortly after the Soviets had launched their first Sputnik in 1957, U Ba Tin married an attractive young village girl and turned up at the Soviet embassy in Yangon. According to Kaznacheev, U Ba Tin showed him and other diplomats a poem he had written in praise of the Soviet Union. It lauded the Sputniks as stars that were leading Myanmar towards communism. The theme was coupled with the idea of the man's own wedding; he likened his young wife to a Sputnik who would lead him to a similar paradise.[14]

But it was obvious that the Soviets could not rely on people like U Ba Tin to maintain some degree of influence in the country and relations were good. U Nu visited Moscow in November 1955 and Khrushchev and premier Nikolai Bulganin came to Yangon on a return visit in December. Khrushchev then promised to build a hotel on the shores of Inya Lake in the capital, a hospital in Taunggyi, and to provide the prestigious Yangon Institute of Technology with new premises. That did happen, but by and large the Soviet Union treated Myanmar with benign neglect verging on discreet sympathy both before and after the 1962 coup.

MYANMAR TODAY—AND TOMORROW

The only major event in post-coup relations came in April 1973, when men loyal to the then imprisoned opium king Zhang Qifu (Khun Sa) kidnapped two Russian doctors at the hospital in Taunggyi. That incident marked a low point in relations between Myanmar and the Soviet Union, but Moscow continued to maintain an active embassy in Yangon. A correspondent for the Russian news agency Tass was also permitted to be based in Yangon, the only other foreign journalist in the capital apart from those from China's Xinhua. All other foreign news services—Reuters, Associated Press, Agence France-Presse, United Press International, Kyodo, Indonesia's Antara and the BBC—were represented by local Burmese journalists, who had to be approved by the government.

Radio Moscow also had a Burmese language service until the Soviet collapse in 1991. Its programming was always rather bland and had few listeners, so many were therefore surprised when in 1989 it began broadcasting commentaries by Dr Vladimir Fedorovich Vasiliev, a prominent historian. He described the 1988 pro-democracy movement in Myanmar as 'a genuine popular uprising against a feudal military system', and said that the military officers who ordered their troops to open fire on the students 'were responsible for driving people into the streets to demonstrate'.[15] Radio Moscow also featured interviews with prominent pro-democracy activists, among them Thakin Chit Maung, who warned that there 'may be bloodshed' if martial law was not lifted before the elections which had been promised for May 1990.

But that was during the *glasnost* ('openness') and *perestroika* ('restructuring') policies of Mikhail Gorbachev, the last leader of the Soviet Union. The Yeltsin years 1991–9 showed minimal interaction between Myanmar and Russia. Then came the Putin era, and the desire to 'make Russia great again'. Russia began to show interest not only in arms sales and military cooperation but also in Myanmar's oil and gas industry. Playing 'religious diplomacy', one of the first companies from the Russian Federation to become involved in Myanmar was from Kalmykia, an autonomous Buddhist republic in European Russia. According to a report on Russian website *Kommersant,* on 20 March 2007, the Kalmykian company Kalmneftegaz 'wins Myanmar's Crude, Gas Tender on Religious Fellowship'.[16]

Russian investment in Myanmar's energy sector is not unimportant, but arms sales have been and will remain the main reason why Russia has established a close relationship with Myanmar's military. The war in Ukraine and Russian losses there has affected Russia's ability to export weapons to other countries, but the friendship remains unshattered. In November 2023, for instance, Myanmar held its first joint naval exercise with Russia. For three days, the navies of the two countries carried out manoeuvres in the Andaman Sea.[17]

Fomin did not return to Naypyitaw in March 2024 out of interest in visiting Buddhist shrines and pagodas. Moscow's deputy defence minister was also there for Armed Forces Day, and Tass reported that he said, on the occasion:

> We have a solid basis for further development of relations between the armed forces of Russia and Myanmar. This year, we have planned more than fifty events of bilateral military cooperation, including reciprocal visits of the commanders-in-chief of branches of the armed forces, as well as joint operational and combat training projects.[18]

But, unlike China, Russia is unable to play a role in Myanmar's internal affairs. While the Chinese have maintained links with several actors in the Myanmar drama and have the manipulative skills to influence domestic developments, the Russians will remain a crude, outside force that can, at best, block Western attempts to raise the Myanmar issue in the UN's Security Council. And, if it can part with any more weapons, serve an alternative source of procurement to make sure that China's influence does not once again become so overwhelming that the country, to quote Lt-Col Aung Kyaw Hla's 2004 thesis, risks losing its independence.

It has been argued primarily in the West that Myanmar's partners in the Association of Southeast Asian Nations, or ASEAN—the regional bloc that it joined in 1997—may be able to influence the SAC and, hopefully, secure a return to pre-coup days. ASEAN's first attempt at addressing the post-coup crisis came on

24 April 2021, when Min Aung Hlaing and leaders of the other nine members of the bloc met in Jakarta. They agreed on what was called a 'five-point consensus', which called for an immediate end to all violence and a 'constructive dialogue' involving 'all parties concerned'.[19]

But ASEAN's two cardinal principles of non-interference and consensus made it impossible to enforce what had been agreed upon. And Min Aung Hlaing and his junta simply ignored it. The 'consensus' principle, though, soon led to splits within ASEAN for the simple reason that its diverse members could not agree on what approach should be taken when engaging with the junta and its opponents. Indonesia and Malaysia issued some critical statements, while the rest of ASEAN did nothing at all.

It is usually forgotten that ASEAN—which is often hailed especially in the West as a successful model of regional cooperation—is actually a gathering of mostly undemocratic regimes. Vietnam and Laos are communist party-ruled dictatorships, while Cambodia remains under the authoritarian rule of the Cambodian People's Party, a former communist party. Brunei is an absolute monarchy without any democratic institutions. Malaysia wavers between oppression of independent thinkers and periods of more openness. Singapore is not known for respect of dissident views. In Thailand, the military has staged several coups against democratically elected governments and manipulated the outcome of elections. The Philippines has democratic institutions but is riddled with corruption and various abuses of power. That leaves Indonesia as the main democratic force in ASEAN, but without the required consensus, there is nothing it can do to implement its vision of a freer Southeast Asia, as the Myanmar crisis has shown.

The reality is that ASEAN is a hodgepodge of nations, which has managed little more than to establish some degree of economic cooperation and to organise exchanges in the fields of sports and music. It has also become easier for citizens of the various member states to travel within the bloc. But it was unable to do anything about the conflict in East Timor, which Indonesia occupied in 1975 and annexed the following year. East Timor was considered an internal Indonesian affair and that meant ASEAN could not interfere. In the end, the United Nations—and Australia—had to intervene, and East Timor became independent.

ASEAN has also been unable to solve issues such as territorial disputes between Cambodia and Thailand, Cambodia and Vietnam, and Malaysia and the Philippines over Sabah and adjacent islands, cross-border insurgency between Malaysia and Thailand's Muslim-majority southern provinces, and frequent incursions by Myanmar troops into Thailand. Furthermore, ASEAN has not managed to articulate a common policy on the South China Sea, one of the region's most important security issues. In fact, it remains divided between members such as Cambodia, Laos and Myanmar, which have sided with China—and Vietnam, the Philippines and Indonesia, which have challenged China's claims.

The United Nations has been as impotent as ASEAN when it comes to influencing the Myanmar military. Since the 1988 uprising, dozens of rapporteurs and special envoys have come and gone, and the military has always ignored their often critical reports. Secretary-general António Guterres pledged at a news conference on 5 February 2021—only four days after the coup—'that the United Nations will do everything it can to unite the international community and create conditions for the military coup in Myanmar to be reversed'.[20]

But the only actions Guterres has taken since then are a series of statements urging the Myanmar military to refrain from using violence against civilians. According to a 3 October 2023 report by the Special Advisory Council-Myanmar, a lobby group consisting of regional human rights advocates, Guterres 'has neglected his responsibilities to the Myanmar people as head of the UN Secretariat'.[21] United Nations agencies continue to cooperate with the SAC, and whatever humanitarian aid they have provided has been channelled through junta-controlled entities.

India, China's main strategic rival in the region, still perceives the access China has gained to the Bay of Bengal as a direct threat to India's security and remains committed to countering Beijing's influence in Myanmar. India, therefore, has sold radar technologies and remote air defence systems to Myanmar since the 2021 coup. But those sales and other exchanges between Myanmar and India are unlikely to rock China's seemingly successful efforts to bring Myanmar back into its orbit. India does not have nearly as much influence over decision making in Naypyitaw, or among the ethnic resistance armies.

On the other hand, India has been severely affected by the coup. Tens of thousands of refugees have streamed into Mizoram and Manipur, which has caused unforeseen problems. Manipur has seen violent clashes between Kukis, of whom many but not all have crossed the border from Myanmar, and the state's own Meitei and Naga population. The outcome has been a virtual civil war in the state.

India's main undertaking on the ground inside Myanmar has been the Kaladan Multi-Modal Transit Transport Project, a strategic response to the Beijing-initiated CMEC. The thought behind the US$484 million project is to establish a secure connection between the port in Kolkata and India's north-east, first by sea to Sittwe in Rakhine State and then by riverboats on the Kaladan River to the town of Paletwa in southern Chin State, from where a road would be constructed to Mizoram.

The thought behind the project was to reduce the need to transport goods via the Siliguri Corridor, the narrow piece of land that connects India's seven north-eastern states of Assam, Meghalaya, Arunachal Pradesh, Tripura, Mizoram, Manipur and Nagaland—eight if Sikkim is included—with the rest of the country. The Siliguri Corridor, or 'The Chicken's Neck', between Bangladesh, Nepal and Bhutan, is only 22 kilometres wide at its narrowest point, and India's security planners believe it could be threatened in the case of a future conflict with China.[22]

The project suffered a serious setback when the Arakan Army (AA), which is active also in southern Chin State, captured Paletwa after heavy fighting in January 2024. The plan to bypass the Chicken's Neck may not be revived unless and until there is peace in western Myanmar—which seems unlikely as the AA continues to make considerable gains and the Myanmar army is retreating from many positions in Rakhine State. Contributing to the chaos in that area is an unexpected move by the Myanmar military: it has recruited and armed Rohingyas to fight the AA, and that could lead to bloody, communal clashes between Muslims and Buddhists. In return for fighting the AA, those Rohingyas would not be granted citizenship but could be allowed more freedom of movement within Rakhine State.[23] Chinese-brokered attempts at a ceasefire in Rakhine State have yet to show results.

Japan is another player, but efforts by the Japanese Nippon Foundation to mediate in Myanmar's civil wars—including the Rakhine conflict—have been unsuccessful. Its local representative, Yohei Sasakawa, has had meetings with Min Aung Hlaing and some representatives of Myanmar's ethnic armed resistance groups, among them the AA. But Sasakawa's influence is at best limited and certainly frowned upon by Chinese leaders who remember the role his stepfather, Ryoichi Sasakawa, played in China during the Sino-Japanese War in the 1930s. Ryoichi Sasakawa was imprisoned as a war crimes suspect by the Allies after the end of the Second World War, but released in 1948.

The Chinese, not surprisingly, have put pressure on the Myanmar military to keep the Nippon Foundation out of Myanmar, especially areas near the border with Yunnan. Ethnic armies such as the KIA have also been told by agents from China's security services not to have anything to do with the Nippon Foundation.[24] And the Chinese have taken over the Nippon Foundation's role as peacemaker in Rakhine State.

The United States has since the 1988 uprising been the strongest supporter of Myanmar's pro-democracy forces and has imposed sanctions on state-owned companies such as the Myanmar Oil and Gas Enterprise, state-owned banks, and businessmen and private firms associated with the SAC.[25] The United States does not support the armed resistance, but a 'bilateral democracy assistance program pivoted to provide emergency support to pro-democracy activists and ethnic support organisations, civil society leaders, journalists, and human rights defenders'.[26]

But Washington's interest in Myanmar is not and never was entirely about democracy and human rights. Security concerns, and then especially the emergence of China as a regional and even global superpower, are more important than domestic conflicts in countries such as Myanmar. And that can be observed in the northern Thai city of Chiang Mai, where the United States is constructing a massive new consulate general at a cost of nearly US$300 million.

The buildings of the new diplomatic mission will sprawl over no less than 26,709 square metres of land in a business park on the outskirts of Chiang Mai. In a colourful online brochure, the United States consul general in Chiang Mai describes the project as 'a concrete sign of our long-term commitment to the people of northern Thailand and the future of our partnership', and then goes on to state that the consulate general is 'dedicated to serving the local American community or those wishing to travel to the United States'.[27]

No one doubts that the American community in Chiang Mai, which consists mostly of NGO workers, missionaries and retirees, needs consular services. But it is not farfetched to assume that the United States also wants to increase and improve its intelligence-gathering capabilities in the region, as covert activity of that kind would fit into the broader picture of geostrategic rivalries. The rise of China has been met by the formation of new alliances locally. The first was the Quad, or the Quadrilateral Security Dialogue, which was set up in 2007 and brings the United States together with Japan, India and Australia. Its clear aim is to monitor and, if possible, counter China's forays into the Indian Ocean, including the CMEC.

Then, on 15 September 2021, the formation of AUKUS, or the Australia-United Kingdom-United States pact, was announced with the specific purpose of coordinating activities in the spheres of 'cyber capabilities, artificial intelligence, quantum technologies and additional underwater capabilities'.[28] Under the terms of the pact, the United States and Britain will help Australia acquire nuclear-powered submarines.

Both pacts are widely seen as efforts to counter China's influence in the contested South China Sea and the Chinese navy's increasingly frequent forays into the Indian Ocean. That was not lost on Beijing, who especially condemned the establishment of AUKUS. Only a day after the announcement of the pact, China's foreign ministry spokesman Zhao Lijian said the alliance 'severely undermined regional peace and stability, intensified the arms

187

race, and damaged global nuclear non-proliferation efforts'.[29] He also criticised what he called 'the outdated Cold War zero-sum mentality' of the pact's members and warned them that 'they will only end up shooting themselves in the foot'.[30]

In an editorial published in the Communist Party of China's mouthpiece *Global Times* on 30 September 2021, the rhetoric was even blunter and more vitriolic:

> The three countries, drawing lines based on ideology, have built a new military bloc that will heighten geopolitical tensions. The international community rejects the Cold War and its divisions, but the US blatantly violates its political claims of not engaging in any new Cold War and gangs up with others to create a small Anglo-Saxon "clique," putting geopolitical self-interest above international solidarity. This is a typical Cold War mentality.[31]

The editorial also warned of the danger of an escalating arms race:

> The move will spur regional countries to accelerate the development of military capabilities, and even seek to break the nuclear threshold and increase the risk of military conflict. The US, on the one hand, hands out sanctions and suppresses some countries to pressure them not to develop nuclear capabilities, while on the other hand flagrantly transferring nuclear technologies to non-nuclear states. This is a typical double standard.[32]

The *Global Times* editorial did not expand on the reference to the possibility of nuclear proliferation, and Australia will certainly not become a nuclear power just because it is about to acquire nuclear-powered submarines. But the harsh rhetoric shows how concerned China's government is, and that the battlelines in the new Cold War are becoming clearer. China is seen as the enemy of a range of countries which consider themselves guardians of democratic values. Needless to say, there are also competing economic interests between China and its adversaries. An increasingly affluent Asia is a huge market for consumer goods and the region is rich in natural and mineral resources which many countries are eager to exploit.

MYANMAR TODAY—AND TOMORROW

That competition can be seen also on land, and Chiang Mai is not a random choice for a strategic listening post in the region. The Americans first set up a diplomatic mission in Chiang Mai in 1950, and it was from there they coordinated their clandestine support for nationalist Kuomintang (KMT) forces that had retreated into the Shan States after their defeat in the Chinese Civil War. Then, in the 1960s, came the wars in Indochina, and the US consulate in Chiang Mai oversaw the gathering of human as well as signals intelligence in the region. Local operatives were sent into Laos and southern China, and the Americans together with the Thais had an extensive network of listening posts in northern Thailand.

The main such facility was located at Ramasun, 20 kilometres south of Udon Thani in north-eastern Thailand. That base was first established in 1966 but then as an outpost for the main facility in Bangkok. In 1970, it was upgraded to an AN/FLR-9 Circular Disposed Antenna Array (CDAA) station, a large, circular array of Wullenweber antennas commonly referred to by the nickname 'Elephant Cage' because its shape resembled an elephant kraal. The Ramasun facility picked up radio traffic from Laos, southern China and North Vietnam and monitored Chinese military movements in the region. Most importantly, it served as a military intelligence terminal for communications between the CIA and its various intelligence sites and allies across Southeast and East Asia.

A similar signals intelligence facility was established near Lampang, 108 kilometres south of Chiang Mai, for the specific purpose of monitoring radio traffic in northern Myanmar and Yunnan. American Chinese language experts translated intercepted messages into English, and Burmese-speaking Shans translated messages in Burmese into Thai and English. A major target at that time was the China-supported CPB. There was always the possibility of a linkup between the CPB and the Communist Party of Thailand and other communist parties in the region, exactly as China's master strategist Kang Sheng envisaged in the 1960s and 1970s.

The 'Elephant Cage' at Ramasun was officially dismantled in 1976, a year after the end of the Indochina wars and, in 1975,

Thailand also switched recognition to the People's Republic of China from the Republic of China (Taiwan). The Americans withdrew and the Thais took over operation of the Ramasun and Lampang facilities. Over the years, the 'Elephant Cages' became obsolete and, in May 1986, the very last of them, in Alaska, was decommissioned. Today, there are more advanced and sophisticated ways of monitoring movements in cyberspace, as well as on the ground.

The current US mission in Chiang Mai is located in old buildings overlooking the banks of the Ping River. Some of them were built over a hundred years ago and then called the Chedi Ngam Palace, or 'the Beautiful Pagoda Palace'. The compound once served as the residence of the last monarch of northern Thailand, Chao Kaew Nawarat, who died in 1939. After that it became government property and, eleven years later, the Americans moved in and turned it into a consulate. But it is important to remember that it remained a consulate until 1986 and only then became a consulate general, or a proper foreign service mission. Until 1986, it was effectively an intelligence station, although it also provided consular services.

It is anybody's guess what roles the United States' new consulate general will play when it opens its doors next year. Apart from the obvious—that people will go there to get visas, for cultural events and to visit its libraries—intelligence gathering will most certainly be a top priority. Myanmar-watching will remain one of the consulate general's main tasks, albeit in a different context, as China no longer exports revolution. But Beijing's expanding economic empire—including the CMEC down to the Indian Ocean—requires political protection and therefore also influence in its neighbouring countries.

Already in 2017, China's then consul general in Chiang Mai, Ren Yisheng, talked about Beijing's multi-trillion-dollar infrastructure project, the Belt and Road Initiative, at the city's university. Two years later, Ren attended a similar conference in Chiang Rai with the emphasis on development in the so-called Greater Mekong Sub-region, which includes parts of southern China, Laos, Myanmar, Cambodia and Vietnam. The Chinese even appear to have made Chiang Mai and their consulate general there a base for their plans for the region.

Chinese patrol boats with armed police are also now for the first time in history venturing down the Mekong River, almost as far as the riverine junction where Myanmar, Laos and Thailand meet. That may not be perceived as a major threat to the region, but it is nevertheless a new development that China's adversaries would be keen to monitor.

In August 2021, China transferred US$6 million to what it for the first time since the coup referred to as 'the Myanmar government' to be used for projects and programmes within Beijing's controversial Lancang-Mekong Cooperation Framework, seemingly a tiny gesture but important in the broader scheme of things.[33] On one side in the area west of the Mekong is China's main ally the UWSA, while its rival, the Restoration Council of Shan State, receives most of its supplies from Thailand—and is seen, rightly or wrongly, by Beijing as a 'pro-Western force'. In other words, China has secured a foothold inside a strategically important riparian area by having a close relationship with the UWSA as well as the SAC.

Since the coup, the geopolitical balance has tilted to the advantage of China, and whether or not that was Min Aung Hlaing's intention when he sent his tanks into Yangon and Naypyitaw, it is the reality of his ill-thought-out action in February 2021. Myanmar is back to square one as an international pariah—and a country that will find it hard to resist the advances of its powerful northern neighbour.

The new Cold War may not yet be as hot as the previous one sometimes was, but it is clear that the Americans and their Quad and AUKUS allies are building a bulwark against China and that the construction of a new US consulate general in Chiang Mai is part of that strategy. But it remains to be seen what that means for the region—and especially for troubled and vulnerable Myanmar. There is still a long way to go before we could see a return to the open confrontations of the 1950s, 1960s and 1970s. But, once again, and even if Ukraine and Gaza are at the top of Washington's security priorities, Myanmar may find itself in the midst of a geopolitical storm.

The old dictator Than Shwe, though, does not seem to be concerned. Like so many Burmese rulers before him, he built his own capital, inaugurated it in 2005, and gave it the royal name Naypyitaw. But 'the Abode of Kings' was not carved out of the jungle, as some Western news reports had it at the time it was being built. It was constructed on the open central plains, which had been denuded in the 1950s to deprive the CPB of the cover its combatants would need if they came down from the mountains to threaten Pyinmana and other nearby towns.

Than Shwe turned ninety-one on 2 February 2024, but nothing in the military hierarchy is likely to change once he has passed away. The warrior-king mentality will also remain the same in the minds of those who command the armed forces. Even the 'reform president' and 'Myanmar's Gorbachev' Thein Sein showed his true colours when, in January 2020, he endorsed the policies of the military, saying that Myanmar faced growing threats to 'territory, race and religion' and called on the people to vote for candidates in the upcoming November general election who would 'protect the country'.[34] Since the coup, Thein Sein has made donations to families of members of the military's proxy Union Solidarity and Development Party (USDP) who have been killed or wounded on suspicion of acting as SAC informants. Needless to say, he has not donated any money to the many families whose loved ones have been gunned down by the military and the police for demonstrating peacefully against the coup.

And the Buddhist monks, the heroes of the 2007 'Saffron Revolution', have become compliant. Ashin Nyanissara, who is best known as Sitagu Sayadaw and was once one of Myanmar's most revered abbots, even accompanied Min Aung Hlaing to Moscow in July 2022. The SAC delegation was there to discuss 'atomic energy cooperation'—and how to enhance military cooperation between Myanmar and Russia. They and the Sitagu Sayadaw then attended a ceremony unveiling a replica of the Shwezigon Pagoda in Kaluga, south-west of Moscow.[35] Other monks are seen in the official Myanmar media receiving donations from military officers and then blessing them. In January 2023, the ultra-nationalist monk U Wirathu was granted the title of 'Thiri Pyanchi', an award recognising 'outstanding work for the good of the Union of Myanmar'.[36]

After the coup, not much remains of the NLD inside the country. As well as its top leaders, such as Aung San Suu Kyi and Win Myint, hundreds of its local leaders—including former ministers in the regional governments—and activists have also been detained and remain in military custody. And two of the icons of the 1988 uprising—former student leaders Min Ko Naing and Ko Ko Gyi—have gone different ways. Min Ko Naing, which means 'conqueror of kings', was born as Paw Oo Tun and assumed his new name during the uprising. He organised student protests, spoke to massive crowds and had a charisma which mesmerised his audience. He had to go underground when the military formed its State Law and Order Restoration Council (SLORC) on 18 September 1988, but the military tracked him down and he was arrested on 24 March 1989. Min Ko Naing was sentenced to twenty years' imprisonment for instigating 'disturbances to the detriment of law and order, peace and tranquillity'.[37]

According to Amnesty International, Min Ko Naing was severely tortured and ill-treated during the early stages of his detention and his health suffered as a consequence.[38] After spending fifteen years in prison, he was released on 19 November 2004. He was rearrested in September 2006, and some of the '88-generation-students', as they called themselves, organised a nationwide campaign called 'White Expression'. People were encouraged to dress in white in a peaceful protest aimed at putting pressure on the military government to release Min Ko Naing and all the other political prisoners.

Min Ko Naing was released in January 2007 and arrested again in August and then released on 13 January 2012 as part of Thein Sein's mass pardon for political activists. He managed to escape from Myanmar after the 2021 coup and his whereabouts are unknown. But he remains a potent voice for the pro-democracy movement and the SAC has charged him in absentia in one of its courts for 'inciting unrest against the state and threatening public tranquillity through their social media post'.[39]

THE GOLDEN LAND ABLAZE

Two other pro-democracy campaigners, veteran student activist Kyaw Min Yu, also known as Ko Jimmy, and Phyo Zeya Thaw, a hip-hop artist who became an NLD MP and one of Aung San Suu Kyi's closest advisers, were charged under the Anti-Terrorism Law and executed by hanging on 23 July 2022. On the same day, Hla Myo Aung and Aung Thura Zaw were hanged for the alleged murder of a woman believed to have been acting as an informer for the military.[40] Although thousands have been extrajudicially executed by the military over the decades, those were the first official executions since Ohn Kyaw Myint was hanged on 27 July 1977 for plotting against the Ne Win government, and Chin Mo, one of the North Korean commandoes who carried out the 1983 bomb attack in Yangon, was led to the gallows on 10 April 1985.

Ko Ko Gyi, a key member of the movement of 1988, who spent over seventeen years in prison on several occasions between 1989 and 2012, decided to follow an entirely different path. Unlike his former comrades in the pro-democracy movement, Ko Ko Gyi has chosen to work with the military. Having failed to be accepted by the NLD as a candidate for the 2015 elections, he formed his own People's Party in 2018 and did not join those who opposed the 2021 coup. Instead, he attended a meeting convened in May 2021 by a SAC-appointed election body and has signalled that the People's Party will take part in the elections the junta has promised to hold as soon as 'peace and tranquility' has been restored.[41] That has led to mass resignations from his party, and it is uncertain whether it remains a viable political entity.

Ko Ko Gyi has also made some controversial statements about the Rohingyas. When Nyan Lin, a spokesman for the NLD said after the Rohingya exodus in August 2017 that 'these Muslims are illegal immigrants from Bangladesh and…this crisis is an infringement of our sovereignty',[42] Ko Ko Gyi stated: 'We have been human-rights defenders for many years and suffered for a long time but we are standing together on this issue because we need to support our national security.'[43] But Ko Ko Gyi is not the only pro-democracy activist who views the Rohingya issue that way. Even the well-respected human rights advocate Min Ko Naing justified the expulsion of the Rohingyas in 2017 by claiming they are not one of the recognised ethnic groups in Myanmar.[44]

Burmese antipathy against the Rohingyas is widespread and deep-rooted and can be explained—but not justified—by the fact that they, unlike urban Muslims who have Burmese names and speak Burmese, are a rural community living next door to over-populated Bangladesh, and they speak a language that is not that different from the Chittagonian dialect spoken across the border. In accordance with a 1982 citizenship law, they are not recognised as citizens of Myanmar—but it is not true that the law, as some Western commentators have argued, 'arbitrarily deprived the Rohingya of their citizenship'.[45]

The 1982 citizenship law states that only those who can trace their family residency prior to 1823, the year before the first Anglo-Burmese War, are recognised as full citizens of Myanmar.[46] And that excludes not only the Rohingyas but also descendants of Indians and Chinese who immigrated during the British colonial era. The enactment of the law led to an exodus primarily of Sino-Burmese, who at that time could be accepted as citizens of the Republic of China, or Taiwan—and that is the reason why there is a 40,000-strong community of Burmese of Chinese descent living in a part of Taipei, which is appropriately called 'Little Burma'.[47]

But there is no denial of the fact that the Rohingyas have been severely victimised and huge numbers of them have been pushed out of the country on several occasions. The first time was in 1978, when more than 200,000 Rohingyas fled to Bangladesh to escape an operation code-named *Naga Min*, or 'King of Dragons', which, according to the authorities, was aimed at 'properly registering every inhabitant of this country, citizen or foreigner'.[48] But even here, it is doubtful whether the Rohingyas were the original and prime targets. *Naga Min* actually began the year before in Shan and Kachin States and, as the name suggests, was meant to track down Chinese who had sought refuge in those areas in the wake of the Cultural Revolution in their homeland. But when the drive reached Rakhine State, the Rohingyas were those who suffered the most. Thousands of people were killed, their homes destroyed, and there were numerous reports of rape.

In 1992, another wave of violence forced 250,000 Rohingyas to flee to Bangladesh, and this time, they were the sole target. Likewise, in 2017 there is nothing to indicate that there was anything other than a drive to force as many Rohingyas as possible to leave Rakhine State. In 1978, diplomatic initiatives led to a repatriation agreement, and the United Nations High Commissioner for Refugees facilitated their return to Rakhine State. That did also happen after 1992, but this time, there has been no serious attempt to repatriate the now more than a million Rohingya refugees who are languishing in camps in Bangladesh.

The plight of the Rohingyas became a diplomatic problem for the NUG when its ministers travelled the world seeking international support. Perhaps so as not to upset supporters at home, they kept silent, but when they were repeatedly asked where they stood on the issue and gave only bland answers, they risked losing support from policy makers in the United States and other Western countries and, eventually, gave in to the pressure. In August 2023, NUG's humanitarian minister, Win Myat Aye, eventually apologised for failing 'to bring justice to the Rohingya in northern Rakhine State'.[49] And the NUG appointed the Rohingya activist Aung Kyaw Moe as its deputy human rights minister. It was a perfect choice, because Aung Kyaw Moe has previously worked for various United Nations agencies and NGOs in Myanmar, Thailand, Afghanistan and Liberia.[50] The NUG then promised to repeal the 1982 law and grant the Rohingyas citizenship.

But the question remains, would any future government accept the return of the Rohingyas and their descendants in the camps in Bangladesh as well as those living in exile in other parts of the world?[51] By now, they are in the millions, and any such move would lead to serious unrest not only in Rakhine State but in the entire country. In Bangladesh officials are concerned that they may be stuck with a Palestine-like permanent refugee population which could result in a state-within-a-state replete with radical elements exploiting the misery and desperation many refugees, especially the young, are experiencing in the camps.[52]

MYANMAR TODAY—AND TOMORROW

An even more acute problem is the economy, which is in a shambles, with ordinary people struggling to survive amid rising prices and shortages of commodities. But the military leadership is not suffering from the economic downturn as much as ordinary citizens. They belong to a privileged elite, and sanctions, smart or otherwise, will remain ineffective for two major reasons. The first, which is mostly overlooked, is the magnitude of Myanmar's parallel, or greyish-black, economy, which does not show up in any official statistics.

The underground economy kept Myanmar alive throughout rigid socialist policies from 1962 to 1988, sanctions and boycotts after that, and until the West changed its policies after the formation of Thein Sein's quasi-civilian government in 2011. Drugs, jade and other precious stones, timber, antiques and various artifacts have been smuggled out of the country for decades while assorted consumer goods and even cars and motorcycles have travelled in the other direction from countries such as China, India, Thailand and Singapore. The exact value of this informal—and illegal—trade is not known, but most probably runs into millions if not billions of dollars.

With an inadequate and largely untrustworthy banking system, many people in Myanmar prefer to utilise the services of dealers in what is called 'hundies', which in the Indian Subcontinent and the Middle East is known as *hawala*. Through this system, money is transferred via a network of private brokers, leaving no paper trail that any authorities can track down and follow. In short, Myanmar will, as it always has, survive another round of punitive measures imposed by the West.

And then there is the fact that countries such as China, Russia, Thailand, India, Malaysia, Vietnam and Singapore—Myanmar's main trading partners—are happy to continue dealing with whoever is in power in Naypyitaw. Most of them may even prefer to deal with a military-run Myanmar rather than having to go through a democratic, transparent and accountable system where the authorities may have the audacity to clamp down on corruption and other malpractices.

And there are some hard realities facing the resistance forces. They may have scored unprecedented successes on the battlefield, but they remain fragmented and disunited, and still do not possess the weaponry that is needed to defeat the well-armed military with all the firepower it has at its disposal, the most devastating, thanks to China and Russia, being air power. And it is far from the first time that the Myanmar army has faced serious threats to its authority. It happened during the years after independence and in the late 1960s and early 1970s, when China poured in weapons to the CPB, which, in turn shared that weaponry with ethnic armed organisations. At that time, the non-communist resistance on the Thai border was also strong, but it fell apart when the Karens and the Burmans could not agree on a common strategy, or what they were actually fighting for. And international peacemakers and conflict-resolutionists have repeatedly shown that their efforts have been a waste of time and money; the generals simply will not listen and, even if they pretend to, they do not take advice from such outsiders. They are determined to stay in power, no matter the cost or the consequences.

That brings us to the sad reality: the military has been running the country under different guises since 1962 and history shows that it cannot be easily dislodged from power. Nothing is likely to change unless and until there is a split at the top or a widespread mutiny within the ranks. That was true when millions of people took to the streets in 1988 and it remains so today. But such a development could also lead to an even bloodier civil war, a potentially devastating scenario for which the outside world and all those involved in Myanmar must be prepared.

Nevertheless, if the military remains united, the decades-long civil wars will continue to bleed the country for years to come—and the main victims will be the people of Myanmar, who for decades have been suffering under the brutal rule of a power-obsessed clique of men in green.

LIST OF ABBREVIATIONS

AA	Arakan Army, armed group in Rakhine State.
ABSDF	All-Burma Students Democratic Front.
AFPFL	Anti-Fascist People's Freedom League. The main political party in the 1940s and 1950s.
ARSA	Arakan Rohingya Salvation Army.
BDA	Burma Defence Army.
BEDC	Burma Economic Development Corporation.
BIA	Burma Independence Army.
BNA	Burma National Army.
BSPP	Burma Socialist Programme Party.
Burifs	Burma Rifles. Unit in the army in the 1950s and 1960s.
CIA	The United States Central Intelligence Agency.
CMEC	China-Myanmar Economic Corridor. A number of infrastructure projects connecting Myanmar with Yunnan in China.
CPB	Communist Party of Burma. In rebellion against the government from 1948 to 1989.
CPC	Communist Party of China. In power in China since 1949.
CP(RF)	Communist Party (Red Flag). Ultra-radical communist group which collapsed in the 1970s.

LIST OF ABBREVIATIONS

DDSI	Directorate of the Defence Services Intelligence.
DSA	Defence Services Academy.
DSI	Defence Services Institute.
DVB	Democratic Voice of Burma.
FACOE	Frontier Areas Committee of Enquiry. Set up before independence to ascertain the views of the frontier peoples.
GCBA	General Council of Burmese Associations.
KIO/KIA	Kachin Independence Organisation/Army. Kachin rebel group set up in 1961.
KKY	Ka Kwe Ye ('defence'). Opium-trading government militia forces in the 1960s and early 1970s.
KMT	Kuomintang (Guomindang in Pinyin). Chinese nationalist forces loyal to the Republic of China (Taiwan).
KNA	Karen National Association. Karen political organisation in the nineteenth century.
KNDO	Karen National Defence Organisation. Early Karen militia.
KNLA	Karen National Liberation Army. The KNU's armed wing.
KNU	Karen National Union. Karen political organisation set up in 1946.
MANPADS	Man-Portable Air Defence Systems.
MIS	Military Intelligence Service.
MNDAA	Myanmar National Democratic Alliance Army. Former CPB force in Kokang.
MNDO	Mon National Defence Organisation. Early Mon rebel movement.
NCGUB	National Coalition Government of the Union of Burma. Government in exile set up in 1990.
NDAA-ESS	National Democratic Alliance Army (Eastern Shan State). Former CPB force in eastern Shan State.

LIST OF ABBREVIATIONS

NDA-K	New Democratic Army-Kachin. Former CPB force in eastern Kachin State.
NDF	National Democratic Front. Front comprising ethnic resistance armies active in the 1970s and 1980s.
NLD	National League for Democracy. Political party formed in 1988.
NUG	National Unity Government. Formed by pro-democracy forces after the 2021 coup.
NULF	National United Liberation Front. Non-communist resistance group in the 1970s.
NUP	National Unity Party.
OTS	Officers' Training School.
PBF	Patriotic Burmese Forces.
PDF	People's Defence Forces. Local forces more or less loyal to NUG.
PDP	Parliamentary Democracy Party. Non-communist resistance group in the late 1960s and 1970s.
PPP	People's Patriotic Party. Non-communist resistance group in the 1970s.
PVO	People's Volunteer Organisation.
RCSS	Restoration Council of Shan State. Group in Shan State set up by opium warlord Khun Sa.
RSS	Rashtriya Swayamsevak Sangh.
SAC	State Administration Council. Junta set up after the 2021 coup.
SLORC	State Law and Order Restoration Council. Junta set up in 1988.
SPDC	State Peace and Development Council. Junta that ruled from 1997 to 2011.
SSA	Shan State Army. Shan rebel army set up in 1964.
SSPP	Shan State Progress Party. The SSA's political wing.
SUA	Shan United Army. Army of opium warlord Khun Sa.

LIST OF ABBREVIATIONS

TNLA	Ta'ang National Liberation Army.
ULFA	United Liberation Front of Asom [Assam]. Rebel group in Assam, India.
UMP	Union Military Police.
UNDP	Union National Democracy Party.
USDP	Union Solidarity and Development Party. Pro-military party.
UWSP/A	United Wa State Party/Army. Political and military wing of the Wa movement.
YMBA	Young Men's Buddhist Association.

NOTES

1. THE COUP

1. Strangio, Sebastian, 'Myanmar Coup Leader Pledges to "Annihilate" Those Opposing His Government', *The Diplomat*, 28 March 2022, https://thediplomat.com/2022/03/myanmar-coup-leader-pledges-to-annihilate-those-opposing-his-government/, last accessed 3 Mar. 2024.
2. Chao Tzang Yawnghwe, who was on the campus on that day, sent several letters to the author in which he described what happened when the army came and opened fire on the students.
3. Steinberg, David, 'Burma Under Military Rule: Towards a Chronology', *Contemporary Southeast Asia*, Vol. 3, No 3, Dec. 1981, pp. 250–1.
4. Steinberg, David, *Burma: A Socialist Nation in Southeast Asia*, Boulder: Westview Press, 1982, p. 76.
5. For an excellent account of the demonstrations in the 1970s, see Selth, Andrew, *Death of a Hero: The U Thant Disturbances in Burma, December 1974*, Brisbane: Griffith University, Australia-Asia Papers No 49, 1989.
6. Interview with Kyaw Gyi, 8 Jan. 1987.
7. Ibid.
8. Interview with Tun Myat, 10 Jan. 1987.
9. 'Burmese take to streets on day of protests', *Associated Press*, 9 August 1988. 'Rangoon' was still used in dispatches at that time. Article not available online.
10. Mydans, Seth, *The New York Times*, 11 Aug. 1988, https://www.sethmydans.com/1988_burma.html and https://web.archive.org/web/20180715012540/https://www.nytimes.com/1988/08/12/world/uprising-in-burma-the-old-regime-under-siege.html?pagewanted=all, last accessed 10 Mar. 2024.
11. Gourley, Richard, 'Troops Fire on Crowds in Rangoon', *The Financial Times*, 10 Aug. 1988. Article not available online.
12. This account of the Sagaing massacre comes from interviews with two frequent visitors from Japan who were there at the time, Bangkok, Sep. 1988.

See also Abbott, Gerry, *Back to Mandalay*, Bromley, Kent: Impact Books, 1990, pp. 171–81 ND 216–18 (with a map of the scene of the massacre). Abbott was teaching at the Mandalay Teacher's Training College at the time.

13. Abbott, interview with *The Times*, 23 Sep. 1988.
14. Summary of World Broadcast FE/0227 B/1, Rangoon home service, 13:30 GMT, 9 Aug. 1988.
15. According to Sai Myo Win Htun, a Shan pro-democracy activist, who stood up and challenged the military's version of the event at a gathering with foreign correspondents in Taunggyi, 19 Jan. 1989. See also White, Helen, 'Burma Gives Outsiders a Rare Glimpse', *The Wall Street Journal*, 23 Jan. 1989 (not available online). This writer was present at that occasion in Taunggyi as well.
16. See Renaud, Egretau, 'The Repression of the August 8–12 (8-8-88) Uprising in Burma/Myanmar', https://www.sciencespo.fr/mass-violence-war-massacre-resistance/en/document/repression-august-8-12-1988-8-8-88-uprising-burmamyanmar.html, last accessed on 5 Mar. 2024, and Huffman. Franklin, 'Military Crackdown in Burma and the Massacres of 8/8/88', https://www.sciencespo.fr/mass-violence-war-massacre-resistance/en/document/repression-august-8-12-1988-8-8-88-uprising-burmamyanmar.html, last accessed 5 Mar. 2024.
17. Summary of World Broadcasts FE/0265 i, 24 Sep. 1988.
18. Ibid.
19. That is what was said after the September 1988 military takeover. Talks about 'a constituent assembly' which had to draft a new constitution came much later. As early as 22 September 1988—four days after the military had formed the SLORC—Burma's powerful intelligence chief and Secretary-1 in the new junta, (then) Brig-Gen Khin Nyunt, had pledged before a meeting with foreign military attachés in Yangon: 'Elections will be held as soon as law and order has been restored and the Defence Services would then systematically hand over power to the party which wins.' (quoted from Summary of World Broadcasts, FE/0265 i, 24 Sep. 1988). He did not say anything about the need to draft a new constitution.
20. According to statistics published by the US State Department's Bureau of International Narcotics Matters on its 'Annual International Narcotics Control Strategy Reports', see https://apps.dtic.mil/sti/tr/pdf/ADA315429.pdf, last accessed 5 Mar. 2024.
21. *The Working People's Daily,* 10 Jan. 1990.
22. *The Working People's Daily*, 11 May 1990.
23. *The Burmese Way: To Where?,* International Commission of Jurists, 1991, p. 32–3, https://www.icj.org/wp-content/uploads/2013/06/Myanmar-Burmese-way-fact-finding-report-1991-eng.pdf, last accessed 10 Mar. 2024.
24. Summary of World Broadcasts FE/0829B/1, 30 July 1990.
25. Ibid.

26. Aung Zaw, 'August is the Cruelest Month', *The Irrawaddy*, 2 Sep. 2013, https://www.irrawaddy.com/opinion/commentary/august-is-the-cruelest-month.html, last accessed on 5 Mar. 2024.
27. 'Recalling Monk Beatings That Sparked the Saffron Revolution', *The Irrawaddy*, 6 Sept. 2013, https://www.irrawaddy.com/news/burma/recalling-monk-beatings-that-sparked-the-saffron-revolution.html, last accessed 5 Mar. 2024.
28. See *Hurricanes: Science and Society*, https://hurricanescience.org/history/storms/2000s/cyclonenargis/index.html (retrieved on 5 Mar. 2024) and 'Natural Catastrophes and Man-made Disasters in 2008', *Sigma*, 2/2009, https://www.preventionweb.net/files/8841_Sigma22009e.pdf, last accessed 5 Mar. 2024.
29. Quoted in 'After the Storm', *New Matilda*, 4 May 2009, https://newmatilda.com/2009/05/04/after-storm/, last accessed 5 Mar. 2024, and Aung Zaw, 'Looking for a Happy Ending? Read the New Light', *The Irrawaddy*, 29 May 2008, https://www2.irrawaddy.com/opinion_story.php?art_id=12368, last accessed 5 Mar. 2024.
30. Quoted in 'When it Comes to Politics, Burmese Say, Government Is All Too Helpful', *The New York Times*, 28 May 2008, https://www.nytimes.com/2008/05/28/world/asia/28delta.html, last accessed 5 Mar. 2024.
31. 'Western States Dismiss Burma's Election', *BBC*, 8 Nov. 2010, https://www.bbc.com/news/world-asia-pacific-11707294, last accessed 4 Mar. 2024.
32. *International Idea Annual Report 2011*, p. 3
33. Lall, Marie, *Understanding Reform in Myanmar: People and Society in the Wake of Military Rule*, London 2016: Hurst Publishers, https://www.hurstpublishers.com/book/understanding-reform-in-myanmar/, last accessed 5 Mar. 2024.
34. See, for instance, Hammer, Joshua, 'Myanmar's Gorbachev?', *The New Yorker*, 14 Jan. 2012, https://www.newyorker.com/news/news-desk/myanmars-gorbachev, last accessed 5 Mar. 2024, and Hunter, Andrew, 'Is Thein Sein Myanmar's Real Champion of Democracy?', *Sydney Morning Herald*, 2 July 2014, https://www.smh.com.au/opinion/is-thein-sein-myanmars-real-champion-of-democracy-20140702-zstai.html, last accessed 5 Mar. 2024.
35. A copy of the document is in the author's possession. The quotes here are the author's translations from the original Burmese.
36. According to civil servants who were present during Hillary Clinton's talks with Myanmar officials.
37. The full text of the 2008 constitution can be downloaded from https://www.myanmar-law-library.org/law-library/laws-and-regulations/constitutions/2008-constitution.html, last accessed 5 Mar. 2024.
38. For instance, on 28 January 2021, only days before the coup, Senior General Min Aung Hlaing said that the Myanmar military 'needs to abide by the constitution', which he described as the 'mother of the law'.

39. Aung San Suu Kyi was married to Michael Aris, who passed away in 1999, and their two sons are not Myanmar citizens. The elder, Alexander, is a US citizen and Kim, the younger, is a citizen of the UK.
40. Shoon Naing, 'Myanmar army warns may "take action" over election dispute', *Reuters*, 26 Jan. 2021, https://www.reuters.com/article/idUSKBN29V1HH/, last accessed 10 Mar. 2024
41. See 'Carter Center Preliminary Statement on the 2020 Myanmar General Elections', https://www.cartercenter.org/news/pr/2020/myanmar-111020.html, last accessed 10 Mar. 2024. 'The 2020 Myanmar General Elections, Democracy Under Attack', and *The Asian Network for Free Elections*, https://anfrel.org/wp-content/uploads/2021/05/ANFREL_Democracy-Under-Attack-F.pdf (retrieved on 10 Mar. 2024), and the EU's figures are referred to in *The University of Melbourne: Asialink*, 'Myanmar's Coup', https://asialink.unimelb.edu.au/insights/Myanmars-coup, last accessed 10 Mar. 2024.
42. *Reuters*, 26 Jan. 2021.
43. 'Timeline of the Coup', *Burma Campaign News*, issue 40, 2021, https://docs.google.com/document/d/1U4NoI9AjZKP8w7LhUL69rHVsT3k0-VEC/edit?pli=1, last accessed 10 Mar. 2024.
44. *The Global New Light of Myanmar*, 26 Feb. 2021, https://www.gnlm.com.mm/reduction-of-fuel-and-cooking-oil-imports-needed-to-decrease-trade-deficiencies-senior-general/, last accessed 10 Mar. 2024.
45. See '*Internet penetration of Myanmar from 2011 to 2020*', https://www.statista.com/statistics/766034/internet-penetration-rate-myanmar/, last accessed 10 Mar. 2024.
46. Among them Marie Lall, a London-based academic, who in a virtual conversation with the UN University in Tokyo on 19 Feb. 2021 said: 'We have to understand that the Tatmadaw [military] is the glue of the nation' and 'is very much perceived by a lot of people as the stalwarts to keep Burma together'. Available at https://www.youtube.com/watch?v=IvX2eHl9sy0, last accessed 10 Mar. 2024. Lall made this astonishing comment less than three weeks after the coup—when tens of millions of people in virtually every city, town and major village across the country were demonstrating against the military takeover. For references to other apologists for military rule, see Kurlantzick, Joshua, *Rangoon Squad: Burma's Wicked Apologists*, Carnegie Endowment for International Peace, 22 Oct. 2007, https://carnegieendowment.org/2007/10/22/rangoon-squad-burma-s-wicked-apologists-pub-19653, last accessed 10 Mar. 2024.
47. Interview: 'Understanding the "old man"', *Frontier Myanmar*, 14 Jan. 2016, https://www.frontiermyanmar.net/en/ne-win-understanding-the-old-man-2/ (retrieved on 10 Mar. 2024).
48. Op. cit., 'Timeline of the Coup'.
49. 'Myanmar Sees Deadliest Day as 38 Protesters Killed', *BBC*, 4 Mar. 2021, https://www.bbc.com/news/world-asia-56265962, last accessed 10 Mar. 2024.

50. Op. cit., 'Timeline of the Coup'.
51. Ibid.
52. See https://www.nugmyanmar.org/en/, last accessed 10 Mar. 2024.
53. Ye Myo Hein, 'Understanding the People's Defense Forces in Myanmar', *The United States Institute of Peace*, 3 Nov. 2022, https://www.usip.org/publications/2022/11/understanding-peoples-defense-forces-myanmar, last accessed 10 Mar. 2024.

2. THE MILITARY

1. Rogers, Benedict, *Than Shwe: Unmasking Burma's Tyrant*, Chiang Mai: Silkworm Books, 2019, p. 167.
2. Interviews with Thakin Ba Thein Tin (the last chairman of the CPB), Panghsang, 21–6 Dec. 1986.
3. Thakin Ba Thein Tin, interviews.
4. Thakin Ba Thein Tin, interviews.
5. Interview with Kyaw Zaw (Thakin Shwe), one of the Thirty Comrades who later joined the CPB, Panghsang, 2 Jan. 1987.
6. Aung Zaw, 'The Man Behind the Burma Independence Army', *The Irrawaddy*, 27 Mar. 2022, https://www.irrawaddy.com/factiva/the-man-behind-the-burma-independence-army.html, last accessed 10 Jan. 2024.
7. Seekins, Donald, *Historical Dictionary of Burma (Myanmar)*, Lanham, Maryland: Scarecrow Press, 2006, p. 354.
8. Interview with Saw Thra Din, a member of that delegation, Sangkhlaburi, Thailand, 4 Jan. 1981.
9. Callahan, Mary, *Making Enemies: War and State Building in Burma*, Ithaca: Cornell University Press, 2003, p. 98.
10. Buchanan, John, 'Security Integration Efforts in Myanmar (1945–2020): A Historical Overview', Institute for Strategy and Policy Briefing Paper, Feb. 2019, p. 5, https://ispmyanmar.com/security-integration-efforts-in-myanmar-1945-2010-a-historical-overview/, last accessed 5 Feb. 2024.
11. Callahan, Mary, 'Rethinking Burmese Military Politics: The Institutional Origins of Postwar Politics', undated paper, Cornell University. In author's possession.
12. *A Collection of Treaties, Engagements and Sanads Relating to India and Neighbouring Countries*, compiled by C.U. Aichison, Vol. XII, Calcutta: Government of India Central Publication Branch, 1931, p. XII. Note that only the Western Karenni states—Kyebogyi and Bawlake—were recognised as 'independent'; the eastern Karenni state of Kantarawaddy had a separate agreement with the British Crown, see Sao Saimong Mangrai, *The Shan States and the British Annexation*, Ithaca, New York: Cornell University Southeast Asia Programme, Date Paper No. 57, 1965, pp. xliii–xlv.
13. For the full text of the Aung San-Attlee Agreement, see https://burmastar1010.files.wordpress.com/2011/06/44172419-aungsan-atlee-agreement.pdf, last accessed 1 Feb. 2024.

14. Ibid.
15. See Kin Oung, *Who Killed Aung San?*, Chiang Mai: Silkworm Books, 1996.
16. Maung Maung, *To A Soldier Son*, Rangoon: Sarpay Beikman Press, 1974, p. 143.
17. U Nu, *Saturday's Son: Memoirs of the Former Prime Minister of Burma*, New Haven: Yale University Press, 1975, p. 192.
18. See McCoy, Alfred W., *The Politics of Heroin in Southeast Asia*, New York: Harper Torchbooks, 1972, pp. 126–35; Gibson, Richard M. and Chen Wenhua, *The Secret Army: Chiang Kai-shek and the Drug Warlords of the Golden Triangle*, Singapore: John Wiley & Sons, 2011; and for Burmese government documents, see *Kuomintang Aggression Against Burma*, Ministry of Information, Government of the Union of Burma, 1953.
19. *Burma: The Eight Anniversary 1956*, Rangoon: Government of the Union of Burma Central Publishing Office, 1956, p. 102.
20. In author's conversations with Burma scholar Josef Silverstein.
21. U Thaung, *Army's Accumulation of Economic Power in Burma (1950–1990)*, paper presented at a Burma seminar in Washington on 20 Oct. 1990.
22. Silverstein, Josef, *Burma: Military Rule and the Politics of Stagnation*, Ithaca: Cornell University Press, 1977, pp. 79 and 153. See also the official publication *Is Trust Vindicated?*, Rangoon: Director of Information, 1960, pp. 223–8.
23. For the development of these militias, see Buchanan, op. cit., p. 8.
24. Maung Maung Dr, *Burma and General Ne Win*, Bombay: Asia Publishing House, 1969, pp. 242–3.
25. Quoted in the foreword to *Is Trust Vindicated?*
26. For the full text of the declaration, see *Is Trust Vindicated,* pp. 533–41.
27. Ibid., p. 535.
28. Ibid., p. 31.
29. Silverstein, op. cit., p. 32.
30. Callahan (2003), op. cit, p. 191.
31. U Thaung, op. cit.
32. Ibid.
33. Yawnghwe, Samara, *Maintaining the Union of Burma 1946–1962: The Role of the Ethnic Nationalities in a Shan Perspective*, Bangkok: Institute of Asian Studies, Chulalongkorn University, 2013, p. 216.
34. For an account of the early days of the Kachin rebellion, see Lintner, Bertil, *The Kachin: Lords of Burma's Northern Frontier*, Chiang Mai: Teak House Publications, 1997, pp. 123–9.
35. For an account of the life and disappearance of Sao Kya Hseng, see Sargent, Inge, *Twilight Over Burma: My Life as a Shan Princess*, Honolulu: University of Hawaii Press, 1994.
36. Quoted in Lintner, Bertil, *Outrage: Burma's Struggle for Democracy*, Hong Kong: Review Publishing, 1989, p. 25.
37. Central Intelligence Agency: *National Intelligence Estimate: Prospects for Survival of a Non-Communist Regime in Burma*, NIE, 1 Aug. 1951.

38. See, for instance, Chakravarti, Nalini Ranjan, *The Indian Minority in Burma: The Rise and Decline of an Immigrant Community*, London: Oxford University Press, 1971, and Roberts, Jayde Lin, *Mapping Chinese Rangoon: Place and Nation among the Sino-Burmese*, Seattle: University of Washington Press, 2016.
39. Seekins, Donald, *Burma and Japan Since 1940: From Co-Prosperity to 'Quiet Dialogue'*, Copenhagen: Nordic Institute of Asian Studies Press, 2007, pp. 14 and 23.
40. McAndrew, James, *From Combat to Karaoke: Burmese Military Intelligence 1948–2006*, Washington: National Defense Intelligence College, 2007, p. 27.
41. Nakanishi, Yoshihiro, *Strong Soldiers, Failed Revolution: The State and Military in Burma, 1962–88*, Singapore: National University of Singapore Press, 2013, p. 229.
42. Interviews with then high-school children who were mobilised to supervise the referendum.
43. Aung Zaw, 'The Enemy Within', *The Irrawaddy*, Mar. 2000, https://www2.irrawaddy.com/article.php?art_id=676&page=1, last accessed 15 Feb. 2024.
44. McAndrew, op. cit., p. 52.
45. Tasker, Rodney, 'Ne Win's No Win Situation', *Far Eastern Economic Review*, 7 July 1983.
46. Choe Sang-hun, 'Forgotten Killer Among the Korean "Erased"', *The New York Times*, 23 Nov. 2013, https://www.nytimes.com/2013/11/24/world/asia/forgotten-killer-among-the-korean-erased.html, last accessed 15 Feb. 2024.
47. For the growth of the Myanmar army, see Selth, Andrew, *Burma's Armed Forces: Power Without Glory*, Norwalk, Connecticut: 2002, Callahan, op. cit. (2003), and Maung Aung Myoe, *Building the Tatmadaw: Myanmar Armed Forces Since 1948*, New Delhi: Knowledge World Publishers, 2011.
48. Seen at the time and quoted in Lintner, Bertil, 'What has Happened to Myanmar's Tatmadaw?', *The Irrawaddy*, 13 Sep. 2021, https://www.irrawaddy.com/opinion/guest-column/what-has-happened-to-myanmars-tatmadaw.html, last accessed 15 Mar. 2024.
49. Interviews with a retired Myanmar army colonel who requested to remain anonymous, Bangkok, Sep. 1995.
50. Interviews with former army officers who requested anonymity, Yangon, Dec. 2014.
51. Mathieson, David Scott, *The Arakan Army in Myanmar: Deadly Conflict Rises in Rakhine State*, Washington: The United States Institute of Peace, Special Report, Nov. 2020, https://www.usip.org/sites/default/files/2021-02/sr_486-the_arakan_army_in_myanmar_deadly_conflict_rises_in_rakhine_state.pdf, last accessed on 15 Mar. 2024.

3. THE ETHNIC JIGSAW

1. See https://en.wikipedia.org/wiki/Kaba_Ma_Kyei from *The Burmese Encyclopaedia* (in Burmese). Rangoon: Burma Translation Society, 1976, Vol. 6, pp. 98–9, link last accessed 12 Mar. 2024.
2. See, for instance, *Myanmar-English Dictionary*, Yangon: Myanmar Language Commission, 1996.
3. *Hobson-Jobson: A Glossary of Colloquial Anglo-Indian Words and Phrases, and Kindred Terms, Etymological, Historical, Gepgraphical, and Discursive*, London: John Murray, 1903 (reprint by Asian Educational Services, New Delhi, 2012), p. 131.
4. *A Brief History of the Dohbama Asiayone* (in Burmese), Rangoon: Sarpey Beikman, 1976, p. 215. See also *The Guardian* monthly (in Burmese), Feb. 1971: 'The word *myanma* signifies only the Burmese, whereas *bama* embraces all indigenous nationalities.'
5. Tarling, Nicholas, *The Cambridge History of Southeast Asia, Volume Two*, Cambridge University Press, 1999, p. 289.
6. Smith, Martin, *Ethnic Groups in Burma: Development, Democracy and Human Rights*, Anti-Slavery International, 1994, p. 18, https://www.burmalibrary.org/docs3/Ethnic_Groups_in_Burma-ocr.pdf, last accessed 12 Mar. 2024.
7. Bennison, J.J., *Census of India, 1931, Volume XI, Burma, Part I. – Report*, Rangoon: Office the Superintendent, Government Printing and Stationery, 1933, p. 224, https://www.burmalibrary.org/sites/burmalibrary.org/files/obl/docs22/1931_Census_of_India-Vol-XI-Burma1.pdf, last accessed 12 Mar. 2024.
8. Houtman, Gustaaf, *Mental Culture in Burmese Crisis Politics: Aung San Suu Kyi and the National League for Democracy*, Tokyo: University of Foreign Studies, 199, p. 55ff. Available at https://www.researchgate.net/publication/272159930_Mental_Culture_in_Burmese_Crisis_Politics_Aung_San_Suu_Kyi_and_the_National_League_for_Democracy_Monograph_Series_No_33, last accessed 12 Mar. 2024.
9. Silverstein, Josef, *Burmese Politics: The Dilemma of National Unity*, New Brunswick, New Jersey: Rutgers University Press, 1980, p. 14.
10. Ibid., p. 14.
11. A brief biography of de Brito can be found in Seekins, Donald, *Historical Dictionary of Burma (Myanmar)*, Lanham, Maryland: The Scarecrow Press, 2006, pp. 119–20.
12. Descendants of those mercenaries are still living in villages in the Mu Valley in Sagaing Region. They are called *bayingyi*, a term derived from *feringhi* or *frank* of Arabic and Persian origin. Similar denotations are widely used in Southeast Asia to refer to white Europeans. In Malay is becomes *ferringhi*, in Thai *farang* and in Khmer *barang*. The majority of the *bayingyi*, who now number around 3,000, are Roman Catholics even today.
13. Seekins, op. cit., p. 62.

14. Crosthwaite, Sir Charles, *The Pacification of Burma*, London: Edward Arnold, 1912. pp. 212–13 (reprinted by Routledge, London, in 1968).
15. Davies, Major H.R., *Yün-nan: The Link Between India and the Yangtze*, Cambridge: Cambridge University Press, 1909 (reprinted by Skilled Books, India), p. 7.
16. Silverstein, op. cit., p. 16.
17. Po, San C., *Burma and the Karens*, London: Elliot Stock, 1928, p. 1.
18. For an account of the meetings in Salem and the first missions to Burma, see Anderson, Courtney, *To The Golden Shore: The Life of Adoniram Judson,* Boston: Little, Brown and Company, 1956.
19. Quoted in Smith-Dun, *Memoirs of the Four-foot Colonel*, Ithaca, New York: Cornell University Southeast Asia Programme, Data Paper no. 113, 1980, pp. 6–7.
20. Andrus, J. Russel, *Burmese Economic Life*, Stanford, California: Stanford University Press, 1948, p. 27.
21. Quoted in Po, op. cit., p. 23.
22. Po, op. cit., p. 77 and 81.
23. For a complete list of all the Shan states, see *Shan and Karenni: List of Chiefs and Leading Families*, Simla: Government of India Press, 1943.
24. Silverstein, op. cit., p. 18.
25. For a succinct history of the Shans, see Yawnghwe, Chao Tzang, *The Shan of Burma: Memoirs of a Shan Exile*, Singapore: Institute of Southeast Asian Studies, 1987 (expanded and reprinted in 2010).
26. *Shan and Karenni: List of Chiefs and Leading Families*, pp. 75–8.
27. Yawnghwe, op. cit., pp. 45–82.
28. Jarvey, G.E., *The Wa People of the Burma-China Border, St. Antony's Papers No III, Far Eastern Affairs*, No. One, London: Chatto & Windus, 1957, p. 129.
29. 'The Young Family's Work Among the Wa People', https://www.humancomp.org/wadict/young_family.html, last accessed 15 Mar. 2024.
30. The origin of the name 'Panthay' is disputed, but it could be of Persian origin. In Thailand, they are called *jin haw*.
31. This Panglong is located south of Kokang, not to be confused with the town with the same name north of Taunggyi, where the Panglong Agreement was signed in 1947.
32. Seidenfaden, Erik, *The Thai Peoples*, Bangkok, The Siam Society, 1968, p. 124.
33. For some excellent studies of the Kachins, see Leach, Edward, *Political Systems of Highland Burma: A Study of Kachin Social Structure*, London: G. Bell, 1954); Tegenfeldt, Herman, *A Century of Growth: The Kachin Baptist Church of Burma*, William Carey Library, California: 1974; and Sadan, Mandy, *Being and Becoming Kachin: Histories Beyond the State in the Borderworld of Burma*, London: Oxford University Press, 2013.
34. Theodorson, George, 'Minority Peoples in the Union of Burma', paper presented at the First International Conference of Southeast Asian Historians,

Singapore, Jan. 1961, https://www.jstor.org/stable/20067473, last accessed 15 Mar. 2024.
35. Vumsom, *Zo History*, Aizawl, Mizoram (self-published and undated), pp. 184–5. The Chin and Mizos are often referred to as 'Zo peoples', hence Mizo in India and Zomi on the Burmese side (*mi* means 'people').
36. Taylor, Robert, *The State of Burma*, London: Hurst & Company, 1987, p. 100.
37. Stevenson, H.N.C., *The Hill Peoples of Burma*, Calcutta: Longmans & Green, 1945, p. 15.
38. When the author trekked through the Naga Hills of Burma in 1985, villagers often asked him if he was 'Indian or Burmese', the only two countries they had heard of. Hardly anyone spoke Burmese, and they clearly considered Burma an alien country. Today, many 'eastern Nagas' have been educated primarily in schools on the Indian side and speak Nagamese, a kind of pidgin Assamese, which is the lingua franca of the Indian Nagas.
39. Theodorson, op. cit., p. 12.
40. For a comprehensive account of the Rohingyas, see Yegar, Moshe, *The Muslims of Burma: A Study of a Minority Group*, Wiesbaden: Otto Harrassowitz, 1972.
41. Ibid., p. 19.
42. South, Ashley, *Mon Nationalism and Civil War in Burma*, London: Routledge Curzon, 2003, p. 101.
43. For a comprehensive history of the Indian community in Burma/Myanmar, see Chakravarti, Nalini Ranjan, *The Indian Community in Burma: The Rise and Decline of an Immigrant Community*, London: Oxford University Press, 1971.
44. For this first round of talks, see Silkverstein, op. cit., pp. 84–5.
45. Ibid., p. 85.
46. Frontier Areas Committee of Enquiry 1947: Part II. Rangoon: Government Printing, 1947, p. 37.
47. Ibid., p. 38.
48. Tinker, Hugh (ed.), *Burma: The Struggle for Independence 1944–1948, Volume II*, London: Her Majesty's Stationery Office, 1984, Vol. 883,
49. For the full text of the Panglong Agreement, see Silverstein, op. cit., 107–8.
50. *The Constitution of the Union of Burma*, Rangoon: Superintendent, Government Printing and Stationery, 1946, reprint 1960, pp. 58–9 (Chapter X: Right of Secession); provisions for a Kachin state 46–8, and for a Karen state, 50–3.
51. This is one of the most controversial subjects in Burma's long history of rebellions and ethnic identification. In order to show that the Rohingyas have lived in their area for centuries, supporters of the Rohingya cause usually quote a 1799 report by Francis Buchanan-Hamilton, where he mentions a people called 'Rooinga' who lived in what is now Rakhine State. Who they were is unclear, and Buchanan-Hamilton met them in Amarapura, the then capital of the Myanmar Empire, not in today's Rakhine State. He was also primarily a botanist and a zoologist, not an ethnographer or anthropologist.

No mention (other than by those quoting Buchanan-Hamilton) of a people called 'Rohingya' or something similar appears for more than 150 years, and then as a political term denoting the Muslims of north-western Rakhine who, throughout the British period were referred to as Chittagonians.

52. Interview with Nai Shwe Kyin, Bangkok, 8 June 1992, a Mon delegate to the secret meetings in Bangkok in 1954.
53. Interview with Sao Nang Hearn Hkam, the Mahadevi of Yawnghwe, Chiang Mai, 7 Jan. 1982.
54. *Weekend Telegraph*, 10 March 1967, and quoted in McCoy, Alfred, *The Politics of Heroin in Southeast Asia*, New York: Harper Torchbooks, 1972, p. 319.
55. For a comprehensive overview of Myanmar's militias, see Buchanan, John, *Militias in Myanmar*, The Asia Foundation, July 2016, https://asiafoundation.org/wp-content/uploads/2016/07/Militias-in-Myanmar.pdf, last accessed 20 Mar. 2024.
56. According to sources close to Khun Sa, who the author met on numerous occasions in the early 1980s.
57. Clymer, Kenton, *A Delicate Relationship: Then United States and Myanmar Since 1945*, Ithaca, New York: Cornell University Press, 2015, p. 229.
58. Martin Smith claims in his *Burma: Insurgency and the Politics of Ethnicity* (London: Zed Press, 1991) that the CIA supported U Nu's and Law-Yone's resistance (pp. 273–8), but that is incorrect. Burma's military intelligence chief, Brig.-Gen. Tin U, was trained by the CIA, and, in the 1970s, the United States clandestinely supplied Ne Win's military with artillery, rocket launchers and carbines which were used in the fight against the CPB.
59. Silverstein, Josef, 'Burma in 1980: An Uncertain Balance Sheet', *Asian Survey*, Vol. 21, No 2, Feb. 1981, pp. 212–22, https://www.jstor.org/stable/2643766, last accessed 15 Mar. 2024.

4. THE CHINA FACTOR

1. 'The Ministry of Foreign Affairs Holds a Briefing for Chinese and Foreign Media on President Xi Jinping's State Visit to Myanmar', https://www.fmprc.gov.cn/eng/gjhdq_665435/2675_665437/2747_663498/2749_663502/202001/t20200114_519197.html, last accessed 25 Mar. 2024.
2. For a chronology of relations between the two countries, see *China's Foreign Relations—a Chronology of Events 1949–1988*, Beijing: Foreign Languages Press, 1989, pp. 207–15.
3. Sino-Burmese relations are described in detail in Choshad Liang, 'Burma's Relationship with the People's Republic of China—From Delicate Friendship to Genuine Cooperation', paper presented at a Burma conference in Oxford, England, 13–15 December 1991 (not available online), and Narayanan, Raviprasad, 'China and Myanmar: Alternating Between "Brothers" and "Cousins"', *China Report*, Vol. 46 (3), 1 Aug. 2010, https://www.deepdyve.

com/lp/sage/china-and-myanmar-hAqe9NDNWf?key=sage, last accessed 25 Mar. 2024.

4. 'Express Letter from the Chief Secretary to the Govt. of Burma, Police Department, No. 173-C-34', 17 Mar. 1934. Reproduced in *Communism in India—Unpublished Documents 1925–1934*, Calcutta: National Book Agency, 1980, pp. 178–9. Although that report was compiled in the 1930s, a Sino-Burmese lady who joined the CPB in 1967 told me at party headquarters in Panghsang in January 1987 she had been a member of a Chinese communist cell in Yangon and that the embassy there had helped her escape from the capital to a CPB-controlled area in northern Shan State.

5. The Namwan Assigned Track refers to a border area between Bhamo in Burma's Kachin State and Namkham in Shan State, that the British had leased from China in 1897.

6. Silverstein, Josef, *Burma: Military Rule and the Politics of Stagnation*, Ithaca and London: Cornell University Press, 1977, pp. 170–3.

7. For an overview of the border dispute and its solution, see Lintner, Bertil, *Cross-Border Drug Trade in the Golden Triangle*, Durham, England: Durham University, International Boundaries Research Unit, 1991. pp. 5–14, http://www.asiapacificms.com/papers/pdf/cross-border-drug-trade-in-the-golden-triangle-1991.pdf, last accessed 25 Mar. 2024.

8. See https://www.reddit.com/r/MapPorn/comments/db1bp3/a_detailed_map_of_the_republic_of_china_including/?rdt=37477 (retrieved on 30 Mar. 2024). Old official maps of the Republic of China also include Tuva in eastern Russia and Mongolia, but those maps are hardly used these days as the pro-independence Democratic Progressive Party has become the island's governing party.

9. The Burmese authorities have always denied that regular Chinese troops took part in the operation, but it is described in detail in this unusually informative Wikipedia entry: https://en.wikipedia.org/wiki/Campaign_at_the_China%E2%80%93Burma_border, last accessed 5 Mar. 2024. See also Gibson, Richard with Wenhua Chen, *The Secret Army: Chiang Kai-shek and the Drug Lords of the Golden Triangle*, Singapore: John Wiley & Sons (Asia), 2011, pp. 171–2.

10. Silverstein, op. cit., pp. 161–2.

11. A copy of that document is in the author's possession.

12. Interview with CPB Chairman Thakin Ba Thein Tin, Panghsang, 24 Dec. 1986.

13. See 10. Those demands are more or less the same as the Myanmar military has put forth in all peace talks since 1963.

14. Interview with Thakin Ba Thein Tin, Panghsang, 24 Dec. 1986. One of Thakin Ba Thein Tin's closest foreign associates was the chairman of the CPA(ML), a Melbourne lawyer called Edward Fowler Hill. Thakin Ba Thein Tin told the author in December 1986: 'Ted Hill and I were together in Beijing. We wrote

appeals against the Soviet Union and for world revolution. He was a fine, cultured kind of man.'

15. Byron, John and Robert Pack, *The Claws of the Dragon: Kang Sheng, the Evil Genius Behind Mao—and His Legacy of Terror in People's China*, New York: Simon & Schuster, 1992, p. 211.
16. *Beijing Review*, 30 July 1976, available at https://www.massline.org/PekingReview/PR1976/PR1976-31.pdf, pp. 20–1, last accessed 25 Mar. 2024.
17. *Beijing Review*, 30 Sep. 1976, available at https://www.massline.org/PekingReview/PR1976/PR1976-40-CondolencesFromParties.pdf, pp. 59–60.
18. *Beijing Review*, 26 Nov. 1976, available at https://www.massline.org/PekingReview/PR1976/PR1976-48.pdf, p. 3., last accessed 25 Mar. 2024.
19. Quoted in Lintner, Bertil, 'The Rise and Fall of the Communists', *Far Eastern Economic Review*, 4 June 1987.
20. The article can be viewed on pp. 22–3 at https://www.massline.org/PekingReview/PR1985/PR1985-34S.pdf, last accessed 25 Mar. 2024.
21. Lintner, Bertil, 'The Busy Border', *Far Eastern Economic Review*, 8 June 1989. That story was based on interviews and observations in Yunnan in May 1989.
22. For full quote, see Burma Press Summary, *Working People's Daily* (Rangoon), Vol. III, No 10, Oct. 1989, p. 17.
23. For lists of Chinese weaponry delivered to Burma/Myanmar, see Selth, Andrew, 'Burma's Arms Procurement Programme', Working Paper No. 289, Strategic and Defence Studies Centre, Australian National University, Canberra, Sep. 1995. See also Lintner, Bertil: 'Lock and Load', *Far Eastern Economic Review*, 13 Sep. 1990, 'Oiling the Iron Fist', *Far Eastern Economic Review*, 6 Dec. 1990, and 'Hidden Reserves', *Far Eastern Economic Review*, 6 June 1991.
24. Interviews with many former CPB cadres in Yunnan, May 1989 and January 1990.
25. Hand-written minutes from this meeting were passed on to the author during my visit to Jinghong, southern Yunnan, in May 1989.
26. According to numerous conversations between CPB soldiers overheard during the author's stay in the CPB's base area from November 1986 to April 1987.
27. Lintner, Bertil, *The United Wa State Army and Burma's Peace Process*. Washington: The United States Institute of Peace, 2019, p. 17, https://www.usip.org/publications/2019/04/united-wa-state-army-and-burmas-peace-process, last accessed 25 Mar. 2024, and Davis, Anthony, 'It's party time for Myanmar's largest armed ethnic faction', *Asia Times*, 9 Apr. 2019, https://www.asiatimes.com/2019/04/article/anthony-davis-wa-story/, last accessed 25 Mar. 2024.
28. Lintner, *The United Wa State Army*, p. 15. See also Davis, Anthony, 'China's Loose Arms Still Fuel Myanmar's Civil Wars', *Asia Times*, 28 Jan. 2020, https://

asiatimes.com/2020/01/chinas-loose-arms-still-fuel-myanmars-civil-wars/, last accessed 25 Mar. 2024.

29. Min Zin, 'When the Chinese *Press* down', *The Irrawaddy*, 14 Aug. 2013, https://www.irrawaddy.com/opinion/guest-column/when-the-chinese-press-down.html, last accessed 24 Mar. 2024.

30. Fishbein, Emily, Hpan Ja Brang, Zau Myet Awng, and Tu Hka Hkawng, 'How the Kachin Public Overturned a Rare Earth Mining Project in KIO territory', *Frontier Myanmar*, 2 May 2023, https://www.frontiermyanmar.net/en/how-the-kachin-public-overturned-a-rare-earth-mining-project-in-kio-territory/ (retrieved on 25 Mar. 2024).

31. Gardiner, Nicholas J., John P. Sykes, Allan Trench, and Laurence J. Robb, 'Tin Mining in Myanmar: Production and Potential', *Resources Policy*, Vol. 46, Part 2, Dec. 2015, pp. 219–33. Quoted and commented in Martov. Seamus, 'Have the Wa Cornered the Global Tin Trade?', *The Irrawaddy*, 25 Feb. 2016, https://www.irrawaddy.com/news/burma/have-the-wa-cornered-the-global-tin-trade.html, last accessed 25 Mar. 2024.

32. Ibid.

33. Fuller, Thomas, 'Myanmar Backs Down, Suspending Dam Project', *The New York Times*, 30 Sep. 2011, https://www.nytimes.com/2011/10/01/world/asia/myanmar-suspends-construction-of-controversial-dam.html, last accessed 28 Mar. 2024.

34. 'Major Cabinet Reshuffle Announced in Myanmar', Xinhua, 1 Feb. 2021, http://www.xinhuanet.com/english/2021-02/02/c_139713877.htm, last accessed 28 Mar. 2024. See also 'Myanmar Just a "Cabinet Reshuffle": Chinese State Media', Agence-France Presse, 2 Feb. 2021, https://www.france24.com/en/live-news/20210202-myanmar-coup-just-a-cabinet-reshuffle-chinese-state-media, last accessed 28 Mar. 2024.

35. 'Myanmar Anti-Coup Protesters Rally at Chinese Embassy', *Reuters*, 11 Feb. 2021, https://www.reuters.com/article/idUSKBN2AB0HG/, last accessed 28 Mar. 2024.

36. Thiha, Amara, 'Unraveling China's Strategic Re-engagement in Myanmar', *Stimson*, 30 June 2023, https://www.stimson.org/2023/unraveling-chinas-strategic-re-engagement-in-myanmar/, last accessed 28 Mar. 2024.

37. Strangio, Sebastian, 'China, Russia, Again Veto UN Statement on Myanmar Conflict,' *The Diplomat*, 30 May 2022, https://thediplomat.com/2022/05/china-russia-again-veto-un-statement-on-myanmar-conflict/, last accessed 28 Mar. 2024.

38. Manimohon, Waikhom, 'Kabo Valley: A Brief History', E-Pao, 11 May 2018, https://www.e-pao.net/epSubPageExtractor.asp?src=manipur.History_of_Manipur.Kabo_Valley_A_brief_history_By_Waikhom_Manimohon, last accessed 28 Mar. 2024.

39. Ibid.

40. Filed under https://chellaney.net/2007/04/ (retrieved on 28 Mar. 2024).

41. Posted on Twitter (now X), https://twitter.com/porbotialora/status/1067693830084804608?lang=en, last accessed 28 Mar. 2024.
42. *International Boundary Study No. 80*, Washington: Department of State, 15 May 1968, p. 6, https://library.law.fsu.edu/Digital-Collections/LimitsinSeas/pdf/ibs080.pdf, last accessed 28 Mar. 2024.
43. Ibid., p. 8.
44. Ethirajan, Anabarasan, 'Tawang: The Indian Monastery Town Coveted by China', *BBC News*, 9 Mar. 2023, https://www.bbc.com/news/world-asia-india-64870707, last accessed 28 Mar. 2024.
45. See, for instance, Chellaney, Brahma, 'Promoting Political Freedoms', in Lagerkvist, Johan (ed.), *Between Isolation and Internationalization: The State of Burma*, Stockholm: The Swedish Institute of International Affairs, 2008, p. 67.
46. Only paper copies exist of the article; it is not available online.
47. Under the Intelligence column, *Far Eastern Economic Review*, 30 Jan. 1994. Not available online.
48. Selth, Andrew, *Burma's Coco Islands, Rumours and Realities in the Indian Ocean*, City University of Hong Kong, Working Papers Series No 101, Nov. 2008, https://www.cityu.edu.hk/searc/Resources/Paper/WP101_08_ASelth.pdf, last accessed 28 Mar. 2024.
49. Based on interviews with survivors of the Coco Island facility. For more about the penal colony and the hunger strike, see Lintner, Bertil, *Burma in Revolt: Opium and Insurgency Since 1948*, Chiang Mai: Silkworm Books, 2011, pp. 272–3.
50. Pollock, John and Damien Symon, *Is Myanmar Building a Spy Base on Great Coco Island?*, Chatham House, 31 Mar. 2023, https://www.chathamhouse.org/publications/the-world-today/2023-04/myanmar-building-spy-base-great-coco-island, last accessed 28 Mar. 2024.
51. Ibid.
52. Quoted in 'China Calls Report About Spy Post on Myanmar Island "Nonsense"', *Bloomberg News*, 10 April 2023, https://www.bloomberg.com/news/articles/2023-04-10/china-calls-report-about-spy-post-on-myanmar-island-nonsense?embedded-checkout=true, last accessed 28 Mar. 2024.
53. 'India Confronts Myanmar About China Spy Post on Remote Coco Islands', *Straits Times*, 7 April 2023, https://www.straitstimes.com/asia/south-asia/india-confronted-myanmar-about-china-spy-post-on-remote-coco-islands, last accessed 30 Mar. 2024.
54. Copies of those delivery reports are in the author's possession.
55. Aung Zaw, 'Burma's Secret Mission to North Korea', *The Irrawaddy*, Vol. 17, No 4, July 2009, https://www2.irrawaddy.com/article.php?art_id=16219, last accessed 30 Mar. 2024. See also 'North Korean Armament on Display', *Radio Free Asia*, 2 July 2000, https://www.rfa.org/english/multimedia/slideshowNKMilitary-07022009151817.html, last accessed 30 Mar. 2024.
56. 'Chinese Ship That Docked At Sri Lanka Port, Leaves After Six Days', *Press Trust of India*, 22 Aug. 2022, https://www.ndtv.com/world-news/chinese-

spy-ship-yuan-wang-5-that-docked-at-sri-lankas-hambantota-port-leaves-after-6-days-report-3275851, last accessed 30 Mar. 2024.
57. For a complete list of missions to China by insurgents from India's northeast, see the appendix to Lintner, Bertil, 'Burma and Its Neighbours', paper presented at a conference at the Nehru Memorial and Library, New Delhi, Feb. 1992, http://www.asiapacificms.com/papers/pdf/burma_india_china.pdf, last accessed 30 Mar. 2024.
58. This is the most common spelling of the name of the king. In proper Shan (Tai) it would be Hsö Kan Hpa, 'a tiger from heaven'. The Ahom kingdom lasted until its territory became British after the first Anglo-Burmese War, 1824–6. But by then it had become Indianised and few could still speak the Ahom dialect.
59. See Chakravarti, Nalini Ranjan, *The Indian Community in Burma: The Rise and Decline of an Immigrant Community*, London: Oxford University Press, 1971.
60. See Lintner, Bertil, 'China and South Asia's East', *Himal South Asia*, October 2002, http://www.asiapacificms.com/articles/china_burma_southasia/, last accessed 30 Mar. 2024. That article was based on numerous interviews with Hindu activists in Kolkata, diplomats and security analysts.
61. Clymer, Kenton, *A Delicate Relationship: The United States and Burma/Myanmar Since 1945*, Ithaca, New York: Cornell University Press, 2015, pp. 121 and 212.
62. *International Communism (Communist Encroachment in the Far East): Consultations with Maj.-Gen. Claire Lee Chennault*, US Congress, House Committee on Un-American Activities, 8th Congress, 2nd sess., 23 Apr. 1958, pp. 9–10.
63. For more about Tin U (Tin Oo), see McAndrew, James, *From Combat to Karaoke: Burmese Military Intelligence 1948–2006*, Washington: National Defence Intelligence College, 2007, pp. 51–3.
64. A typed transcript of Burton Levin's speech is in the author's possession.
65. Ott, Marvin, 'Don't Push Myanmar Into China's Orbit', *The Los Angeles Times*, 9 June 1997, https://www.latimes.com/archives/la-xpm-1997-06-09-me-1645-story.html, last accessed 30 Mar. 2024.
66. Articles about the relationship first appeared in the *Far Eastern Economic Review* of 10 July 2003 ('Intelligence') and Lintner, Bertil and Shawn Crispin, 'Dangerous Bedfellows', 20 Nov. 2003. Later, minutes and photographs from Thura Shwe Mann's 2008 visit have appeared on social media.

5. THE POLITICIANS

1. Shway Yoe, *The Burman: His Life and Notions*, New York: Norton and Company, 1963, p. 286.
2. Quoted in *Colonial Policy and Practice: A Comparative Study of Burma and the Netherlands India*, https://dokumen.pub/colonial-policy-and-practice-a-

comparative-study-of-burma-and-netherlands-india-gm80hv49r.html, last accessed 28 Mar. 2024.
3. Ibid.
4. Smith, David Eugene, *Religion and Politics in Burma*, Princeton, New Jersey: Princeton University press, 1965, p. 85.
5. Ibid., p. 93.
6. Becka, Jan, 'Buddhist Revival in Post-Independence Burma: A Study of Interaction of religion and Politics', in Vavrouskova, Stanislava (ed.), *Religion and Society in India and Burma*, Prague: The Oriental Institute of the Czechoslovak Academy of Sciences, 1991, pp. 10–12.
7. Ibid.
8. Tipton, C.B., 'Monks, Monasteries and Western Education in Colonial Burma, 1865–1930', *Journal of Educational Administration and History*, Vol. 37, No 2, 1981, pp. 22–32, posted online: 7 July 2006, https://www.tandfonline.com/doi/pdf/10.1080/0022062800130103, last accessed 29 Mar. 2024.
9. Smith, op. cit., p. 88.
10. U Lay Pe Win, *History of the 1920 University Boycott (Rangoon)*, Yangon: Student Press, 1970, pp. 29–30.
11. For an excellent account of the Saya San rebellion, and similar uprisings against British rule, see Ghosh, Parimal, *Brave Men of the Hills: Resistance and Rebellion in Burma, 1825–1932*, Honolulu: University of Hawaii Press, 2000.
12. Smith, op. cit., p. 115.
13. U Ba Swe, *The Burmese Revolution*, Yangon: Information Department, Union of Burma, 1952, p. 7.
14. Sarkisyanz, E., *Buddhist Backgrounds of the Burmese Revolution*, The Hague: Martinus Nijhoff, 1965, pp. 192–3.
15. Ibid., p. 126.
16. Thein Pe Nyint, *Tet Pongyi (The Modern Monk)*, Yangon: New Light of Burma Press, 1935 and 1937. See also Smith, op. cit., p. 208.
17. It is not unusual that Burmese change names several times during their lifetime. While in Japan, Htein Lin/Aung San became 'Bo Teza' (officer + fire). He also used the Japanese name Omoda Monji, and, in the resistance, his code names were Myo Aung, U Naung Cho and Ko Set Pe.
18. Aung San Suu Kyi, *Aung San*, St Lucia, Queensland: University of Queensland Press (Leaders of Asia Series), 1984, p. 1.
19. Ibid., p. 1.
20. Shway Yoe, op. cit., p. 5.
21. Aung San Suu Kyi, op. cit., p. 1.
22. Ibid., p. 6. The article was written by Nyo Mya, who later became a prominent author and a member of parliament.
23. Silverstein, Josef (ed.), *The Political Legacy of Aung San*, Ithaca, New York: Cornell University South East Asia Program, 1993, p. 20.

24. Houtman, Gustaaf, 'Aung San's *lan-zin*, the Blue Print and the Japanese Occupation of Burma', in Nemoto, Kei, *Reconsidering the Japanese Occupation in Burma (1942–35)*, Tokyo: Tokyo University of Foreign Studies, 2007, p. 185.
25. Ibid., p. 187.
26. Aung San Suu Kyi, op. cit., p. 19.
27. U Nu, *Saturday's Son*, New Haven, Connecticut: Yale University Press, 1975.
28. Callahan, Mary, 'The Sinking Schooner: Murder and the State in Independent Burma, 1948–1958', in Trocki, Carl (ed.), *Gangsters, Democracy and the State in Southeast Asia*, Ithaca, New York: Cornell Southeast Asia Program, 1998, p. 19.
29. Ibid., p. 27.
30. U Thaung, *A Journalist, a General and an Army in Burma*, Bangkok: White Lotus, 1995, p. 3.
31. Lintner, Bertil, 'Burma, Laos and Cambodia, Status of Media in', in *Encyclopedia of International Media and Communications*, Elsevier Science (USA), 2003, pp. 139–52, https://www.sciencedirect.com/science/article/abs/pii/B0123876702000170?via%3Dihub, last accessed 30 Mar. 2024.
32. U Thaung, op. cit., p. 31.
33. Lintner (2003).
34. Sargent, Inge, *Twilight Over Burma: My Life as a Shan Princess*, Honolulu: University of Hawaii Press, 1994, p. 141.
35. Sanjay Gandhi died when his private air plane crashed on 23 June 1980. Rajiv Gandhi served as prime minister of India from 1984 to 1989, and was assassinated on 21 May 1991.
36. The author was shown those letters during a visit to Michael Aris in Oxford in June 1989. See also introduction by Michael Aris to Aung San Suu Kyi, *Freedom from Fear and Other Writings*, London: Penguin, 1993, p. xvii.
37. Aung San Suu Kyi, op. cit. (1984).
38. Aung San Suu Kyi, *Burma and India: Some Aspects of Intellectual Life Under Colonialism*, New Delhi: Allied Publishers, 1990.
39. A transcript of the speech is in the author's possession.
40. Ibid.
41. 'Norway: Consul Tortured in Myanmar, Oslo Says', *The Los Angeles Times*, 12 July 1996, https://www.latimes.com/archives/la-xpm-1996-07-12-mn-23360-story.html, last accessed 30 Mar. 2024.
42. Taylor, Robert, 'The Evolving Military Role in Burma', *Current History*, March 1990.
43. The author was interviewed by several international TV and radio stations in May 1990, and was criticised for saying that there was no way the military would honour the outcome of the election.
44. 'We'll Play Fair. Interview, Kyi Maung', *Asiaweek*, 13 July 1990.
45. A full transcript of her speech can be found at 'Aung San Suu Kyi's Speech at the ICJ in Full', *Al Jazeera*, 12 Dec. 2019, https://www.aljazeera.com/

news/2019/12/12/transcript-aung-san-suu-kyis-speech-at-the-icj-in-full, last accessed 28 Mar. 2024.
46. Amnesty International, press release, 12 November 2018, https://www.amnesty.org/en/latest/press-release/2018/11/amnesty-withdraws-award-from-aung-san-suu-kyi/, last accessed 28 Mar. 2024.
47. See, for instance, 'Aung San Suu Kyi: Myanmar Democracy Icon Who Fell From Grace', *BBC*, 6 Dec. 2021, https://www.bbc.com/news/world-asia-pacific-11685977, last accessed 28 Mar. 2024.
48. Al Jazeera, 12 Dec. 2019.
49. Lintner, Bertil, 'Domestic Politics Drives Suu Kyi's Genocide Denial', *Asia Times*, 20 Dec. 2019, https://asiatimes.com/2019/12/domestic-drivers-behind-suu-kyis-genocide-denial/, last accessed 30 Mar. 2024.
50. 'In a Letter From Prison, Former Myanmar Leader Writes of Suffering', *Voice of America*, 10 Feb. 2024, https://www.voanews.com/a/in-letter-from-prison-former-myanmar-leader-writes-of-suffering/7482036.html, last accessed 30 Mar. 2024.
51. 'Citizens Perception of Current Political and Armed Conflicts', *Blue Shirt Initiative*, March 2024, p. 41, https://blueshirtinitiative.org/en/polls/1, last accessed 4 Apr. 2024.
52. Ibid., p. 41.
53. See https://web.archive.org/web/20140428181428/http://www.state.gov/s/gwi/programs/iwoc/2012/bio/, last accessed 30 Mar. 2024.
54. 'Crowdfunding a War: The Money Behind Myanmar's Resistance', *Reliefweb*, 20 Dec. 2022, https://reliefweb.int/report/myanmar/crowdfunding-war-money-behind-myanmars-resistance, last accessed 30 Mar. 2024.
55. Lieberman, Victor B., *Burmese Administrative Circles: Anarchy and Conquest, c.1580–1760*, Princeton, New Jersey: Princeton University Press, 1984, p. 213.

6. MYANMAR TODAY—AND TOMORROW

1. 'Statement on Operation 1027 and Related Operations', National Unity Government, 27 Oct. 2023, https://gov.nugmyanmar.org/statement-on-operation-1027-and-related-operations/, last accessed 3 Apr. 2024.
2. According to information the author received from well-placed sources in Yangon after the coup.
3. 'Myanmar Junta Leader Min Aung Hlaing Thanks Russia for Boosting its Military', *Agence France-Presse*, 23 June 2021, https://www.scmp.com/news/asia/southeast-asia/article/3138372/myanmar-junta-leader-min-aung-hlaing-thanks-russia, last accessed 28 Mar. 2024.
4. Strangio, Sebastian, 'Pariah Solidarity: Myanmar-Russia Relations Blossom Amid Western Sanctions', *The Diplomat*, 5 Aug. 2022, https://thediplomat.com/2022/08/pariah-solidarity-myanmar-russia-relations-blossom-amid-western-sanctions/, last accessed Mar. 2024.

NOTES

5. Ludmila, Lutz-Auras, 'Russia and Myanmar—Friends in Need?', *Journal of Current Southeast Asian Studies*, Vol. 34, No 2, 2015, https://journals.sub.uni-hamburg.de/giga/jsaa/article/view/877.html, last accessed 28 Mar. 2024.
6. 'Myanmar's Military Council Supports Russia's Invasion of Ukraine', *Voice of America*, 25 Feb. 2022, https://www.voanews.com/a/myanmar-s-military-council-supports-russia-s-invasion-0f-ukraine/6458527.html, last accessed 28 Mar. 2024.
7. This list of training facilities was compiled from information available on the trainees' Facebook pages. Since then, it appears that Myanmar's military leadership has forbidden them from posting such information on social media.
8. 'Russia to Build Nuclear Reactor in Myanmar', *Reuters*, 10 Aug. 2007, https://www.reuters.com/article/us-russia-myanmar-nuclear-idUSL1565024820070515/, last accessed 28 Mar. 2024.
9. 'Myanmar, Russia Sign Pact on Developing Nuclear Power', *Associated Press*, 8 Feb. 2023, https://apnews.com/article/politics-russia-government-myanmar-min-aung-hlaing-5c44b944599eecdab15a0c40b9e9608, last accessed 28 Mar. 2024.
10. For that and other exchanges of visits by Myanmar and Russian military officials, see 'A timeline of Russia's Relations With Myanmar Since the Coup', *The Irrawaddy*, 15 Feb. 2023, https://www.irrawaddy.com/specials/a-timeline-of-russias-relations-with-myanmar-junta-since-the-coup.html, last accessed 28 Mar. 2024.
11. 'Russian Deputy Defence Minister, Military Attachés Visit Maravijaya Buddha Image', *The Global New Light of Myanmar*, 28 Mar. 2024, https://www.gnlm.com.mm/russian-deputy-defence-minister-military-attaches-visit-maravijaya-buddha-image/, last accessed 28 Mar. 2024.
12. 'UEC Chair-led Delegation Arrives back from Russian Federation', *The Global New Light of Myanmar*, 22 Mar. 2024, https://www.gnlm.com.mm/uec-chair-led-delegation-arrives-back-from-russian-federation/, last accessed 30 Mar. 2024.
13. Kaznacheev, Alexandr (and edited by Simon Wolin), *Inside a Soviet Embassy: Experiences of a Russian Diplomat in Burma*, London: Robert Hale Limited, 1962, p. 63.
14. Ibid., p. 155.
15. Lintner, Bertil, 'Radio Moscow's Misstep', *Far Eastern Economic Review*, 12 Apr. 1990. The article is based on transcripts of those broadcasts into English.
16. Article no longer available on the Internet.
17. Peck, Grant, 'Military-ruled Myanmar Hosts Joint Naval Exercise With Russia, Its Close Ally and Top Arms Supplier', *Associated Press*, 8 Nov, 2023, https://apnews.com/article/russia-myanmar-navy-andaman-sea-1d0f0c692a4583a0c449e6c8cc3b620b, last accessed Apr. 2024.

18. 'Russia Myanmar Plan to Hold Over 50 Military Events in 2024—Top Brass', *Tass*, 28 Mar. 2024, https://tass.com/defense/1767141, last accessed 30 Mar. 2024.
19. 'Chairman's Statement on the ASEAN Leaders' Meeting, 24 April 2021, ASEAN Secretariat, Jakarta, Republic of Indonesia', https://asean.org/wp-content/uploads/Chairmans-Statement-on-ALM-Five-Point-Consensus-24-April-2021-FINAL-a-1.pdf, last accessed 28 Mar. 2024.
20. Lederer, Edith M., 'UN Chief: UN will Seek to Unite World, Reverse Myanmar Coup', *Associated Press*, 6 Feb. 2021, https://apnews.com/article/aung-san-suu-kyi-global-trade-myanmar-elections-antonio-guterres-e15c06b4fce06621f4651466cad6e458, last accessed 30 Mar. 2024.
21. 'New SAC-M Report: How the UN is Failing Myanmar', https://specialadvisorycouncil.org/2023/10/report-un-failing-myanmar/, last accessed 30 Mar. 2024.
22. Singh, Mohinder Pal, 'What if China Wrings India's "Chicken Neck"—the Siliguri Corridor? Here are Some Countermeasures', *The Times of India*, 9 Oct. 2019, https://timesofindia.indiatimes.com/blogs/toi-edit-page/what-if-china-wrings-indias-chickens-neck-the-siliguri-corridor-here-are-some-countermeasures/, last accessed 30 Mar. 2024.
23. 'Myanmar Military Recruiting Rohingyas at Displaced Camps', *Radio Free Asia Burmese*, 22 Feb. 2024, https://www.rfa.org/english/news/myanmar/recruiting-02222024174652.html, last accessed 30 Mar. 2024).
24. According to what KIA officers have told the author.
25. For a complete list of US sanctions, see 'U.S. Department of State: Burma Sanctions', https://www.state.gov/burma-sanctions/, last accessed 30 Mar. 2024.
26. 'Burma: Human Rights in the Aftermath of the Coup', the United States Agency for International Development, 13 Sep. 2013, https://www.usaid.gov/news-information/congressional-testimony/sep-13-2023-burma-human-rights-aftermath-coup, last accessed 2 Apr. 2024.
27. Brochure about the new consulate general can be downloaded here: https://www.state.gov/wp-content/uploads/2021/05/United-States-of-America-Consulate-General-Chiang-Mai-Design-Monograph.pdf, last accessed 2 Apr. 2024.
28. 'The White House: Joint Leaders Statement on AUKUS', 15 Sep. 2021, https://www.whitehouse.gov/briefing-room/statements-releases/2021/09/15/joint-leaders-statement-on-aukus/, last accessed Apr. 2024.
29. 'U.S., Britain Exporting Nuclear Submarine Technology to Australia "extremely irresponsible": FM Spokesperson', *Xinhua*, 16 Sep. 2021, http://www.xinhuanet.com/english/2021-09/16/c_1310191989.htm, last accessed 2 Apr. 2024.
30. Ibid.

31. 'AUKUS Threatens Regional Peace, Stability, International Order: FM', *Global Times*, 30 Sep. 2021, https://www.globaltimes.cn/page/202109/1235519.shtml, last accessed 2 Apr. 2024.
32. Ibid.
33. 'China Starts Calling Myanmar Junta "Government"', *The Irrawaddy*, 11 Aug. 2021, https://www.irrawaddy.com/news/burma/china-starts-calling-myanmar-junta-government.html#google_vignette, last accessed 2 Apr. 2024.
34. San Yamin Aung, 'Myanmar's Ex-President Tells Voters to Protect Race, Religion, Military in 2020 Election', *The Irrawaddy*, 7 Jan. 2020, https://www.irrawaddy.com/news/burma/myanmars-ex-president-tells-voters-protect-race-religion-military-2020-election.html, last accessed 2 Apr. 2024.
35. Tin Htet Paing, 'Myanmar's Outcast Junta Chief Pursues Russian Support and Fierce Resistance at Home', *Myanmar Now*, 13 July 2022, https://myanmar-now.org/en/news/myanmars-outcast-junta-chief-pursues-russian-support-amid-fierce-resistance-at-home/, last accessed 3 Apr. 2024.
36. Strangio, Sebastian, 'Why Did Myanmar's Junta Grant Wirathu a National Award?', *The Diplomat*, 9 Jan. 2023, https://thediplomat.com/2023/01/why-did-myanmars-junta-grant-wirathu-a-national-award/, last accessed 3 Apr. 2024.
37. 'Myanmar: Min Ko Naing, Student Leader and Prisoner of Conscience', *Amnesty International*, Jan. 2001, https://www.amnesty.org/en/wp-content/uploads/2021/06/asa160012001en.pdf, last accessed 3 Apr. 2024.
38. Ibid.
39. 'Veteran Student Leaders, Rocker, Social Influencers on Myanmar Military's Arrest Warrant', *The Irrawaddy*, 13 Feb. 2021, https://www.irrawaddy.com/news/burma/veteran-student-leaders-rocker-social-influencers-myanmar-militarys-arrest-warrant.html, last accessed Apr. 2024.
40. 'Myanmar: First Executions in Decades Mark Atrocious Escalation in State Repression', *Amnesty International*, 25 July 2022, https://www.amnesty.org/en/latest/news/2022/07/myanmar-first-executions-in-decades-mark-atrocious-escalation-in-state-repression/, last accessed 3 Apr. 2024.
41. 'People's Party Sees Mass Resignations Over Decision to Attend UEC Meeting', *Myanmar Now*, 23 May 2021, https://myanmar-now.org/en/news/peoples-party-sees-mass-resignations-over-decision-to-attend-uec-meeting/, last accessed 3 Apr. 2024.
42. Beech, Hannah, 'Across Myanmar, Denial of Ethnic Cleansing and Loathing of Rohingya', *The New York Times*, 24 Oct. 2017, https://www.nytimes.com/2017/10/24/world/asia/myanmar-rohingya-ethnic-cleansing.html, last accessed on 3 Apr. 2024.
43. Ibid.
44. Nachemson, Andrew and Lun Min Mang, 'Activists Championed by Rights Groups Have History of Anti-Rohingya Messaging', *Frontier Myanmar*, 24

45. See, for instance, 'The Rohingya: The World's Largest Stateless Population', Médecins Sans Frontières/Doctors Without Borders, https://msf.org.au/rohingya-worlds-largest-stateless-population, last accessed 3 Apr. 2024. Another common mistake seen in many writings about the Rohingyas is that the 1982 citizenship law listed the '135 national races' of the country and excluded the Rohingyas. The 1982 law does not contain any such list. The notion of '135 national races' is much more recent and was first floated by the military in the early 1990s. But, even so, no official list of those '135 national races' was made public until 2014 (see link at footnote 4 and chapter three).
46. For the full text of the 1982 Citizenship Law, see https://www.legal-tools.org/doc/d3e586/pdf, last accessed 3 Apr. 2024. It does not mention the Rohingyas, nor does it have a list of 135 'national races'.
47. Prentice, David, 'Taiwan's "Little Burma"', *The Diplomat*, 18 Mar. 2017, https://thediplomat.com/2017/03/taiwans-little-burma/, last accessed 3 Mar. 2024.
48. *Forward* (magazine, Yangon), Aug. 1978. Not available online.
49. Ingyin Naing, 'Myanmar Shadow Government Official Apologizes to Rohingya', *Voice of America*, 17 Aug. 2023, https://www.voanews.com/a/myanmar-shadow-government-official-apologizes-to-rohingya/7230216.html, last accessed 3 Apr. 2024.
50. For a profile, see Myanmar's Civilian Government Appoints Rohingya Activist as Deputy Minister', *The Irrawaddy*, 1 July 2023, https://www.irrawaddy.com/news/burma/myanmars-civilian-government-appoints-rohingya-activist-as-deputy-minister.html, last accessed 3 Apr. 2024.
51. There are sizable Rohingya communities in Malaysia, Pakistan, India, Saudi Arabia and Sharjah in the United Arab Emirates, as well as smaller refugee communities in Thailand, Indonesia, the United States, Australia and other countries. The total number of Rohingyas who are not living in camps in Bangladesh could be as many as two million.
52. According to what Bangladeshi officials have told the author.

ADDITIONAL READING

Books

Abbott, Gerry, *Back to Mandalay: An Inside View of Burma*, Bromley, Kent: Impact Books, 1990.
Anderson, Courtney, *The Golden Shore: The Life of Adoniram Judson*, Boston: Little, Brown and Company, 1956.
Aung San Suu Kyi, *Burma and India: Some Aspects of Intellectual Life Under Colonialism*, Shimla: Indian Institute of Advanced Study, 1990.
———, *Freedom From Fear and Other Writings*, London: Viking, 1991.
———, *Letters from Burma*, London: Penguin Books, 1997.
Aung Zaw, *The Face of Resistance: Aung San Suu Kyi and Burma's Fight for Freedom*, Chiang Mai: Mekong Press and Silkworm Books, 2013.
Ball, Desmond, *Burma's Military Secrets: Signals Intelligence (SIGINT) from 1941 to Cyber Warfare*, Bangkok: White Lotus, 1998.
Becka, Jan, *The National Liberation Movement in Burma during the Japanese Occupation Period (1941–1945)*, Prague: The Oriental Institute, 1983.
Bhatia, Rajiv, *India-Myanmar Relations: Changing Contours*, New Delhi: Routledge, 2016.
Cady, John, *A History of Burma*, Ithaca, New York: Cornell University Press, 1958.
Callahan, Mary, *Making Enemies: War and State Building in Burma*, Ithaca: Cornell University Press, 2003.
Clymer, Kenton, *A Delicate Relationship: The United States and Burma/Myanmar Since 1945*, Ithaca: Cornell University Press, 2015.
Director of Information, *Is Trust Vindicated? A Chronicle of the Various Establishments of the Government Headed by General Ne Win During the*

ADDITIONAL READING

Period of the Tenure from November 1958 to February 6, 1960, Rangoon: Government of the Union of Burma, 1960.

Ferguson, Jane, *Repossessing Shanland: Myanmar, Thailand, and a Nation-State Deferred*, Madison: The University of Wisconsin Press, 2021.

Ghosh, Parimal, *Brave Men of the Hills: Resistance and Rebellion in Burma, 1825–1932*, Honolulu: University of Hawaii Press, 2000.

Houtman, Gustaaf, *Mental Culture in Burmese Crisis Politics: Aung San Suu Kyi and the National League for Democracy*, Tokyo: Tokyo University of Foreign Studies, 1999.

Kin Oung, *Who Killed Aung San?*, Bangkok: White Lotus 1993 and (updated and expanded) 1996.

Kyaw Zwa Moe, *The Cell, Exile, and the New Burma: A Political Education amid the Unfinished Journey toward Democracy*, Yangon: New Myanmar Publishing House, 2018.

Lehman, F.K. (ed.), *Military Rule in Burma Since 1962*, Singapore: Maruzen Asia, 1981.

Lieberman, Victor B., *Burmese Administrative Circles: Anarchy and Conquest, c.1580–1760*, Princeton, New Jersey: Princeton University Press, 1984.

Lintner, Bertil, *Outrage: Burma's Struggle for Democracy*, Hong Kong: Review Publishing, 1989, and London: White Lotus UK, 1990.

———, *The Rise and Fall of the Communist Party of Burma*, Ithaca: Cornell University Southeast Asia Program, 1990.

———, *Burma in Revolt: Opium and Insurgency Since 1948*, Boulder: Westview Press, 1994, and Chiang Mai: Silkworm Books, 1999, 2003 and 2011.

———, *The Kachin: Lords of Burma's Northern Frontier*, Chiang Mai: Teakhouse Publications, 1997.

———, *Aung San Suu Kyi and Burma's Struggle for Democracy*, Chiang Mai: Silkworm Books, 2011.

———, and Michael Black, *Merchants of Madness: The Methamphetamine Explosion in the Golden Triangle*, Chiang Mai: Silkworm Books, 2009.

———, *The Wa of Myanmar and China's Quest for Global Dominance*, Copenhagen: Nordic Institute of Asian Studies Press, 2021.

Marshall, Andrew, *The Trouser People: Burma in the Shadows of the Empire*, London: Viking Books, 2002.

Maung Aung Myoe, *Building the Tatmadaw: Myanmar Armed Forces Since 1948*, New Delhi: Knowledge World Publishers, 2011.

—, *In the Name of Pauk-Phaw: Myanmar's China Policy Since 1948*, Singapore: Institute of Southeast Asian Studies, 2011.

ADDITIONAL READING

Maung Maung, Dr, *Burma's Constitution*, The Hague: Martinus Nijhoff, 1961.
———, *Burma and General Ne Win*, Bombay: Asia Publishing House, 1969.
———, *To a Soldier Son*, Rangoon: Sarpay Beikman Press, 1974.
Maung Maung, U, *Burmese Nationalist Movements 1940–1948*, Edinburgh: Kiscadale Publications, 1989.
McAndrew, James, *From Combat to Karaoke: Burma's Military Intelligence 1948–2006*, Washington: National Defense Intelligence College, 2007.
Nakanishi, Yoshihiro, *Strong Soldiers, Failed Revolution: The State and Military in Burma, 1962–88*, Singapore: National University of Singapore Press, 2013.
Nu, U, *Saturday's Son*, New Haven: Yale University Press, 1975.
Popham, Peter, *The Lady and the Peacock: The Life of Aung San Suu Kyi*, London: Rider, 2011.
Rogers, Benedict, *Than Shwe: Unmasking Burma's Tyrant*, Chiang Mai: Silkworm Books, 2010.
Rotberg, Robert (ed.), *Burma: Prospects for a Democratic Future*, Washington: Brookings Institution Press, 1998.
Sadan, Mandy, *Being and Becoming Kachin: Histories Beyond the State in the Borderworlds of Burma*, London: Oxford University Press, 2013.
Seekins, Donald, *Historical Dictionary of Burma (Myanmar)*, Lanham, Maryland: The Scarecrow Press, 2006.
———, *Burma and Japan Since 1940: From 'Co-Prosperity to 'Quiet Dialogue'*, Copenhagen: Nordic Institute of Asian Studies Press, 2007.
Selth, Andrew, *Burma's Armed Forces: Power Without Glory*, Norwalk, Connecticut: East Bridge, 2002.
———, *Secrets and Power in Myanmar: Intelligence and the Fall of Khin Nyunt*, Singapore: Institute of Southeast Asian Studies, 2019.
Shway Yoe, *The Burman: His Life and Notions*, New York: Norton and Company, 1963.
Silverstein, Josef, *Burma: Military Rule and the Politics of Stagnation*, Ithaca: Cornell University Press, 1977.
———, *Burmese Politics: The Dilemma of National Unity*, New Brunswick, New Jersey: Rutgers University Press, 1980.
——— (ed.), *The Political Legacy of Aung San*, Ithaca: Cornell University Southeast Asia Program, 1993.
Smith, David Eugene, *Religion and Politics in Burma*, Princeton, New Jersey: Princeton University press, 1965.

ADDITIONAL READING

Smith, Martin, *Burma: Insurgency and the Politics of Ethnicity*, London: Zed Books, 1991.

Smith Dun, *Memoirs of the Four-Foot Colonel*, Ithaca, New York: Cornell University Southeast Asia Program, Data Paper, No. 113, 1980.

South, Ashley, *Mon Nationalism and Civil War in Burma*, London: Routledge Curzon, 2003.

Steinberg, David, *Burma's Road Toward Development: Growth and Ideology Under Military Rule*, Boulder: Westview Press, 1981.

———, *Burma: A Socialist Nation of Southeast Asia*, Boulder: Westview Press, 1982.

———, *The Future of Burma: Crisis and Choice in Myanmar*, Lanham, Maryland: University Press of America, 1990.

———, *Burma: The State of Myanmar*, Washington: Georgetown University Press, 2001.

———, and Hongwei Fan, *Modern China-Myanmar Relations: Dilemmas of Mutual Dependence*, Singapore: National University of Singapore Press, 2012.

Taylor, Robert, *The State in Burma*, London: Hurst & Company, 1987, reprinted as *The State in Myanmar* in 2009.

———, *General Ne Win: A Political Biography*, Singapore: Institute of Southeast Asian Studies, 2015.

Thant Myint-U, *The Making of Modern Burma*, Cambridge: Cambridge University Press, 2001.

———, *The Rivers of Lost Footsteps: Histories of Burma*, New York: Farrar, Straus and Giroux, 2006.

———, *The Hidden History of Burma: Race, Capitalism and the Crisis of Democracy in the 21st Century*, London: Atlantic Books, 2019.

Thida, Ma, *Prisoner of Conscience: My Steps Through Insein*, Chiang Mai: Silkworm Books, 2016.

Tinker, Hugh, *The Union of Burma: A Study of The First Years of Independence*, London: Oxford University Press, 1957.

———, *Burma: The Struggle for Independence: Constitutional Relations Between Britain and Burma*, London: Her Majesty's Stationery Office, 1983 (Vol. I) and 1984 (Vol. II).

Vavrouskova, Stanislava (ed.), *Religion and Society in India and Burma*, Prague: The Oriental Institute of the Czechoslovak Academy of Sciences, 1992.

Ware, Andrew and Monique Skidmore (eds), *After the Coup: Myanmar's Political and Humanitarian Crises*, Canberra: Australian National University Press, 2023.

ADDITIONAL READING

Yawnghwe, Chao Tzang, *The Shan of Burma: Memoirs of a Shan Exile*, Singapore: Institute of Southeast Asian Studies, 1987, 1990 and 2010.

Yawnghwe, Samara, *Maintaining the Union of Burma 1946–1962: The Role of the Ethnic Nationalities in a Shan Perspective*, Bangkok: Institute of Asian Studies, Chulalongkorn University, 2013.

Yegar, Moshe, *The Muslims of Burma: A Study of a Minority Group*, Wiesbaden: Otto Harrassowitz, 1972.

Select Research Papers

Buchanan, John, *Militias in Myanmar*, The Asia Foundation, July 2016, https://asiafoundation.org/wp-content/uploads/2016/07/Militias-in-Myanmar.pdf, last accessed 20 Mar. 2024.

Callahan, Mary, *Rethinking Burmese Military Politics: The Institutional Origin of Postwar Politics*, undated Cornell University research paper. Not available online.

———, *The Origins of Military Rule in Burma*, Ph.D. dissertation, Cornell University, May 1996.

Lintner, Bertil, *The Shans and the Shan States of Burma*, Institute of Southeast Asian Studies, Singapore, Mar. 1984, http://www.asiapacificms.com/papers/pdf/the_shans_and_shan_state.pdf, last accessed 20 Mar. 2024.

———, *Cross-Border Drug Trade in the Golden Triangle*, International Boundaries Research Unit, 1991, http://www.asiapacificms.com/papers/pdf/cross-border-drug-trade-in-the-golden-triangle-1991.pdf, last accessed 20 Mar. 2024.

———, *The Golden Triangle Opium Trade: An Overview*, research paper, http://www.asiapacificms.com/papers/pdf/gt_opium_trade.pdf, last accessed 20 Mar. 2024.

———, *The Staying Power of the Burmese Military Regime*, paper presented at a public forum on Burma at Aichi Gakuin University, Nagoya, Japan, 11–17 Mar. 2009, https://www.academia.edu/70968953/The_Enigma_of_Military_Power_in_Burma, last accessed 20 Mar. 2024.

———, *The Resistance of the Monks*, Human Rights Watch, 22 Sep. 2009, https://www.hrw.org/report/2009/09/22/resistance-monks/buddhism-and-activism-burma, last accessed 20 Mar. 2024.

———, *Burma's WMD Programme and Military Cooperation Between Burma and the Democratic People's Republic and Korea*, research paper, Mar. 2012, http://www.asiapacificms.com/papers/pdf/burma_dprk_military_cooperation.pdf, last accessed 25 Mar. 2024.

ADDITIONAL READING

———, *The People's Republic of China and Burma: Not Only Pauk-Phaw*, Project 2049 Institute, 9 May 2017, http://www.asiapacificms.com/papers/pdf/ThePeoplesRepublicofChinaandBurmaNotonlyPauk-Phaw.pdf, last accessed 20 Mar. 2024.

———, *The United Wa State Army and Burma's Peace Process*, United States Institute of Peace, April 2019, http://www.asiapacificms.com/papers/pdf/the_united_wa_state_army_and_burmas_peace_process.pdf, last accessed 20 Mar. 2024.

———, *Burma's Path to Peace, Lessons from the Past and Paths Forward*, Researchers Republic, June 2023, http://asiapacificms.com/papers/pdf/burma-path-to-peace.pdf, last accessed 25 Mar. 2024.

Mathieson, David Scott, *The Arakan Army in Myanmar: Deadly Conflict Rises in Rakhine State*, Washington: The United States Institute of Peace, Special Report, Nov. 2020, https://www.usip.org/sites/default/files/2021-02/sr_486-the_arakan_army_in_myanmar_deadly_conflict_rises_in_rakhine_state.pdf, last accessed 20 Mar. 2024.

Selth, Andrew, *Burma's Arms Procurement Programme*, Working Paper No. 289, Strategic and Defence Studies Centre, Australian National University, Canberra, Sep. 1995.

———, *Burma's North Koream Gambit: A Challenge to Regional Security?*, Canberra Papers on Strategy and Defence No. 154, Strategic and Defence Studies Centre, Australian National University, Canberra, 2004.

———, *Burma's Coco Islands: Rumours and Realities in the Indian Ocean*, City University of Hong Kong, Nov. 2008, https://www.cityu.edu.hk/searc/Resources/Paper/WP101_08_ASelth.pdf. last accessed 20 Mar. 2024.

———, *Myanmar: An Enduring Intelligence State or a State Enduring Intelligence?*, Asia Policy Paper, Washington DC: Stimson Centre, April 2021, https://www.stimson.org/wp-content/uploads/2021/04/China-2021-1393-Selth.pdf. last accessed 20 Mar. 2024.

———, *Myanmar's Military Mindset: An Exploratory Survey*, Brisbane: Griffiths Asia Institute, Griffith University, 30 Sep. 2021, https://blogs.griffith.edu.au/asiainsights/myanmars-military-mindset/. last accessed 20 Mar. 2024.

———, *Intelligence and Intelligence Agencies in Myanmar Since the 2021 Coup*, Brisbane: Griffith Asia Institute, Griffith University, 2023, https://www.griffith.edu.au/__data/assets/pdf_file/0028/1774531/Selth-Post-coup-intelligence-in-Myanmar.pdf. last accessed 20 Mar. 2024.

ADDITIONAL READING

Smith, Martin, *Ethnic Groups in Burma: Development, Democracy and Human Rights*, Anti-Slavery International, 1994, https://www.burmalibrary.org/docs3/Ethnic_Groups_in_Burma-ocr.pdf, last accessed 12 Mar. 2024.

———, *Arakan (Rakhine State): A Land in Conflict on Myanmar's Western Border*, Transnational Institute, 18 Dec. 2019, https://www.tni.org/en/publication/arakan-rakhine-state-a-land-in-conflict-on-myanmars-western-frontier, last accessed 20 Mar. 2024.

Steinberg, David, *The Military in Burma/Myanmar: On the Longevity of Tatmadaw Rule and Influence*, Yusof Ishak Institute, Singapore, 2021, https://www.iseas.edu.sg/wp-content/uploads/2021/04/TRS6_21.pdf, last accessed 20 Mar. 2024.

Thaung, U, *Army's Accumulation of Economic Power in Burma (1950–1990)*, paper presented at a Burma seminar in Washington on 20 Oct. 1990. Not available online.

Yawnghwe, Chao Tzang, *Ne Win's Tatmadaw Dictatorship*, MA thesis, University of British Columbia, 1990, https://open.library.ubc.ca/soa/cIRcle/collections/ubctheses/831/items/1.0098440, last accessed 20 Mar. 2024.

INDEX

Abel, David, 121
'the Abode of Kings', 37
Act East Policy, 138
AFPFL. *See* Anti-Fascist People's Freedom League (AFPFL)
Agence France-Presse, 181
Ahom kingdom, 137
Air Force Engineering Academy, 178
Alaska, 190
Alaungpaya, 79–80
Allahabad, 154
All-Burma Federation of Student Unions, 154
All-Burma Students Democratic Front (ABSDF), 16, 17, 18, 20, 166, 171
'All-States Conference', 54–5
Amarapura, 81
America, 51
American Board of Commissioners for Foreign Missions, 85
Amnesty International, 169, 193
Amoy, 38–9
Anawrahta, King, 78

Andaman and Nicobar Islands, 132
Andaman Sea, 132, 182
Anglo-Burmese War I, 81
Anglo-Burmese War II, 82
Anglo-Burmese War III, 83–7
Antara, 181
Anti-Fascist People's Freedom League (AFPFL), 41, 44, 98
  split, 52
  U Nu government, 153–5
Anti-Terrorism Law, 194
Arakan Army (AA), 31, 32, 70, 126, 185–6
Arakan coast, 88, 95
Arakan kingdom, 42, 48, 79, 80–2
Arakan mountains, 48
Arakan Rohingya Salvation Army (ARSA), 168
Arakan Yoma, 180
Aris, Alexander, 160
Aris, Kim, 160, 170–1
Aris, Michael, 159–60
Armed Forces Day, 30–1, 37–8
Arunachal Pradesh, 88, 131, 185

INDEX

Asia Society in New York, 141
Asia, 57, 61
Asian Age (newspaper), 130
Asian Network for Free Elections, 27
Asiaweek (magazine), 166
Assam, 81, 185
Associated Press (News agency company), 12, 181
Association of Southeast Asian Nations (ASEAN), 182–4
Attlee, Clement, 43, 153
August 1988 uprising and massacre, 22, 161
AUKUS. *See* Australia-United Kingdom-United States pact (AUKUS)
Aung, U, 157
Aung Gyi, 53, 57, 114, 164
Aung Kyaw Hla, 24, 25, 128, 182
Aung Kyaw Moe, 196
Aung Min, UWSA, Chinese support, 125–6
Aung Myo Min, 171–2
Aung San Chit, 158
Aung San Lin, 158–9
Aung San Oo, 158–9
Aung San Suu Kyi, 2, 14–16, 20, 25–7, 128, 142, 168–70, 193, 194
    Nobel Peace Prize, 167, 169
    politics, 158–65
    revolutions, 27–31
Aung San, 2, 20, 38–42, 62, 99, 149, 151
    assassination of, 43-44, 99
    ethnic Burman Divisions, 76–7
    Panglong Agreement, 152–3
Aung Thura Zaw, 194

Australia, 61, 63, 128, 160, 168, 172, 184, 187
Australia-United Kingdom-United States pact (AUKUS), 187, 191
Ava Bank, 50
Ava, Kingdom of (Inwa), 78–81, 144
Aw Chu Kin, 97
Aya House, 50
Ayutthaya, Kingdom of, 78, 79, 80, 100

Ba Choe, 43–4
Ba Maw, 62
U Ba Swe, 52, 149
Ba Tin, U, 180
Ba Win, 20, 44
Ba Yin, 149
Bago, 12, 14, 18
Bagyidaw, 81
Ban Hin Taek, 105
Ban Kin Yu, 97
Bandoola Journal (newspaper), 156
Bandoola Square, 13
Bandung Conference, 154
Bangkok, 80, 100, 104, 106
    Japanese vs. Chinese, 39–42
Bangladesh, 168, 185, 195–6
Baptism, 85
Barr Street, 38
Bassein, 87
Bawlake, 43
Bay of Bengal, 134, 135, 184
Bayinnaung, 78–80
Becka, Jan, 145
Beijing Review (newspaper), 117–18, 120
Beijing, 92, 109–10, 115, 118, 138, 176, 187, 191

INDEX

boundary treaty, 112
Rangoon and Beijing, relations, 116–19
UWSA, Chinese support, 124–6
Belgium, 89
Bhamo, 90, 93
Bharatiya Janata Party, 139
Bhopal, 157
Bhutan, 159–60, 185
BIA. *See* Burma Independence Army (BIA)
'big Shan', 76
Bingley, John, 44
'Blue Print for Burma', 151
Blue Shirt Initiative, 171
Bo Aung Kyaw Day, 151
Bo Aung Kyaw Street, 151
Bo Balanew Myanmar army, 70
Bo La Yaungnew Myanmar army, 70
Bo Let Ya, 10, 11, 70, 107, 157
Bo Mya, 108
Bo Ni, 66
Bo Setkya, 70
Bo Tayanew Myanmar army, 70
Bo Yan Aungnew Myanmar army, 70
Bo Yan Naing, 70
Bo Ye Htut, 45
Bo Zeya, 114
Bodawpaya, King, 80–1
Bodh Gaya, 139
Bohmu Aung, 70
Bombay Burmah Trading Company, 83
Brahmaputra valley, 137
Britain, 3, 33, 61, 82, 172
Anglo-Burmese War, 82
Burmese Empire III, 79–82

British Bengal, 81
British Broadcasting Corporation (BBC), 131–2, 181
British Burma, 38
British colonialism, 40
British India, 82, 83, 87
Brito, Felipe de, 79
Brotherhood Alliance, 33–4, 70, 175
Brunei, 183
BSPP. *See* Burma Socialist Programme Party (BSPP)
Buddhism, 55, 87, 96, 139
adoption, 78
in Burma, 144–7
Shans adopted, 92
Bulganin, Nikolai, 180
Burma Asiatic Company, 50
Burma Broadcasting Service, 14, 64
Burma Campaign, 30
Burma Defence Army (BDA), 40, 42
Burma Economic Development Corporation (BEDC), 54
Burma Five Star Shipping Line, 50
Burma Herald (newspaper), 155
Burma Independence Army (BIA), 40, 42, 46
Burma National Army (BNA) Japanese vs. Chinese, 39–42
Burma Socialist Party, 149
Burma Socialist Programme Party (BSPP), 12, 14–15, 18, 21, 58, 63, 158
Burma Territorial Force, 51
Burmanisation, 77
Burmese Air Force, 46
Burmese Empire I, 78, 89
Burmese Empire II, 78–9

237

INDEX

Burmese Empire III, 79–83
'Burmese Way to Socialism', 64
Buru Island concept, 133
Bush, George W., 141–2

Calcutta, 41, 81, 85, 97, 132
California, 159
Callahan, Mary, 42, 154–5
Cambodia, 77, 116, 118, 179, 183, 184, 190
Cambodian People's Party, 183
Cameron, David, 2
Canada, 168, 169
Caretaker Government, 52–7
Carter Center, 27
Ceylon. *See* Sri Lanka
Chahi Taret Khuntakpa, 81
Chakri Dynasty, 80
Chang, Ronald, 105
Chao Kaew Nawarat, 190
Chao Phraya, 80
Chao Tzang, 56
Chatham House, 133–4
Chauk, 8
Chedi Ngam Palace, 190
Chellaney, Brahma, 130
Chengdu, 60
Chennault, Claire, 140
Chiang Kai-shek, 109, 140
Chiang Mai, 187–91
'The Chicken's Neck', 185
Chin Hills, 94
Chin Mo, 194
Chin State, 185
Chin tribes, 31, 42, 46–7, 93–4
 ethnic Burman Divisions, 76
'China Lobby', 140
China, 16, 24, 25, 33–4, 38–9, 48, 57–9, 65, 68, 86, 97, 108, 111, 188–90, 197

boundary treaty, 112–13, 120–2;
vs. British, 83–4
Brotherhood Alliance, 175–6
Hsinbyushin's kingdom, 80
Japanese vs. Chinese, 39–42
militaries friendship, 176–9
Myanmar's naval bases, 132–6
new policies, 123
Rangoon and Beijing, relations, 116–19
relations, 109
Sino-Burmese declaration, 110–11
U Nu's relation, 154
UWSA support, 124–6
Washington's Myanmar policy, 139–42
See also Russia
China-Myanmar Economic Corridor (CMEC), 127, 129, 136, 139, 176, 185, 187
Chindwin River, 95
Chinese civil war, 110, 189
Chinese Communist Party, 112
Chinese communists, 38
Chinese Kuomintang (KMT) forces, 48–9, 101, 109, 189
 Washington's Myanmar policy, 139–40
Chittagong, 96
Christianity, 79, 93–4
Churchill, Winston, 152
CIA. *See* United States Central Intelligence Agency (CIA)
Circular Disposed Antenna Array (CDAA) station, 189
Civil Disobedience Movement, 28
'Clean AFPFL', 52
Clift, Tommy, 106

INDEX

Clinton, Bill, 141
Clinton, Hillary, 2, 25, 142
CMEC. *See* China-Myanmar Economic Corridor (CMEC)
Cochran Stevenson, Henry Noel, 94
Coco Islands, 132–6
Colonel Suzuki, 40
Columbia University, 171
communism, 107, 116
'communist conspiracy', 16
Communist Party (Red Flag), 100
Communist Party of Australia (Marxist- Leninist), 116
Communist Party of Burma (CPB), 8–9, 11, 16–17, 31, 38, 43, 45–9, 59–61, 108–9, 180, 189
   alliances and opium trafficking, 100–6
   border agreement, 120–2
   exiles, 113–15
   Japanese vs. Chinese, 39–42
   vs. Military, 111
   new Myanmar army, 70
   Rangoon and Beijing, relations, 116–19
   Thein Pe Myint in, 150
   UWSA, Chinese support, 124–5
Communist Party of China (CPC), 116–17, 188
Communist Party of Thailand, 189
Communist Party of the Soviet Union, 180
'The Constitution of the Union of Burma', 52
Convention on the Prevention and Punishment of the Crime of Genocide (1948), 168

Court of Ava, 172–3
Cox's Bazar, 96
Craddock, Reginald, 146
Crime Against the State and High Treason Act, 64
Crosthwaite, Charles, 83
Cuba, 118
Cultural Revolution, 60
Current History (Robert Taylor), 165–6
Cyclone Nargis, 141
Czech Republic, 172

Dagon, 80
Dai, 88
Dalai Lama, 138
Dali, 92
Danubyu, 81
Daw Mying Myint Khin, 163
Daw Saw Khin, 153
Daw Su, 150
Dawei, 12, 79
Deedok (journal), 44
Defence Services Academy (DSA), 51
Defence Services Institute (DSI), 49–50, 54, 57
Democracy and Peace Party, 157
Democratic Alliance of Burma, 107
Democratic Voice of Burma (DVB), 167
Deng Xiaoping, 16, 116–19, 121–2
Denmark, 165
Directorate of the Defence Services Intelligence (DDSI), 17, 19, 66–7
Dissanayake, C.S., 145
Djibouti, 136

INDEX

Dohbama Asiayone ('Our Burma Association'), 74–5, 149–50, 153
'the domino theory', 116
'Dtai', 88
Duan Xiwen, 103–4
Dublin, 169
Dufferin, Lord, 83
Dundee, 169
Duwa Lashi La, 31

East Asia, 92
East Asiatic Company, 50
East Bengal, 96
East Pakistan (Bangladesh), 48
East Timor, 183–4
Eastern Europe, 57
Edinburgh, 169
Egypt, 147
'Elephant Cage', 189–90
Elie Wiesel Award, 169
Enriquez, Colin Metcalfe, 87
E-Pao, 130
Equality Myanmar, 172
Europe, 168
European Union's Election Observation Mission, 27
exmeitei (Manipuri blog), 130

Far Eastern Economic Review (weekly), 65, 132
Federal Movement, 55, 101
Federal National Democratic Front, 106
Federated Shan States, 90
Fedorovich Vasiliev, Vladimir, 181
Financial Times (newspaper), 13
Finland, 165
'Five Principles of Peaceful Co-existence', 111

'the five twos revolution', 29
Fomin, Alexander Vasilyevich, 178
Formosa (Taiwan), 39–40
Forsyth, T.D., 43
Fort Leavenworth, 166
"Four Cuts" policy, 62–3
4th Burma Rifles, 45–7, 49, 53, 57, 58, 70–1
France, 82, 147, 172
Free Burma (newspaper), 156
Freedom of the City awards, 169
Frontier Areas Committee of Enquiry (FACOE), 98–9
Fujian province, 38–9

Galons, 149
Galway, 169
Gambia, 168
Gandhi, Mahatma, 147, 159
Gandhi, Rajiv, 138, 159
Gandhi, Sanjay, 159
Gauri, 76
Gawlum, 111
Gaza, 128, 191
General Council of Burmese Associations (GCBA), 147, 148–9
General Council of Sangha Sammeggi, 147
Generation Z, 2, 29–30
Germany, 151
Ghoshal, Hamendranath, 117
Gilbert Swell, George, 129
Glasgow, 169
Global Times (newspaper), 188
'globalisation', 24
'the Golden Land', 141
Golden Triangle, 92, 122
Google Earth, 135
Gorbachev, Mikhail, 181

INDEX

Gore-Booth, Lord, 159–60
Gourley, Richard, 13
Guangxi, 89
Guardian (newspaper), 50, 58, 158
Guizhou province, 60, 89, 110, 115
Guterres, António, 184

Hainan, 40
Hakka, 97
Hambantota, 135
Hamburg, 20
Hanson, Ola, 93
Hanthawaddy, 96
Haris Nasution, Abdul, 53
Harvey, G.E., 91
Havana summit, 118
hawala, 197
'Hell Hound at Large', 151, 153
Henry Craddock, Reginald, 148
Henson Kya Doe, 46, 106
Henzada, 87
Himalayas, 93
Hinduism, 139
Hinthada, 12, 14
Hkakhu, 76
Hkun Sai, 98–9
U Hla Aung, U, 19
Hla Myo Aung, 194
Hmawbi, 51
HN-5A Man-Portable Air Defence Systems (MANPADS), 124–5
Homöng, 105
Hong Kong, 97
Hopang-Panglong area, 92
Hopin, 90
Horn of Africa, 128, 136
Houtman, Gustaaf, 77, 152
Hpimaw, 111

Hsawnghsup, 90
Hsenwi, 77
Hsinbyumashin, 82–3
Hsinbyushin, 80
Hsipaw, 56, 77, 157
Htay, *yebaw,* 117
Htein Lin. *See* Aung San
Htein Lin. *See* Aris, Kim
Hua Guofeng, 118
Hukawng Valley, 93
Human Rights Education Institute of Burma, 172
Hungary, 111

Imperial Japanese Army, 150
India, 20, 38, 47, 48, 57, 85, 107, 121, 128–9, 157, 168, 184–7, 197
 border, 138
 and Burma agreement, 130–1
 Burma, Buddhism in, 144–7
 Burmese Empire III, 79–82
 rebellions, 137
 Soviet Union and, 179
 Suu Kyi in, 161
 U Nu government, 153–5
 See also China
Indian civilisation, 78
Indian National Congress, 87, 147
Indian Ocean, 22, 33, 120, 127, 128, 135, 136, 187
 CMEC, 176
Indonesia, 24, 53, 57, 116, 133, 154, 181, 183
Inlay Lake, 30
Inside a Soviet Embassy (Aleksandr Kaznacheev), 180
Internal Unity Advisory Board, 157

INDEX

International Court of Justice, 168
International Monetary Fund, 24
International Trading House, 50
Inya Lake, 58, 180
Iran, 128
Irrawaddy (magazine), 166–7
Irrawaddy delta, 12, 22, 41, 47, 116, 153
    Danubyu, battle at, 8
    ethnic Burman Divisions, 76
    Karens migration, 87
Irrawaddy River, 96
Israel, 68, 128
Italy, 82, 151

Jakarta, 183
Jane's Defence Weekly (magazine), 132
Japan, 97, 127–8, 147, 151, 165, 168, 172, 186–7
Japanese allies, 38
Jesus, 21
Jimmy Yang (Yang Kyin-sein), 106
Jubilee Hall, 146
Judson, Adoniram, 85
Judson College, 87
Judson, Nancy, 85

Ka Kwe Ye ('defence'), 104
Kabaw Valley, 129–31
Kachin army, 32
Kachin Hills, 40
Kachin Independence Army (KIA), 2–3, 17–18, 33, 55, 107, 126–7, 137, 175, 186
    ceasefire agreements, 68–9
Kachin rebels, 48
Kachin Rifles, 47

Kachin State, 31, 33, 40, 42, 46, 61
    ceasefire agreements, 68–9
    ethnic Burman Divisions, 76
    Panglong Agreement, 152–3
    U Nu's concessions, 112
    UWSA, Chinese support, 124–6
Kaladan Multi-Modal Transit Transport Project, 185
Kaladan River, 185
Kalmykia, 181–2
Kandy, 42
Kang Sheng, 116, 121, 127, 128
Kanran, 95
Kansas, 166
Karen National Association (KNA), 87
Karen National Defence Organisation (KNDO), 41, 46, 100, 106
Karen National Liberation Army (KNLA), 106
Karen National Union (KNU), 2–3, 18, 59, 106
Karen rebel headquarters, 20
Karen rebels, 47
Karen, 40, 42, 46, 84, 88
    Burmese vs., 84–7
    ethnic Burman Divisions, 76
    ethnic minorities and, 154
    Panglong Agreement, 152–3
Karenni ('Red Karen'), 42–3, 48, 88, 99–100, 103
Kawthaung, 12
Kawthoolei, 41
Kayah (Karenni), 47
    ethnic Burman Divisions, 76
Kayah Rifles, 47
Kayah State, 30

INDEX

Kayah, 31, 88
Kayan (Padaung), 17, 88, 103
Kazan Military Command Academy, 178
Kaznacheev, Aleksandr, 180
Keiji Suzuki, 39
Kempetai, 62
Kengtung, 77, 89, 91, 112, 124
Kenya, 20
Kettaya, U, 146
Khasi, 129
Khathing', Ralengnao 'Bob', 129
Khin Kyi, 44, 158–9, 161, 164
Khin Maung Gyi, 59
Khin Nyunt, 17, 18, 19, 121
  arrest, 66–7
  ceasefire agreements, 68–9
Khin Thida Htun, 162
Khmer Rouge, 118
Khrushchev, Nikita, 114, 180
Khun Sa (alias Zhang Qifu), 104–5, 181
'the King of Arakan', 42
'King of Dragons', 195
Kinwun Mingyi U Khaung, 43
Ko Jimmy, 194
Ko Ko Gyi, 193, 194
Ko Ko, 178
Ko Yu, U, 163–4
Kokang KKY, 104
Kokang, 34, 70, 92, 103, 106, 123, 124, 126, 177
Kolkata, 185
Kommersant (website), 181–2
Konbaung Dynasty, 79
Korean War, 140
Kriangsak Chamanan, 105
Kublai, Khan, 92
Kulangsu (Gulangyu), 39
Kunming, 124

Kuomintang, 109
Kyaington, 77
Kyauk Taw Kyi Temple, 80
Kyaukphyu, 127
Kyaw Gyi, 10
Kyaw Htin, 64
Kyaw Min Yu, 194
Kyaw Nyein, 52, 154
Kyaw Soe, 53, 57
Kyaw Swa Myint, 63
Kyaw Zaw, 14, 48–9, 65
  new Myanmar army, 70
Kyebogyi, 43
Kyemon ('the Mirror') (newspaper), 156
Kyi Maung, 166, 170
Kyiv, 178
Kyoto, 161, 181

Lahu, 91
Laihka, 77, 98
Lall, Marie, 23, 205, 206
Lan Na Kingdom, 79
Lancang-Mekong Cooperation Framework, 191
'the Land of the Bama', 73
Laos, 79, 83, 90, 112, 115–16, 125, 179, 183–4, 189–91
Lashio, 46, 104, 120
Lavrov, Sergey, 177
Law-Yone, Edward, 106–7, 156, 157
Laycha, 77
Levin, Burton, 141
Le Pe Win, U, 147
LGBT rights, 172
Li Xiannian, 119
Liars, Johnny. *See* Kyaw Swa Myint
Liberation Daily, The (newspaper), 158

INDEX

Liberia, 196
Liberty (newspaper), 156
Light Infantry Divisions, 61
Light of Dawn, The (newspaper), 158
Likhachev, Alexey Evgenievich, 178
line of actual control, 131
Little Coco, 132, 134
Lo Hsing-han, 104, 107
Loi Maw KKY, 104, 105
Loikaw, 30
Lokhta Pyithu Nezin (the *Working People's Daily* in English) (newspaper), 58, 156, 167
Lon Htein, 12
London, 41, 43, 160, 169
Look East, 138
Los Angeles Times (newspaper), 141
Lu Fang mountain range, 125
Luther King Jr, Martin, 159

Mae Hong Son, 105
Magwe region, 31
Magwe, 30
Maha Bandula, 81
Maha Muni ('Great Sage'), 81
Mahn Ba Khaing, 44
Mahn Ba Zan, 106
Mainichi Daily (newspaper), 165
Majoi Shingra Bum, 93
Malaya, 111, 116, 121, 183–4, 197
Mali Hka River, 76
Man Maw, 127
Mandalay Gazette (newspaper), 155
Mandalay, 12, 28, 46, 81, 83, 125, 144, 146–7, 155, 167
Mandalay Hill, 82

Manerplaw, 20
Manipur, 81-82, 129–30, 137, 185
Manipuri rebels, 137–8
Mao Zedong, 16, 39, 48, 109, 114, 127–8
   China's new policies, 123
   Communist Party of China (CPC), 116–17
Martyrs Day, 161
Marxism, 149
   in Burma, 153
Massachusetts, 84
Maulmain Chronicle (newspaper), 155
Maung Aye, 132, 138–9
Maung Maung Kha, 15, 46, 119
Maung Nu. *See* U Nu
Maung Thaw Ka, 161–5
Mawlamyine, 12, 14
Maxar Technologies, 133–4
Maymyo (Pyin Oo Lwin), 46, 51, 99
McKendree Key, David, 139–40
Meghalaya, 129, 185
Meiktila, 12, 46, 52
Meio University, 62
Meitei population, 137, 185
Mekong, 83, 191
Menglian, 91
Mergui, 88
Methodist English High School, 158
Middle East, 127, 197
Military Intelligence Service (MIS), 10, 61, 66
Min Aung Hlaing, 7–8, 67, 129, 172, 183, 186, 191–2
   movement, 28–9
Min Ko Naing, 193–5

INDEX

Minbu, 12
Min Yaung, U, 150
Mindon, King, 82, 155
Mingaladon airport, 61
Minkyinyo, King, 78
Mizoram, 137, 185
Mizzima (news organisation), 167
MNDAA. *See* Myanmar National Democratic Alliance Army
Modern Burma (newspaper), 156
Moe Thu, U, 161
Mogaung, 93
Moksobomyo, 79
Mon kingdom, 80
Mon National Day, 96
Mon National Defence Organisation, 100
Mon rebels, 47, 77–9, 84, 88, 96
    ethnic Burman Divisions, 76
Mon State
    ethnic Burman Divisions, 76
Möng Ko, 48, 59–60
Möng Lun, 92
Mong Pa Liao, 112
Möng Pawn, 44
Mong Yang, 112
Mongol empire, 78
Mongolia, 111
Monywa, 125
Moscow, 111, 115, 177, 178
Moulmein (Mawlamyine), 155
Mountbatten, Louis, 41–2, 152
mujahids, 42
Muslims, 42
Mya Thwe Thwe Khaing, 28
Myanma Alin (newspaper), 156, 167
'Myanmafication', 77
Myanmar Air Force, 177

'Myanmar Naing-Ngan', 73
Myanmar National Democratic Alliance Army (MNDAA), 31, 32, 70, 124, 126
Myanmar Oil and Gas Enterprise, 186
Myanmar's Defense Services Academy, 24
Myaungmya, 87
Myay Nu Street, 38
Mydans, Seth, 13
Myeik, 12
Myint San Aung. *See* Aris, Alexander
Myitkyina, 12, 14, 120
Myitsone, 128

Naga Hills, 94–5, 137
Naga Min, 195
Naga Ni ('Red Dragon') book club, 153
Naga population, 93, 185
    Panglong Agreement, 152–3
Naga tribes, 94–5, 137–8
Nagaland, 185
Namkham, 30, 46, 65
Namtok, 89
Namwan Assigned Tract, 111
Nargis (Cyclone), 22
Nation (newspaper), 106, 156
National Coalition Government of the Union of Burma (NCGUB), 20, 166, 172
National Council of the Union of Burma, 107–8
National Democratic Alliance Army- Eastern Shan State (NDAA-ESS), 124
National Democratic Front (NDF), 106

INDEX

'The National Ideology of the Defence Services', 52
National League for Democracy (NLD), 2–3, 16, 18, 29, 107, 163–6, 171, 193–4
  election victory, 19–20
  election, boycotting, 232;
  movements, 27–9
National Liberation Front, 116
National United Liberation Front (NULF), 106–7
National Unity Consultative Council, 108
National Unity Government (NUG), 3, 31–2, 108, 171–2, 175
National Unity Party (NUP), 15, 21, 165
Nationalities Liberation Alliance, 106
Nationalities United Front, 106
Natmauk, 150
'Naturally Flat Mountain', 93
Naungdawgyi, 80
Naw Seng, 46, 48, 59–60, 109-10, 115
Naypyitaw, 27, 28, 29, 30, 37, 108, 129, 131, 135, 170, 185
  Lavrov visits, 177
  ceasefire, 75
Ne Win, 8, 15, 30, 44, 47, 49, 53, 57, 61
  Aung Gyi, 164
  Burma newspapers, 155–8
  death, 21
  "Four Cuts" policy, 62–3
  Japanese vs. Chinese, 39–42
  military vs. democratic system, 51–2
  Ne Win government, 194

new Myanmar army, 70
PDP, formation of, 106–7
Rangoon and Beijing, relations, 116–19
Suu Kyi politics, 158–63
Washington's Myanmar policy, 139–42
See also U Nu
Nehru, Jawaharlal, 130, 132, 154, 157
Nemoto, Kei 15
Nepal, 185
Nestorian Christians, 86
New Burma (newspaper), 156
New Delhi, 138–9, 159
New Democratic Army-Kachin (NDA-K), 124
New England, 85
New Light of Burma, The (newspaper), 156
New Light of Myanmar (newspaper), 22, 23, 167
New Victory (newspaper), 158
New York Times (newspaper), 13
New York, 9, 160, 171
Newcastle, 169
Newsletter, The (newspaper), 158
Nichols, James 'Leo' Leander, 165
  1988 uprising, 141, 193
  1962 coup, 139, 180
  alliances and opium trafficking, 100–6
  1960 border agreement, 120
Nippon Foundation, 186
Nizhniy Novgorod Command Academy, 178
NLD. *See* National League for Democracy (NLD)
Nmai Hka River, 76
Non-Aligned Movement, 118

INDEX

Noom Suk Harn, 101
North Korea, 25, 57, 134, 179
    partnership, 140–2
    See also Russia
North Vietnam, 57, 189
northern Shan States, 46
northern Wa Hills, 127
Norway, 2, 165, 172
Nu, U, 44–7, 49–50, 52, 60
    Burma newspapers, 155–8
    on Burmese, 98
    Moscow visit, 180
    Nehru and, 138
    Panglong Agreement, 152–3
    PDP, formation of, 106–7
    as prime minister, 153–5;
    Sino-Burmese border,
        111–13
    Sino-Burmese declaration,
        110–11
Nu-Attlee Treaty, 153
Nyan Lin, 194
Nyanissara, Ashin, 192

Obama, Barack, 2, 23, 142
Observer (newspaper), 156
Ohn Kyaw Myint, 64, 194
    arrest, 65
Ohn Maung, 44
Okinawa, 62
'the Old Opium Pipe', 116
Omsk Armor Engineering
    Institute, 178
135 'national races', 75–6
Ontario, 169
Operation (1027), 31, 126,
    175
'opportunism', 114
Organisation of Islamic
    Cooperation, 168

'Organisation Rules for the
    Burma Socialist Programme
    Party', 63
Ott, Marvin, 141
Oway (magazine), 151
Oxford, 159, 169

Pacific islands, 65, 140
Padaung, 88
Pagan (Bagan), 78
Pakistan, 42, 68
Palaung Ta'ang National
    Liberation Army, 126
Palaung, 17, 91
Palaung army, 32, 70
Paletwa, 185
Pali, 144
Pamfilova, Ella, 179
Pan Qi, 120, 122
Pang Tara, 77
Panghsai, 120
Panghsang, 16, 60, 103, 118, 123,
    125
Panglong Agreement, 99, 152–3
Pangwa, 123–4
Panthay, 97
Pa-O rebels, 17, 32–3, 103
Paris, 169
Parliamentary Democracy Party
    (PDP), 106–7
Pathein, 12, 14
Patriotic Burmese Forces (PBF).
    See Burma National Army
    (BNA)
pauk-phaw concept, 111
Paw Oo Tun, 193
Paw Tun Aung, 147
Pegu Yoma, 47–8, 60, 78, 79, 80,
    113, 114–15
Pemberton, Boileau, 130

247

INDEX

Pemberton Line, 130
Penang, 97
People's Comrade Party, 52
People's Defence Forces (PDF), 31–2, 108, 175
People's Liberation Army Strategic Support Force, 135
People's Patriotic Party (PPP), 107
People's Republic of China, 190
People's Republic, 109
People's Voice of Burma, 60
People's Volunteer Organisation (PVO), 42, 45, 47, 52
Pha, U. *See* Aung San Suu Kyi
Philippines, 184
Phnom Penh, 118
Phyo Zeya Thaw, 194
Pindaya, 77
Ping River, 190
PLA, 125
Plaek Phibunsongkhram, 100
Pongyi, 145
Prakash Malik, Ved, 138
Putao (Hkamti Long), 90
Putin, Vladimir, 179
Pwo, 88
Pyidaungsu Hluttaw (Union Parliament), 28
Pyidaungsu Lane, 56
Pyin Oo Lwin, 24
Pyinmana, 12
Pyithu Hluttaw, 18
Pyongyang, 135

Quadrilateral Security Dialogue, 187

Radio Moscow, 181
Radio Rangoon, 52

Raju (Ne Win's cook), 58–9
Rakhine Democratic League, 19
Rakhine State, 70, 127, 148, 176, 185–6, 195
  ethnic Burman Divisions, 76
Ramasun, 189
Rangoon (Yangon), 80
Rangoon Chronicle (newspaper), 155
Rangoon Gazette (newspaper), 155
Rangoon Mail (newspaper), 156
Rangoon University, 8, 149, 151
Rangoon
  border agreement, 120–2
Rangoon and Beijing, relations, 116–19
Raschid, U, 154
Rashtriya Swayamsevak Sangh (RSS), 139
Razak, U, 44
Red Flag communists, 48
'Red Flags', 114
'Red Guards', 42, 60, 113
Red Sea, 128, 136
Rees-Williams, David, 99
'regionalism', 24
Religion and Politics in Burma (Donald E. Smith), 144
Ren Yisheng, 190
Republic of China (Taiwan), 190
Resources Policy (newspaper), 127
Restoration Council of Shan State (RCSS), 33, 191
Reuters (news agency company), 19, 181
Revolutionary Council (1962), 57–8, 164, 166
Revolutionary Nationalities Alliance, 106

INDEX

Rohingyas, 185–6, 194–6
Rohingya crisis, 168
Roman Catholics, 87, 88
Rowe & Co., 50
Rudolph Davies, Henry, 84, 127
Ruili, 137
Russia, 129, 197
    invasion, 176–8
    Myanmar's relations with, 179–81
Russian Air Force, 178
Russian Aircraft Corporation MiG, 177
Russian State Atomic Energy Corporation, 178

SAC. *See* State Administration Council (SAC)
Saffron Revolution (2007), 21–2, 29, 141, 166, 192
Sagaing Division People's Council, 14
Sagaing Division, 48
Sagaing Region, 12, 13, 31, 137
Sai Myee, 56
Saipan, 65, 140
Sakharov Prize, 169
Salem, 84–5
Salween River, 49, 89
Salween Village, 104
Samuel Shi Sho, 46
San C. Po, 84, 87
San Diego, 159
San Thu, 115
San Tun, U, 153
San Yu, 15, 118
Sanchaung, 38
Sao Kya Hseng, 56, 156–7
Sao Nang Hearn Hkam, 59
Sao Sam Htun, 44

Sao Shwe Thaik, 45, 55, 56, 59, 101
Sasakawa, Ryoichi, 186
Sasakawa, Yohei, 186
Saturday's Son (U Nu), 153
Saw, U, 44, 156
Saw Ba U Gyi, 154
Saw Maung, 15, 19, 20–1
Saya San, 148–9
Scoop (newspaper), 158
Scott Bank, 50
Scott, James George, 143
Seagrave, Gordon, 98
'Secret KMT Army', 48
Seekins, Donald, 62, 80
Sein Da, U, 42
Sein Lwin, 8, 15
Sein Win, 20
Sein, Thein, 26
Selth, Andrew, 132–3
'the Seven Years of Devastation', 81
Shan army, 32
'Shan Gyi', 76
Shan Hills, 83, 86
Shan Literary Society, 101
Shan Nationalities League for Democracy, 18–19
Shan Sao Shwe Thaik, 154
Shan State Army (SSA), 17–18, 32–3, 59, 103, 104
Shan State Progress Party, 32
Shan State, 30–4, 47–8, 61, 70, 78, 83–4, 97–8, 101
    ethnic Burman Divisions, 76–7
    Panglong Agreement, 152–3
    Washington's Myanmar policy, 139–42
Shan Student Association, 101

INDEX

Shan United Army (SUA), 105
Shan valleys, 91
Shanghai, 38
Shenzhou spacecraft, 135
Shillong, 138
Shimla, 161
Shoigu, Sergei, 177
Shway Yoe. *See* Scott, James George
Shwe Dagon, 9, 14, 162
Shwe Mann, 21
Shwe Zedi, 148
Shwebo, 12, 79–80
Shweli River, 116
Siam, 80
Siamese kingdom, 78
Siamese royal family, 80
Sichuan, 60, 110
Sikkim, 185
Siliguri Corridor, 185
Silverstein, Josef, 89
Singapore, 57, 68, 97, 111, 121, 197
Singkaling Hkamti, 90, 95, 137
Sinmalaik Dockyard, 9
Sitagu Sayadaw, 192–3
Sittwe, 148
Sitwundan, 47
Smith Dun, 46
Smith, Donald Eugene, 144
Smith, Martin, 75
Socialism, 15
'Some Facts about Ne Win's Military Government', 113
South China Sea, 127, 184
South Korea, 172
South Pacific Ocean, 135
'South Tibet', 131
Southeast Asia, 41, 92, 116, 122
Soviet Union, 57, 111, 115–16, 154, 179

Sputnik, 180
Sri Lanka, 20, 42, 135
SSA. *See* Shan State Army (SSA)
St Hugh's College, 159
'Stable AFPFL', 52
Stalin Peace Prize, 111
Stalin, Joseph, 114, 180
State Administration Council (SAC), 2, 8, 28, 29, 33, 34, 171, 182, 184
 Brotherhood Alliance, 175–6
State Law and Order Restoration Council (SLORC), 15–18, 21, 75, 157–8, 163, 165, 193
 NLD's election victory, 19–20
'the State of Myanmar', 73
State Peace and Development Council (SPDC), 21, 23
Steinberg, David, 8
Strait of Malacca, 127, 128
'A Study of Myanmar–US Relations', 24
Suez Canal, 128, 136
Suharto, 24
Sukaphaa, 137
Sule Pagoda Road, 49
Sule Pagoda, 13
Sumprabum, 40
Supayagyi, 82–3
Supayalat, Queen, 150
Supayalay, 82, 83
Supreme Soviet Presidium, 111
Suu Kyi. *See* Aung San Suu Kyi
Switzerland, 165
Sydney Peace Foundation for Human Rights, 172
Syriam, king of, 79
Syriam, port of (Thanlyin), 79

INDEX

Ta'ang National Liberation Army (TNLA), 31, 32, 70
Tabernacle Church, 85
Tabinshwehti, 78–9
Tai Dam ('Black Tai'), 88
'Tai Long', 76
Taipei, 195
Taiwan, 57
Talaings, 77
Tasker, Rodney, 65
Tass, 182
'Tatmadaw officer', 75
Tatmadaw, 62, 68, 70
Taunggyi, 12, 14, 54, 90, 101, 105, 180
Tavoy, 83
Taylor, Robert, 30, 165–6
'Ten Thousand Golden Oil', 97
Tenasserim (Tanintharyi), 79, 81–2, 88
Tet Pongyi ('The Modern Monk') (Thein Pe Myint), 150
Tha Kyaw, 18
Thailand, 18, 20, 42, 55, 57–63, 90, 116, 121, 157, 166, 168, 184, 189–91, 196–7
    alliances and opium trafficking, 100–5
    Chakri Dynasty, 79–80
    Japanese vs. Chinese, 39–42
Thakin Aung San. *See* Aung San
Thakin Ba Hein, 38
Thakin Ba Thein Tin, 114–15, 117–18, 123–4
Thakin Bo, 114
Thakin Chit Maung, 181
Thakin Hla Myaing, 39
Thakin Kodaw Hmaing, 11, 111, 149–50
    movement, 11–12
Thakin Mya Hlaing, 38
Thakin Mya, 43–4
Thakin Nu. *See* U Nu
Thakin Shu Maung. *See* Ne Win
Thakin Soe, 41, 48, 107, 114, 180
Thakin Than Tun, 45, 152–4
Thakin Thein Pe. *See* Thein Pe Myint
Thakin Tin Shwe, 41
Thamaing Spinning Mill, 9
Than Shwe, 20–1, 26–7, 37, 121, 192
Thant, U, 9, 154, 159
Thaung, U, 50, 54, 156
The Hague, 168–70
Thein Pe Myint, 41, 150
Thein Sein, 1, 3, 21, 128, 142, 167, 192–3
    government, 197
Theinli, 77
Theravada Buddhism, 78, 90
Thibaw, King, 77, 82–3, 144, 150
Thimphu, 160
3rd Burma Rifles, 57
'Thiri Pyanchi', 192–3
Thirty Comrades, 10, 114, 157, 161
Thonburi, 80
Thura Kyaw Zwa, 14, 18
Thura Shwe Mann, 134–5
Thuriya ('the Sun') (newspaper), 156
Tiananmen Square massacre, 121
Tiananmen Square, 109
Tibet, 21, 91, 93
Tiger Balm, 97
Tin Pe, 53, 57
Tin, U, 156, 167
Tin U, 15–16, 64–5, 140, 164
Tin U (MI Tin U), arrest of 65-7

INDEX

TNLA. *See* Ta'ang National Liberation Army (TNLA)
Tokyo, 39, 102
Toungoo Dynasty, 79
Toungoo, 12, 78, 83, 88
Tripura, 185
Tun Myat, 11
2021 coup, 128, 142, 172, 184, 193

U Ottama, 147–8
U Wirathu, 192–3
U Wisara, 148
Udon Thani, 189
Ukraine, 177, 182, 191
UN Security Council, 179, 182
Union Day, 99
Union Military Police (UMP), 45, 47
Union National Democracy Party (UNDP), 164
Union Solidarity and Development Party (USDP), 1, 21, 26–7, 192
  movements, 27–9
United Aircraft Corporation, 177
United Karenni Independent State, 42–3
United Kingdom, 128
United Liberation Front of Asom [Assam] (ULFA), 137–8
United Nationalities Front, 106
United Nations High Commissioner for Refugees, 196
United Nations Security Council, 129
United Nations, 9, 22, 140, 154, 184
United Press International, 181
United States Central Intelligence Agency (CIA), 48, 189
  Washington's Myanmar policy, 139–40
United States Holocaust Memorial Museum, 169
United States Institute of Peace, 32, 70
United States, 24, 25, 61, 64, 82, 107, 128, 134, 168, 171–2, 186
  Washington's Myanmar policy, 139–42
United Wa State Army (UWSA), 17, 32, 34, 191
  Chinese support, 124–6
University Avenue, 8, 161–2
University of Calcutta, 146
University of Kyoto, 161
University of Queensland Press, 160
University of Rangoon, 64, 87
University of Sydney, 172
'Upper Burma Campaign', 46
US Army, 140
USDP. *See* Union Solidarity and Development Party (USDP)

Vanguard (newspaper), 58
Vietnam, 24, 88, 116, 118, 179, 183–4, 190, 197
Vivian, David, 44
Vumsom, 94

Wa Hills, 32, 91–2, 98, 103, 112, 122
Waingmaw, 90
Wakema, 153
Was, 91, 152–3
Washington, 24, 139, 186, 191

INDEX

Webb, Jim, 142
West Africa, 168
West German G-3, 8
West Germany, 61
Western Pacific Ocean, 135
Win Myat Aye, 196
Win Myint, 29, 31, 171, 193
Win Tin, U, 161, 163
Working People's Daily (newspaper), 22, 58, 75–6, 158, 167
World Bank, 24, 122
World War II, 42, 46–7, 60, 98, 161, 162, 186

Xinhua News Agency, 128–9, 181
Xinxing ('New Star'), 124–5

Yadana-bon Nay-pyi-taw (newspaper), 155
Yandabo, Treaty of, 81
Yangon Institute of Technology, 180
Yangon School of Political Science, 171
Yangon University of Foreign Languages, 179
Yangon, 9–14, 17, 20–1, 28, 38, 64, 100, 110, 122
  army, 173
  border agreement, 120–2
  boundary treaty, 112
  Burma newspapers, 155–8
  Burmese invasion, 79
  ceasefire agreements, 68–9
  India's relationship, 138
  Japanese vs. Chinese, 39–42
  Khun Sa in, 105
  pauk-phaw concept, 111
  Rangoon and Beijing, relations, 116–19
  Washington's Myanmar policy, 139–42
Yangon massacre, 121
YMBA, 146
Yangtze River, 89
Yawnghwe *saohpa*, 101
Yawt Seik, 105
Yay Kyi Aing ('Clearwater Pond'), 61
Yeltsin, Boris, 179
Yemen, 128
'Yodia people', 80
Young Men's Buddhist Association (YMBA), 145–6
Young Men's Christian Association, 145
Yuan Wang 5 (ship), 135
Yuan Wang 6 (ship), 135
Yuan Wang spy ships, 136
Yuan Wang tracking ships, 135
Yunnan, 48, 84, 88, 91–2, 137–8
  CPB, 113–14
Yunnan border, 16

Zagarnar' ('forceps', or 'tweezer'), 164
Zau Dan, 55
Zau Seng, 55
Zau Tu, 55
Zaw Min Tun, 27, 134, 178
Zhang Qifu. *See* Khun Sa
Zhao Lijian, 187–8
Zhou Bo, 131
Zhou Enlai, 112
  Sino-Burmese declaration, 110–11
Zin Mar Aung, 171